Real Estate Valuation

Real Estate Valuation: A Subjective Approach highlights the subjective valuation components of residential and commercial real estate, which can lead to a range of acceptable property value conclusions.

It discusses the causes of housing booms and goes in depth into the heterogeneity of commercial real estate property valuation via examples from owner-occupied, multifamily residential, hotel, office, retail, warehouse, condo conversion, and mortgage-backed security areas of real estate. Other topics explored include the role of machine learning and AI in real estate valuation, market participant value perceptions, and the challenge of time in the valuation process. The primary theoretical basis for the range of acceptable values and the subjectivity of property valuation focuses on the work of G.L.S. Shackle from the Austrian School of Economics.

This illuminating textbook is suitable for undergraduate and master's students of real estate finance, and will also be useful for practitioners in residential and commercial real estate.

G. Jason Goddard is adjunct professor at Wake Forest University and University of North Carolina at Greensboro, USA.

Real Estate Valuation

A Subjective Approach

G. Jason Goddard

Routledge
Taylor & Francis Group

LONDON AND NEW YORK

First published 2022
by Routledge
2 Park Square, Milton Park, Abingdon, Oxon OX14 4RN

and by Routledge
605 Third Avenue, New York, NY 10158

Routledge is an imprint of the Taylor & Francis Group, an informa business

British Library Cataloguing-in-Publication Data
A catalogue record for this book is available from the British Library

Library of Congress Cataloging-in-Publication Data
Names: Goddard, G. Jason, author.
Title: Real estate valuation : a subjective approach / G. Jason Goddard.
Description: New York, NY : Routledge, 2021. | Includes bibliographical references and index.
Identifiers: LCCN 2021031308 (print) | LCCN 2021031309 (ebook) | ISBN 9780367539085 (hardback) | ISBN 9780367539078 (paperback) | ISBN 9780367539078 (ebook)
Subjects: LCSH: Real property—Valuation. | Information technology—Management. | Artificial intelligence—Economic aspects.
Classification: LCC HD1387 .G63 2021 (print) | LCC HD1387 (ebook) | DDC 333.33/20285—dc23
LC record available at https://lccn.loc.gov/2021031308
LC ebook record available at https://lccn.loc.gov/2021031309

ISBN: 978-0-367-53908-5 (hbk)
ISBN: 978-0-367-53907-8 (pbk)
ISBN: 978-1-003-08367-2 (ebk)

DOI: 10.4324/9781003083672

Typeset in Sabon
by codeMantra

Access the Support Material: https://www.routledge.com/9780367539078

This book is dedicated to those white squirrels of Brevard, North Carolina.

Brevard's natural wonders provided much writing solitude and inspiration.

Contents

Author

G. Jason Goddard is vice-president at Wells Fargo, where he has been a commercial lender for over 25 years. Jason is credit team manager for Real Estate Portfolio Services (REPS), and works in Winston-Salem, NC. Mr. Goddard has been adjunct associate professor of practice at Wake Forest University since 2008, teaching real estate finance. He obtained his MBA from the Bryan School at the University of North Carolina at Greensboro. He has taught various undergraduate and MBA courses in international business and finance at UNC-G since 2003. Jason is co-author of the following text books: *International Business: Theory and Practice, Second Edition* (M.E. Sharpe Publishers, September 2006), *Customer Relationship Management: A Global Perspective* (Gower Publishing, May 2008), *The Psychology of Marketing: Cross-Cultural Perspectives* (Gower Publishing, October 2010), *Real Estate Investment: A Value Based Approach* (Springer, July 2012), *International Business: A Course on the Essentials* (M.E. Sharpe, October 2013), and *Global Business: Competitiveness and Sustainability* (Routledge, October 2017). *Follow him on Twitter @GJasonGoddard.*

Preface

During the months while I was writing this book, there was much talk about the "new normal" everywhere and in every conceivable situation. Old beliefs were being uprooted, or this was at least the tone of the rhetoric. Rather than focusing on the new normal, this book instead helps answer an old question: *Why is real estate an illiquid asset whereby it takes longer for a hopeful seller to connect with a willing buyer?* The answer to that question has always been that it takes time for two market participants to agree on a final purchase price. The reason that this takes so long is that there must be a range of possible values for which a property could theoretically be sold. Disagreement causes delay in transfer. Rather than assuming away such differences, in the pages that follow, we will deliberate on these valuation inflection points together. After finding an old (and mostly forgotten) academic model which helped to explain the range of possible values, I produced a series of papers in the Risk Management Association (RMA) Journal and elsewhere over the last few years dealing with the subjectivity of value in commercial real estate. Each of these papers has been referenced in this book. The fun part for me was to take a model originally theorized by G.L.S. Shackle as the foundation for this book, and link it into the larger framework of real estate.

I believe that this book will be of interest to students and academics associated with real estate as well as the vast army of practitioners in the real estate industry across the globe. My work generally tends to pull from varied sources rather than an insistence on a silo approach which so grips the academic community presently. After the basic chapter content was written, I stumbled across the idea of the "market vignettes" which complete each chapter. These are essentially short plays that help explain where the inflection points of valuation subjectivity can arise in market situations.

Perhaps decades after my passing, some interested scholar will find some of my published work and attempt to resurrect it as I have done for G.L.S. Shackle here. Hopefully, this book inspired by him will instead be read and discussed by a large readership in the present day. I leave that to the vagaries of time to decide. Some would say that the solitary opinion of value for a commercial property is sacrosanct. I am reminded of the words of Voltaire in this regard when he said, "If you want to know who controls you, look at who you are not allowed to criticize".

In any event, the writing of this book, coupled with frequent trips to Brevard, North Carolina, allowed me to remain productive during a difficult time for us all. I hope that you enjoy the fruit of my efforts.

G. Jason Goddard, August 2021
Winston-Salem, NC, USA

From Austrian value subjectivity to Shackle's Possibility Curve

Chapter highlights

- The range of values for real estate
- The spectrum of valuation
- Austrian value subjectivity: historical origins
- Shackle's Possibility Curve: original model and modern context
- Investor choice example: land development

> We are prisoners of the present who must choose in the present on the basis of our present knowledge, judgments, and assessments.
>
> GLS Shackle

1.1 The range of values for real estate

It has been said that beauty lies in the eyes of the beholder. In no asset class is this better exhibited than in real estate. Sometimes people's assessment of real estate value is based on empirical evidence, and at other times, this evidence is somewhat (or completely) clouded with emotional ties or feelings of nostalgia. Regardless of the method, real estate is an illiquid asset class. In other words, it takes quite a bit of time to sell a property as compared to other assets such as stocks and bonds, or even smaller things such as bologna sandwiches. One reason for this time difference is the legal determination of the ability of the seller to adequately convey the property to the buyer. Another reason is the length of time it takes for an appraiser to provide an official value of record for the transaction. While these time pressures indubitably exist, the purpose of this book is to explore why it takes so long for a buyer and seller to agree on a price.

DOI: 10.4324/9781003083672-1

Let's return to bologna sandwiches for a moment. If you desire to purchase one of these at your local restaurant, there really is no price negotiation. Right there on the menu you can plainly see the price for bologna sandwiches, with the only real price variability consisting of side items and beverages. Thus, the seller lists their determination of the current market price and you can take it or leave it. Within the bologna sandwich spectrum, I am sure there could be higher priced luxury versions (with fancier bread for example) as well as lower priced more standard versions, but in each case, the price is stated and the buyer can take it or leave it. If no restaurant customers purchase a bologna sandwich on a given day, this may not mean that the price is excessive; however, if this situation persists, the price will inevitably come down. Maybe customers just don't like bologna sandwiches anymore owing to perceived health risks, or maybe the price offered in the particular restaurant is just too high. "Jimmy makes a great bologna sandwich, but at that price I think I will just stay home and make it myself". For this one restaurant in the bologna sandwich selling universe, the supply was too great relative to demand, so the price came down.

The concept of subjective price is related to the supply and demand charts exhibited in classical economics. Under the scenario just described, the surplus of bologna sandwiches led to the price decline. At some magical point, the quantity of the supply and the quantity of the demand meet, achieving equilibrium. While this represents convenient theory, the process by which equilibrium is achieved is rarely mentioned and often ignored. Equilibrium is so celebrated that you would think that once it is achieved that there would be some ceremony where the sandwich makers and the sandwich buyers come together in song, or at least come together with prepared speeches. The pathway to equilibrium for any asset price represents the period where there is disagreement among market participants as to the value for a stated asset.

Returning to real estate, given the length of time typically required for a buyer and seller to agree on a price (i.e., the time that the property is offered for sale on the open market), there is obviously a difference of opinion between the purchase price that a seller desires and what prospective buyers who decide not to pay this price believe is the appropriate amount. We have all seen the residential or commercial property that is initially offered at one price, but then after a few months when the seller is unsuccessful in finding a willing buyer at the offering price, the price is subsequently dropped. In fact, sometimes rather than a price drop, the property is taken off the market for a period of time, only to be offered for sale as a new listing at a reduced price soon thereafter. What is going on from a pricing standpoint during this period of time? Apparently the market process is not able to locate a buyer willing to pay the indicated price. The tacit assumption is that if demand exists for the subject property, would-be buyers are only interested in purchasing the property at a strike price lower than what is currently being offered. The implication of all of this is that there is a range of acceptable values for the subject property as determined by various market participants.

The range of values for real estate is highly influenced by the valuation method employed. The three most common forms of valuation for real estate are the sales approach, the cost approach, and the income approach. Each of these methodologies has a combination of objective and subjective value considerations. As shown in Exhibit 1.1, embedded in all valuation are subjective and objective components.

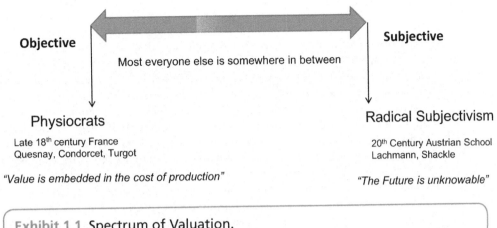

Exhibit 1.1 Spectrum of Valuation.

1.2 The spectrum of valuation

The **sales approach** involves the use of objective, empirical data such as consummated sales of properties deemed similar to the subject property. These "comparable properties" form the basis for the asking price of the property being sold, as a rational market participant would not expect to pay more than other rational market participants have paid for a like or similar property. While this sounds almost entirely objective, the sales approach does have a significant level of subjectivity, especially as the comparable properties deviate in some form or fashion from the subject property being valued. As we will discuss more in Chapter 3, home sales have a perceived objectivity in valuation as long as there are recent sales of similar homes in the market. But what if the subject property consists of a brick structure with three bedrooms and two bathrooms, but that exact paradigm is not found in the comparable properties surveyed? There must be some mechanism to obtain an "apples to apples" comparison, whereby the historical comparable properties' sales prices are increased or lowered based on whether the subject property is deemed inferior or superior in some component of value. The sales approach is the most common appraisal method for owner-occupied homes and owner-occupied commercial properties.

The **cost approach** has historically been viewed as the most objective form of value, as it consists of a determination of how much it would cost to reproduce the subject property should it be razed to the ground. The cost approach owes its origins to a group of economists in 18th-century France who were known as the physiocrats. They believed that the source of all wealth was in agriculture and that value is embedded in the cost of production. As alluded to in Exhibit 1.1, some famous members of this economic school were Francois Quesnay, Anne Robert Jacques Turgot, and Marie Jean de Caritat, Marquis de Condorcet. As a generalization, these gentlemen believed that value is embedded in the cost of production. In other words, a determination of value for a given object is ultimately related to how much it costs to produce. In the landmark *"Tableau êconomique"* of 1758, Quesnay developed the notion of economic equilibrium and the term laissez-faire (i.e., "allow to do" without government intervention) among other well-known ideas. In this book, the first circular diagram for how a national economy works was devised, and the groundwork for the cost approach was theorized. Today, the cost approach is utilized in newly constructed properties to determine the insurable value of a residential or commercial property and the effective age of a property which, in turn, is helpful for determining how long a lender might consider amortizing a loan secured with the subject property. Additionally, the current cost approach includes more subjective elements such as "entrepreneurial profit", as a real estate developer would not be motivated to build a property and sell it for the cost of construction alone. Other subjective elements in the cost approach include the assumed cost of components (i.e., the cost of appliances in an apartment building) and the various adjustments to the subject property's valuation based on differences in layout, size, and type of construction. Examples of the cost approach in the context of this book will be discussed in Chapter 3.

The income approach is utilized for commercial properties where the tenant is different from the owners of the property, and a lease has been negotiated whereby net income can be capitalized to estimate value. I have written on the income approach extensively (Goddard & Marcum 2012), so this book will discuss how the income approach fits into the subject of valuation subjectivity, a mark that it consistently achieves. Exhibit 1.2 illustrates the basic IRV formula which sits at the base of the income approach.

The three basic components of the IRV formula are income, rate, and value. Income is traditionally viewed as net income, and the rate employed is known as a capitalization rate (a.k.a. "cap rate"). The capitalization rate takes the net income and converts it to a value. The equation can be written differently to solve for the element that is unknown:

- Income = rate * value
- Rate = income/value
- Value = income/rate

As baseball announcer Vin Scully used to say, "for those of you scoring at home", if we assume a net income of $150,000 annually and a cap rate of 7.00%, you can back into a property value of $2,142,857. This exact looking value would typically be rounded to $2,150,000, or perhaps $2,200,000. Thus, subjectivity exists in even the simplest of calculations! Exhibit 1.3 allows the opportunity for the reader to explore their inner Vin Scully and "score from home". Just take the two knowns and back into the answer for each of the three IRV components. This is where Vin meets IRV.

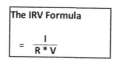

The IRV Formula

$$= \frac{I}{R * V}$$

Exhibit 1.2 IRV Formula.

Income = Rate (cap) * Value	$150,000
Rate = Income/Value	7.00%
Value = Income/Rate	$2,142,857

Exhibit 1.3 Various IRV Iterations.

Appraisal theory suggests that each of the three valuation approaches should wind up in about the same place. While this is a great concept, we often do not live in an M.C. Escher world of symmetry. The assumptions contained in each of these approaches can be massaged to ordain a certain unison result that makes the range of values appear moot. In the United States, an appraisal by an independent third party is required for most loans secured by real estate. A popular definition for an appraisal is an opinion of value, of which apparently there could be many opinions if not for supremacy of one opinion by government fiat. While the "independent third party" has a nice ring to it, one of the first questions that the appraiser of record asks when taking on an assignment is what the purchase price is that has (finally) been negotiated between a buyer and seller. This reminds me of a Kierkegaard line, "*in case he who should act was to judge himself according to the result, he would never get to the point of beginning*". What would happen if the independent third party approached the assignment like the characters in an Agatha Christie novel, and didn't lead with the answer required at the outset? Taken to its extreme, market chaos could ensue, whereby appraisers arrive at very different value conclusions than two market participants (a buyer and a seller). Shown in a different light, if the third-party evaluation was not required for the majority of purchases requiring a loan from a financial institution, the sales contract between two market participants would be all that was required. If that was the case, neither a book like this nor the real estate appraisal industry would be necessary. So let's not wish that situation into existence!

As will be elucidated in the chapters that follow, each of these three elements has a subjective component that contributes to possibilities of different opinions of market value for a given property. In order to calculate net income, we must first start with the gross potential income of the subject property. What if a space is vacant? Do we include this space in our calculation? Do we simply value the property based on its specific performance, or must we also consider how the property's rents, vacancies, and expenses compare to other properties in the market? When deriving a cap rate, should we simply use the IRV formula, or should we compare what other investors have received when purchasing similar properties? Finally, how does the value per square foot compare with similar consummated sales in the recent past? All of these are good questions which we will explore in depth later, but for now, let us recognize the subjectivity which enters into the valuation model when these questions are considered.

The one element of Exhibit 1.1 not yet explored is the right-hand side of the valuation spectrum. While subjectivity exists in all valuation as the future is not known, there is a wing of the Austrian school of economics which takes the prize for the "most subjective" on our valuation spectrum. The Austrian school of economics differs from the Keynesian and Classical schools on many fronts, but the one of primary import for this book is value subjectivity. The most famous of the Austrian school (think "libertarian") economists were Ludwig von Mises and Friedrich von Hayek. While this school of economic thought originated in Austria with Carl Menger, not all proponents of this school hail from the nation of Austria, but a lot of the most famous economists in this school are native Austrians. The most radical of this school as related to the subjectivity of value were (conveniently) known as the radical subjectivists. Two of the most well-known members of this school were Ludwig Lachmann and, most importantly for our book, G.L.S. Shackle (a Brit, not an Austrian!). The radical subjectivists believe that "the future is unknowable", which essentially relegates econometric or economic prediction as essentially useless. If the future is unknowable, the present decisions that we make are all the more important. While it would seem that this school would be a brief stop in our valuation spectrum, in fact there is a model created in this school which serves as the hallmark of this book.

If classical economics utilizes equilibrium theory to illustrate how the world works, and if econometrics utilizes statistical modeling to explain away the "road to price variability", then the radical subjectivist school provides a road map for the *why* in the question –Why do market participants often lead to different valuation conclusions. To be clear, I do not have an issue with equilibrium theory or statistical modeling, but I believe that the subjectivity of value has an interesting story to tell in the real estate valuation context, and this was my motivation for writing this book.

1.3 Austrian value subjectivity: historical origins

The subjectivity of value has been much explored in Austrian economic thought. One of the foundational differences between classical economics and the Austrian school of economics is the Austrian focus on individual human actions rather than the assumption of market equilibrium and the rational actor as emphasized in classical economics. The Austrian focus on individuality fits well with existential philosophy as theorized by Kierkegaard. Given the individual tastes and preferences, Austrian theory per Menger and existentialist thought per Kierkegaard both state that the same object can be valued quite differently by different actors given the individual ordering of subjective and objective factors. Subjective factors regard subtle categorizations of the value components of a given object, while objective factors deal with more concrete variables whereby the satisfaction of these variables leads to a higher level of satisfaction for a particular individual. To quote Mises, *"use-value in the objective sense is the relation between a thing and the effect it has the capacity to bring about"*. Said another way, an objective value would be the utility which an object provides to its user.

Regarding commercial real estate, subjective factors may consist of the aesthetic appeal for a particular property, externalities associated with a given location, or the general risk tolerance of the investor. Objective factors in commercial real estate would consist of concrete benefits received by the owner. While you might consider specifically measurable items such as projected cash flows and resale values to be objective values, these are themselves subjective and a main point of this book. Objective values for real estate have traditionally dealt mainly with the shelter and convenience provided from ownership. Even within variables of value that are considered objective, there exists the possibility of individual perception differences. One man's certainty is another man's anxiety. To quote Menger, *"value is nothing inherent in goods, no property of them, but merely the importance that we first attribute to the satisfaction of our needs"*.

1.3.1 Menger's contribution

The subjectivity in value owes its origin to Austrian economist Carl Menger. He envisioned trade occurring when two parties exchange for items whereby they feel that the item obtained is of higher value to them than the item exchanged. Individuals may value a particular good for its use (i.e., an owner-occupied property) or its exchange potential (i.e., a series of rental homes). If a good is valued higher for its use than for its exchange, the individual is more likely to retain that particular item. From a commercial real estate perspective, an investor may hold a property that others covet, but the current owner may have a desire to retain the asset owing to the cash flow being received from the property, or some other factor. This is not to say that a future price (or sales offer) might not change the individual's perception whereby the property is more readily sold than retained. This subjective ranking depends on the relative satisfaction that a given item provides to its owner. Exhibit 1.4 was adapted from Menger to illustrate the individual satisfaction rankings whereby trade might occur.

Carl Menger: Numerical Representation of Satisfaction of Wants									
Good I	Good II	Good III	Good IV	Good V	Good VI	Good VII	Good VIII	Good IX	Good X
10	9	8	7	6	5	4	3	2	1
9	8	7	6	5	4	3	2	1	0
8	7	6	5	4	3	2	1	0	
7	6	5	4	3	2	1	0		
6	5	4	3	2	1	0			
5	4	3	2	1	0				
4	3	2	1	0					
3	2	1	0						
2	1	0							
1	0								
0									

Notes:
Goods ranked 10 are things on which life depends
Goods ranked 9-0 are less and less important

Exhibit 1.4 Menger Satisfaction Scale.

As shown in Exhibit 1.4, the higher ranked the goods are, the more the satisfaction felt by the owner. Goods ranked ten are things on which our life depends. Goods ranked from nine down to zero are less important – with zero being the least important – to the individual making the assessment. If Good I is food and Good V is entertainment, entertainment is desired only when the need for food has been satisfied, whereby future consumption would only register as a six on the importance scale. Trade occurs in this model when two parties exchange for items where they feel the item obtained is higher than for what the item was exchanged.

For our purposes, the salient points in this nascent theory of value subjectivity are that value is related to the person making the assessment, and that the value of a given object is not immutable and can change with circumstances and time. In our real estate example, a given property could be valued for its use until such time as this use is exceeded in value by another good, whereby exchange occurs.

1.3.2 Hayek and Mises: bridging the gap

Following Menger's contribution, both economists and psychologists have played a role in further developing the idea that individual market participant perception can change based on the accumulated experience and knowledge of the actor in question. The concept of perception in valuation casts a fairly wide net, with the most relevant branches for our purposes being from market psychology generally and for real estate valuation specifically. The concept of perception is understood to be a process of information assimilation or processing utilized by an individual to obtain insight into themselves and their environment. The processing of items relevant to the perception of value is influenced by subjectivity, selectivity, and activity. Subjectivity means that every person individually perceives their own environment, while selectivity and activity involve how people select and process those variables that they deem most crucial to the object being valued. Gestalt psychology is based on six principles that help people perceive the world around them: similarity, continuation, closure, proximity, figure/ground, and symmetry. The rules of perception that are most closely linked to real estate are the law of similarity, the law of figure/ground, and the law of proximity. These rules relate fairly well with the idea of using the most relevant properties in the market in order to compare to the subject property. The characteristics deemed most important for the determination of property value can be seen as a composite of brand, beauty, and utility. The brand is a function of the assessment of the appeal of the location, beauty encompasses the improvements to the building and the site, and utility concerns access proximity, the functionality of the property, and the opportunity for future returns.

Returning to the Austrian school of economics, economic titans Hayek and Mises have contributed to furthering the concept of perception as related to the subjectivity of value. Hayek specifically dealt with perception and the inter-workings of the human mind in *The Sensory Order*, while Mises explored the origins of subjectivity in his opus *Human Action*.

In *The Sensory Order*, Hayek coined the term "linkage" to describe the formation of new connections by the simultaneous occurrence of several afferent impulses. These connections create a lasting effect, which gives rise to memory and learning. He theorized that all experience and all memory are based on the creation of physiological events representing stimuli which shape the organization of the central nervous system. Memory is thus "stored", as with every experience some new mental entity presenting sensations or images enters the mind or the brain and is there retained until it is retrieved at the appropriate moment. Hayek's sensory order theory centered on the previous occurrence of linkages between different impulses, which are constantly being modified by new linkages. The connections formed by linkages between different impulses will reproduce certain regularities in the occurrence of the external stimuli acting on the individual. These connections create the gradual formation of a map relating to classes of events in the environment. As a result of its own operations, the map will continuously change its structure and alter the range of operations of which it is capable. The individual will, as a result of experience, acquire the capacity of performing entirely new actions. The actions of the mind will appear self-adaptive and purposive, and will be active in the sense that at any given moment the character of its operations will be the preexisting state of its internal processes as much as the external influences acting on it.

The concept of a sensory order "map" helped bridge the gap between the foundations of theoretical psychology and economic thought. Given the constant change, storage, and linkages of the individual mind, the correct anticipation of future events in the environment can rarely be based on a single event, but will instead have to take account of a combination of numerous present events. This will involve not only different responses to individual events but also different combinations of future events. Individual perception is thus always an interpretation, the placing of something into one or several classes of objects. All that we can perceive of external events is guided by how similar events have been classified based on past linkages. Every sensation (or thought) must be regarded as an interpretation of an event in light of the experience of the individual. The apparatus by which we learn about the external world is itself the product of experience which changes over time. It is shaped by conditions prevailing in the environment in which we live, consists of a reproduction of what we have experienced in the past, and is utilized to interpret any new event in light of that experience. Different external events may evoke one of several responses which will affect the "color of perception" and the responses to external events. All of this makes the prediction of the future problematic as the market should be seen as an aggregation of individuals with different experiences, risk tolerances, and preferences, rather than as a solitary and predictable whole. The subjectivity of value is pervasive given the extant differences among individuals themselves.

In Mises' *Human Action*, it was made clear that the ultimate goal of human action is always the satisfaction of the acting person's desire. While people appear as a being driven by various innate instincts and dispositions, every instinct is an instinct to happiness. While valuation is personal and subjective, "*inflamed with passion, man sees the goal as more desirable and the price he has to pay for it as less burdensome than he would in cool deliberation*". This helps explain how market participants can become so enamored with a specific tract of land, whereby they are willing to get into a price war to purchase the property or are unlikely to lower their price when considering offering the property for sale.

When an individual is contemplating an action in the marketplace, they must consider all that is going on in their body and mind along with factors present in the external environment. This includes market data and the actions of other market participants. Thus, Mises' *Human Action* described that both inheritance and environment help shape the actions of people. Each person has their own internal, subjective value scale in mind when they are arranging their priorities and actions. Similar to Menger, this value scale satisfies the more urgent (or highly valued) wants before less urgent wants and needs. The difference between the price paid and the goal attained is viewed as profit, while a loss is defined as when the value attained is less than what was originally desired. These value judgments are not immutable, such that as value changes, so do actions.

Regarding market prices, Mises theorized that all prices are historical, and that present prices reflect the assumption that the prices of the immediate future will not differ from those of the immediate past. The ultimate source of the determination of prices is the value judgments of market participants. The ratios of exchange, which are for real estate primarily monetary based, are determined on the basis of the narrow margins between the valuations of the marginal potential buyer and the seller who abstains from selling, and the marginal potential seller and the marginal potential buyer who abstains from buying. "Each individual, in buying or not buying and in selling or not selling, contributes their share to the formation of the market prices".

1.3.3 Radical subjectivism

These foundations were followed by the radical subjectivist school of Austrian economic thought. Subjectivism is a research program of the social sciences, which aims at elucidating social phenomena in terms of their inherent meaning to individual actors. In this context, even when different actors possess an identical knowledge about the same object, they will not necessarily make the same use of it, since knowledge exists for each actor within a different frame of reference. Thus, the past differs for each actor whereby different weights are applied when making value judgments. Additionally, different actors will hold divergent expectations about the same future events. Ludwig Lachmann, a leading advocate of the radical subjectivist approach, stated that "in a world of unexpected change, investment is necessarily governed by expectation, not past results". The past is important as it provides us with points of comparison that make our present problems intelligible to us. Lachmann believed that we are living in a "*kaleidic society interspersing its moments or intervals of order, assurance, and beauty with sudden disintegration*", which will then "*cascade into a new pattern*".

Given these divergent patterns, "*equilibrium analysis is hard to apply where the dependent variables of the system take a long time to respond to changes in data occurring frequently*". One could venture to assume that this view lends credence to the idea that the value of a given object can vary depending on who is doing the valuing.

These thoughts lead us directly to a primary point of this book, that is, the illustration of how subtle value judgments can sway the final valuation whereby a range of possible values could represent a given property. What remains is the inclusion of an Austrian economic model that helps explain this range in potential values.

1.4 Shackle's Possibility Curve: original model and modern context

The work of George Lennox Sharmin Shackle further contributed to our understanding of why human minds might differ on issues of valuation. Shackle, an English economist, spent considerable time in illustrating that the future is unknowable given the actions of other market participants, which may or may not resemble patterns of the past. Shackle conceived *"time to come as the void needing to be filled by work of imagination using suggested elements but not bound as to their arrangement"*. In other words, as we have heard on countless investment marketing campaigns, past performance is not necessarily indicative of future results. Shackle believed that any choice involves valuation and that *"we are prisoners of the present who must choose in the present on the basis of our present knowledge, judgments, and assessments"* (Shackle, 1979). The past is helpful for interpreting present decisions, but often there exists a knowledge gap given the presence of other actors and variables which remain outside the control of the decision maker. Shackle called this knowledge gap "un-knowledge" that *"liberates imagination which seizes and occupies the void of time to come"*. Enterprising individuals embrace "un-knowledge" whereby innovation is possible given a plurality of possible outcomes.

Thus, Shackle stated that the *"process of valuation is beyond the reach of analysis by any apparatus which the formal theoretician as such disposes of"*. This reminds me of the quote from J.K. Galbraith, certainly not an Austrian economist, *"the only function of financial forecasting is to make astrology look respectable"*. The Shackle Possibility Curve helps illustrate why this is the case.

Exhibit 1.5 depicts the situation facing anyone needing to make a choice for a given problem in the present. Let us assume for our purposes that G_N represents the initial neutral position for someone assessing the value of an asset. The entirety of the graph represents all of the possible choices that might exist for a given situation. The G axis represents "desiredness" such that the individual's prior experience is perfectly suited in making the present decision. In Shackle's terminology, no "un-knowledge" exists. Even in this perfect (and often unrealistic) situation, shocks may be present that might cause the near-term path which is entirely predictable by the recent past to veer off the course.

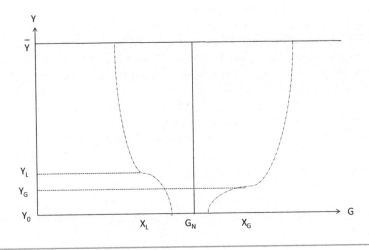

Exhibit 1.5 Shackle Possibility Curve.

As an example of this, assume you are contemplating two very different activities. On the one hand, there is a nice glass of cold beer sitting on the table in front of you that you wish to drink. On the other, you have been inspired to attempt figure skating jumps as you venture out onto the ice after watching some professionals on television. Drinking beer is certainly not new for me, so the variability in the result of my picking up the glass and placing it on my lips is very narrow indeed. On the other hand, I might be lucky enough to manage my first attempt at a toe loop, but when I then try the triple Lutz maneuver, the odds are that I would wind up square on my behind! Variability is more common as the experience level of the individual is further and further removed from the task at hand. Placing this in a real estate context, it would be the difference between owning a few rental homes and trying to transition to ownership of a 300-unit apartment complex. It's possible, but the experience just does not match the activity. This gap between the task at hand and the experience of the market participant is reviewed next.

The Y axis represents disbelief, such that the further up the Y axis you venture, the larger the gap is between the chooser's existing knowledge and the theoretical leap needed to reach a particular choice (that triple Lutz!). The wider this gap (or un-knowledge) is, the more there is for variability in choice and result. Y_0 represents perfect possibility in the judgment of the investor, or where the individuals feel that they have all the necessary information to make a rational choice, which sets the upper limit on the amount of un-knowledge that is seen as being too great for a pathway (or choice) to be selected. Thus, the variability in response to a given choice is dependent upon the gap between the decision maker's knowledge and the knowledge required to make an informed choice. Temporary shocks, or "news from the field" in Shackle's terminology, are positive (Y_G) or negative (Y_L) information which may sway the decision maker from the initial G_N position. For example, in the aftermath of the COVID-19 health and resultant economic crisis, investors were much more risk-averse when valuing retail properties than before the crisis, as there existed a lack of knowledge concerning which retail tenants could withstand the recession and which would in fact reopen after forced closure by the government. A positive shock could be the willingness to accept more risk given the desire to obtain a good return for the investor in an otherwise lackluster yield environment.

These shocks, when combined with the decision maker's existing knowledge base and their risk tolerance, help set points X_L and X_G on the graph above. These points help determine the boundaries of acceptability for the investor. This bound of acceptability reveals itself in the marketplace in the range of possible values for a given property. In Exhibit 1.5, the range of acceptable values appears to take the shape of a roll of toilet paper on the graph, such that a marketing slogan comes to mind: Don't squeeze the Sharmin (Shackle)!

A few years ago, I was invited to speak at a breakfast meeting for the local commercial real estate association. Since I teach real estate at Wake Forest, they allowed me to choose the topic for my presentation. Rather than going with the typical economic overview approach, I decided to unload the Shackle Possibility Curve on the unsuspecting breakfast crowd. The "news from the field" element of Shackle's model resonated with some of the participants. Astronomer Stephen Hawking's parallel universe theory was referenced in the following example. Assume that an inhabitant of universe A is going to evaluate a commercial retail property. On the way to the appointment, they hear the following news on the radio: "*retail vacancies are at an all-time high and retail lease rates are plummeting given the impact of ecommerce on an already dilapidated retail environment".* Another individual lives in universe B. As they are driving to see the very same property, they hear on the radio how *retail occupancy rates have soared recently as have market lease rates.* This new information may be incorporated into the interpretation of the market data collected as part of the valuation process. At the end of my presentation, about eight of the participants swarmed me like when the Beatles arrived in the U.S.A. for the first time. The other participants weren't as excited, but this helped with confirmation that I might have been onto something useful!

1.5 Investor choice example: land development

During this first chapter discussion, we have provided support to confirm that a range of possible values for real estate are possible given the different experience levels of market participants. The examples discussed so far have assumed that the use of the property in question was known at the time of valuation. In other words, a home was a home, and a retail property was a retail property. But what if the property in question only consisted of land and a dream?

See the tract of raw land as depicted in Exhibit 1.6. For years this tract of land has had a for sale sign on it, which in and of itself is not noteworthy. What is interesting is that the adjacent property consists of a psychic's office. There is a grocery store that I frequent weekly across the street, so for many years I saw the for sale sign for this property (not pictured) and wondered if the psychic could tell us what might become of the parcel of land next to her home office. While tempted, I did not call to find out as I was sure there would have been a fee involved. Recently, after years of advertising, news came that a paint supply store would

Exhibit 1.6 Land Development Dream Scene.

construct a property at this location. It makes one wonder how long the psychic knew of this new paint supply construction project.

More importantly for our inquiry, how did the eventual purchaser of the raw land come to decide on which type of tenant to attract? Maybe the paint supply store performed a market study and concluded that the visibility from the road (and from the psychic!) would be helpful in generating necessary customer foot traffic into the new store. In other words the paint supply store owners bought the land for the purposes of constructing the new location. Another possibility is that the owner of the land and the owner of the building are different. In that case, the land was purchased not simply to house an owner-occupied business but also for investment purposes.

Take another land development example. Let's assume that there is a busy road and that near the traffic signal a bank is located at one corner. Directly next to the bank is a parking lot for bank customers. Adjacent to that is a coffee shop and drug store multi-tenant retail property. Behind the bank parking lot sits a parcel of land listed for sale. The parcel of land is not particularly visible from the busy road and is entirely dependent on the bank parking lot for access. Said another way, should the eventual buyer decide to construct a building on site, an easement would be required which would allow customers to pass through the bank parking lot in order to access the new property.

In either land development example, if the land is considered by a buyer for its investment potential, a myriad of options exist. Let's assume that both land parcels are not large enough for an industrial property, and that zoning ordinances would more than likely prohibit construction of an industrial type property. What other possible uses exist? Given the dependence on the bank parking lot easement, it can be assumed that property use such as multifamily, hotel, and multi-tenant retail is probably not possible. The size of either site would appear likely to support a single-tenant structure, and a personal residence would also be ruled out owing to zoning rules. The two most likely candidates for tenancy would be retail and office.

1.5.1 Highest and best use

Now that we have narrowed down our possible uses to either single-tenant retail or office, the next question is which one would be considered the highest and best use. Suppose that as the swarming herd of commercial brokers approached you after your scintillating Shackle lecture, you asked them for some market data in order to help you along on your quest. The information that you obtained is shown in Exhibit 1.7.

	Office	Retail
Rentable Square Feet	10,000	8,000
Rent per Square Foot	$ 24.00	$ 30.00
Operating Expense Ratio	40%	50%
Avg. NOI Growth per Annum	3%	3%
Required Return	10%	10%
Total Construction Cost per Sq. Ft.	$ 200.00	$ 200.00

Exhibit 1.7 Highest and Best Use Market Data.

You decide that based on the size of the vacant lot, you can build an office building of 10,000 square feet or an 8,000-square-foot retail property. The difference in the size of the building is owing to wider ingress and egress access lanes for the retail location. The brokers were able to provide the market rent per square foot along with what a typical property would produce in terms of an operating expense ratio. You then inquired about average investor return expectations for these types of properties in your market and utilized that information. Assuming a constant level of inflation (i.e., the average NOI growth per annum), once you obtained a construction cost estimate per square foot, you were able to move to the second phase of your projection for the highest and best use of the proposed site.

Exhibit 1.8 illustrates the process of determining which of these site proposals makes the most economic sense. Both sites are projected to generate revenues of $240,000, but the difference in operating expenses leads the office property to come out of the gates quicker as it shows a higher estimated cash flow relative to the retail site proposal. This value surplus also translates to a higher value for the office property relative to the retail project, but since there is more to build in the office project (i.e., the building is larger), the resultant residual economic project is projected to be higher for the retail location than for the office site.

What would the physiocrats make of this situation? The office has a higher cost to build, but since the return is expected to be the same for either project, the retail location appears to generate a higher estimated profit than the office property. Maybe there is something to this "profit thing" after all!

Of course the devil is in the details when determining which site use makes the most economic sense. What if the cap rate estimate provided by the brokers was a bit low (perish the thought!)?

Exhibit 1.9 highlights that if the assumed cap rate is only 50 basis points higher, the office property is projected to lose money and the retail property only produces a break-even result. In fact, changing a good number of the assumptions in this example could produce a different result. This end-of-chapter example provides a hint for the direction we will take in this book. On the one hand, real estate valuation is subjective. On the other hand, given that subjectivity, the winners and losers in the market will best be determined by those who have the best market data and the best operating plan.

	Office	Retail
Rent	$ 240,000	$ 240,000
Expenses	$ 96,000	$ 120,000
Cash Flow	$ 144,000	$ 120,000
Cap Rate	7.00%	7.00%
Property Value	$ 2,057,143	$ 1,714,286
Cost	$ 2,000,000	$ 1,600,000
Residual	$ 57,143	$ 114,286

Exhibit 1.8 Highest and Best Use Profit Comparison.

	Office	Retail
Rent	$ 240,000	$ 240,000
Expenses	$ 96,000	$ 120,000
Cash Flow	$ 144,000	$ 120,000
Cap Rate	7.50%	7.50%
Property Value	$ 1,920,000	$ 1,600,000
Cost	$ 2,000,000	$ 1,600,000
Residual	$ (80,000)	$ -

Exhibit 1.9 Highest and Best Use Revised Estimates.

Questions for discussion

1. Describe the three forms of value. How does each methodology contain subjective elements?
2. Describe the Shackle Possibility Curve in your own words. How is this model helpful in describing why real estate values can differ depending on the market participant?
3. What are the components of the spectrum of valuation? Provide examples of two schools of thought at either end of the spectrum. Describe where you might see yourself on this spectrum.
4. Elaborate on the components of IRV. Describe how each term is dependent on the other two variables.
5. Provide other examples of the highest and best use methodology. In what situations other than real estate could this model also be employed?
6. Research the physiocrats on the internet. What other interesting ideas did they have?
7. Provide an example of a recent trade that you made (real estate or otherwise) using the Menger satisfaction scale framework.
8. Does either the Austrian or Keynesian schools claim Shackle as one of their own? Research and discuss.
9. As you drive around your home community, what are some good examples of real estate investment properties?
10. Describe when news from the field made you change your mind on a purchasing decision. How far did your final price change and for what reasons?

Chapter 1 Market vignette

Cast of characters: Archie (seller's appraiser), Betty (seller), Reggie (buyer's appraiser), Veronica (buyer), Radio announcer

   Act: Two distinct appraisal engagements for a multi-tenant retail property in Hasbrouck Heights, NJ

Scene one: seller appraisal engagement

BETTY: Hello Archie! I was hoping that you could help me with an appraisal for a property that I wish to sell. I have owned a three-tenant retail property on the Boulevard for the last ten years. It seems like a good time to sell, and I have an interested buyer, but we are not able to agree on the price. Before she goes to the bank for a loan, I thought it made sense for me to validate with you if my asking price was reasonable. I am hoping to sell the property for $2.2 million.

ARCHIE: Hi Betty! Thank you for contacting me directly. So you said that you have a three-tenant property on the market. Is it fully leased and at what rental and expense rates?

BETTY: Yes, it is a 10,000-square-foot property leased at $21 per square foot annually for each tenant. It is fully occupied, and operating expenses typically run about 30% of the effective gross income.

ARCHIE: That is very helpful. I just appraised a similar property last month, so I believe that I can provide you a value indication fairly quickly once I do a bit of research and visit the property.

BETTY: The prospective buyer thinks my rental rates are a bit high relative to the market and that my cap rate is a bit too low.

ARCHIE: Based on what you have told me the cap rate would need to be 6% to achieve the asking price that you desire. Please send me the specifics on the property, and I will be back in touch after I complete my analysis.

Archie and Betty part and agree to speak again in one week.

Scene two: buyer appraisal engagement

VERONICA: Hello Reggie, I have heard great things about you and would like for you to help me ascertain a value for a retail property in Hasbrouck Heights that I am interested in purchasing. You were referred to me by a close friend and you come highly recommended.

REGGIE: Hi Veronica, I would be happy to help you with this transaction. Can you share some specifics on the property?

VERONICA: This is a 10,000-square-foot, three-tenant retail property located on the Boulevard. The seller has fairly short-term leases signed at $21 per square foot annually, but my research indicates that the lease rates are closer to $20 per square foot today. Since I am new to this market and to retail properties generally, I am not questioning the seller's estimates for the market vacancy of 10%, or that of the operating expenses running at about 30% of effective gross income. From what I have seen, I think this property is a good buy at $1.8 million, which is currently $400,000 shy of the asking price.

REGGIE: Thank you for that information. Please send me what you have and I can take a look at the property and get back to you in the next few days.

VERONICA: That would be great Reggie. Before I go to the bank to ask for a loan, we really need to get this purchase price ironed out. I know the market very well and feel like this is the property for me.

Scene three: seller appraiser

Archie has reviewed the market and property information and heads to his car to visit the property.

RADIO ANNOUNCER: Turning to commercial real estate, property continues to escalate in value, as it's a great time to sell, especially in the retail sector. Occupancy rates are at all-time highs, and given the health of the economy, rental rates are on an upward trajectory.

ARCHIE: Hi Betty. I took a look at your property and the information that you sent. The market seems to echo your thoughts on market rental and cap rates and fits right into my analysis of getting to a property value of $2.2 million. This is a great part of the Boulevard and I can certainly see your point of view for this property.

BETTY: That is great news Archie. I look forward to the receipt of your final appraisal and will inform my prospective buyer that I will be keeping my asking price right where it is!

Scene four: buyer appraiser

Reggie has reviewed the market and property information and heads to his car to visit the property.

RADIO ANNOUNCER: In other news, the Central Bank announced today a new plan for economic stimulus and held firm on their pronouncement of keeping rates low long-term. E-commerce continues to takes its toll on retail properties, as existing product is beginning to stay longer on market in hopes of attracting buyers willing to pay current asking prices.

REGGIE: Hi Veronica. I took a look at your property and the information that you sent. The market seems to echo your thoughts on market rental and cap rates and fits right into my analysis of getting to a property value of $1.8 million. While the property is in good shape, the leases are short and it would seem that the market is starting to turn downward a bit and I don't want you to over pay for this property.

VERONICA: That is great news! I just knew that asking price seemed too high, so thank you for confirming it. I will stick to my guns at an offer price of $1.8 million and not a penny more!

Questions for discussion

1. Itemize some factors that might sway the appraisers in this case in their opinions of value?
2. Construct a direct capitalization model that shows how the seller and buyer came to their value conclusions.
3. Explain how this market vignette is the Shackle Possibility Curve in action.
4. What would you advise Betty and Veronica to do in this case?

5. How does this case illustrate the point that the lending institution should be ordering the final appraisal for this transaction as opposed to either the buyer or the seller?

Bibliography

Ajami, R. A. & Goddard, G. J. (2018) *Global Business: Competitiveness and Sustainability*. Routledge, London.

Cypher, M., Price, S. M., Robinson, S., & Seiler, M. J. (2017) Price Signals and Uncertainty in Commercial Real Estate Transactions. *The Journal of Real Estate Finance and Economics*, 57(2), 246–263. doi: 10.1007/s11146-017-9617-0

Felser, G. (1997) *Advertising and Consumer Psychology*. Springer Verlag: Stuttgart.

Goddard, G. J. (2014) Kierkegaard and Valuation in a Business Context. *Business and Economics Journal*, 5(2), 1–7.

Goddard G. J. & Marcum, B. (2012) *Real Estate Investment: A Value Based Approach*. Springer, Heidelberg.

Hayek, F. A. (2014) *The Sensory Order*. Martino Publishing, Mansfield Centre, CT.

Kebeck, G. (1994) *Perception: Theories, Methods, and Research Results of Perception Psychology*. Springer Verlag, Weinheim.

Kroeber-Riel, W. & Weinberg (1999) *Consumer Behavior*, 7th ed. Springer Verlag, Munich.

Lachmann, L. (1986) *The Market as an Economic Process*. Basil Blackwell Ltd., Oxford & New York.

La Voie, D. (1994) *Expectations and the Meaning of Institutions: Essays in Economics by Ludwig Lachmann*, edited by Don La Voie. Routledge, London.

Menger, C. (1971) *Principles of Economics*. English Translation of original German *Grundsatze der Volkswirthschaftslehre* (1871). New York University Press, New York and London.

Mises, L. (1949) *Human Action: A Treatise on Economics*. Yale University Press, New Haven, CT.

Mises, L. (2006) *The Ultimate Foundation of Economic Science*. Liberty Fund, Inc., Indianapolis, IN.

Papastamos, D., Matysiak, G., & Stevenson, S. (2018) A Comparative Analysis of the Accuracy and Uncertainty in Real Estate and Macroeconomic Forecasts. *The Journal of Real Estate Research; Sacramento*, 40(3), 309–345.

Roulac, S. E. (2007) Brand + Beauty + Utility = Property Value. *Property Management*, 22, 428–446.

Shackle, G. L. S. (1966) *The Nature of Economic Thought*. Cambridge University Press, London and New York, pp. 162–186.

Shackle, G. L. S. (1969) *Decision, Order and Time in Human Affairs*, 2nd ed., pp. 277–296. Cambridge University Press, London and New York.

Shackle, G. L. S. (1970) *Expectation, Enterprise, and Profit*. Aldine Publishing Co., Chicago, IL, pp. 122–169.

Shackle, G. L. S. (1979) *Imagination and the Nature of Choice*. Edinburgh University Press, Edinburgh.

Chapter 2

The role of machine learning and artificial intelligence in real estate valuation

Chapter highlights

- A brief history of the credit decision
- Existing models for assuming away variability in valuation
- Artificial intelligence in real estate property valuation
- Machine learning in real estate property valuation
- Algorithm subjectivity

> All the desperate efforts to reduce thinking and valuing to mechanical principles have failed
>
> Ludwig von Mises

2.1 A brief history of the credit decision

In Chapter 1, we introduced the concept that a real estate can consist of a range of values. We also introduced the Shackle Possibility Curve to describe a method for how value perceptions can be subtly changed by both the experience of the market participant and current news from the field. In this chapter, we expand our coverage to include the latest technological attempts at arriving at valuation (as well as commercial lending) decisions. Since we know that different market actors can arrive at divergent valuation conclusions, what does this forebode for the ability of machines to adequately imitate value conclusions via algorithms? Said another way, how does subjectivity and the experience of the model adapt to the reality of changing market values? Further questions to explore are if artificial intelligence

DOI: 10.4324/9781003083672-2

algorithms should be subjective, and is the goal to assume away the variability in valuation to arrive at one distinct "best fit" value valid?

Since the basis of Shackle's model for explaining the possible divergence in property values among different market participants is based on the human mind, it is helpful that we begin this chapter with a history of how commercial lenders have historically assessed individual commercial borrowers for lending opportunities. While lending is only one facet of property valuation (i.e., a buyer of a commercial property comes to a bank for a loan), it may shed light on the path that artificial intelligence has taken over the past few decades. For starters, before the advent of credit scoring algorithms, commercial lenders would utilize both objective and subjective factors when reviewing a new loan request. Objective factors would include review of relevant financial information, credit checks, and credit reports. Subjective factors would include personal interviews and in-person assessments of the prospective borrower's willingness to repay.

2.1.1 The five Cs of credit

One of the first lessons for any new commercial lender is the five Cs of credit. This has been around so long it is tough to tell where it originated, but generally the five Cs are seen as:

- Character
- Capacity
- Collateral
- Capital
- Conditions

When I was in commercial lending school, it was stressed that character (now sometimes referred to as credit history) was the most important of the five Cs of credit. The underlying philosophy was that since a foundation of the lender–borrower relationship is trust, if someone has poor character the other components of the five Cs just don't matter. A person of good character is more likely to repay their loans than one of poor character. While this is something easy to understand, very few people advertise their poor character, so the paradigm of character assessment is important. How character is defined depends on the individual predilections of the lender or of those that trained them. A lender would look for certain clues to the "true nature" of a borrower, which could consist of a multitude of things. On the one hand, it could be the kind of car that they drive or the company that they keep. On the other hand, character assessment could be based on more subtle clues like how they treat the bank staff when they come to the bank. You can see how things can quickly unravel here, as one person's sustainable lifestyle is another's red flag. Additionally, character can be utilized to exclude borrowers that you don't like, for reasons that can exhibit discriminatory biases. Some lenders would determine that borrowers located in certain areas of town were deemed unsuitable for loans simply because of their home address. This was called redlining, which allows us to envision a town map somewhere in the lending office, with red circles around prohibited areas. As time went on, credit reports became an important facet of character assessment, as these reports provide documented proof of a prospective borrower's loan repayment ability.

Another element of the five Cs is capacity. Here is where the more objective elements of character, such as the credit report, are utilized along with a borrower's employment and income history. The basic idea here is that having good character is a good first step, but does this borrower have the ability to repay their debts when annual income is compared with annual debt service and other living expense obligations?

A third element of the five Cs is collateral. From a real estate perspective, a lender will require a certain minimum amount of equity going into the purchase of the property. Depending on the type of property, the loan to value percentage can range between 50% to upwards of 80%. In the latter case, the borrower would have to pony up 20% of the purchase price in order to fulfill the bank's prescribed loan to value requirements.

A fourth component of the five Cs of credit is capital. If we view capacity as the primary source of repayment for a loan (i.e., residual income), capital represents a secondary source of repayment as if the income level of a given borrower drops, then their next move might be to liquidate savings and other investments to pay their debt obligations. One of the fun terms that I remember from my early days in lending was a "deep pockets" borrower. This fortunate individual had a more than adequate level of savings and investments, which is certainly a plus from a lending perspective. If this is the only characteristic considered, a lender might find themselves in trouble if a borrower proves to have short arms. In other words, their deep pockets might be lined with silver and gold, but when the going gets tough the individual just can't seem to find a way to plunder their nest egg to repay the loan!

A final element of the five Cs is conditions. This final category consists of a litany of items ranging from the economic condition at the time the loan was made, to the conditions placed on the borrower in terms of the usage of the loan proceeds, to the financial covenants that the lender requires during the loan term, and to the other conditions as further elaborated in the loan documentation. The primary areas of concern in loan documentation are the evidence of a debt between the borrower and the lender (i.e., a "note"), the evidence of security of an asset to the indebtedness (i.e., the mortgage or deed of trust in real estate), and the evidence of a personal endorsement of the principals of a corporate borrower with accompanying provisions (i.e., the guarantee agreement).

2.1.2 Early examples of credit scoring algorithms

The point of discussing the five Cs of credit is to highlight exactly the variables that an algorithm would be attempting to reproduce. Some of the areas of concern are objective and more easily reproduced, while others are more subjective and require more thought. As the financial services industry has progressed through time, credit scoring algorithms have become more complex in an attempt to become all-encompassing.

My first commercial lending experience consisted of business credit cards. The application process consisted of a customer obtaining an application in a branch and mailing it in to the office where I worked. The application itself was the size of an index card if you take out the marketing materials and instructions on where to mail it. The only information that was required was for the customer to disclose the following things: annual income, total liquidity, total assets, and total net worth. The customer was instructed to sign on the dotted line and submit the application.

Once the application was received, a personal and a business credit report were obtained. This helped check the "character" box based on the historical repayment record. Then basic calculations were made regarding debt to income ratio to ensure that the capacity and capital were considered as the lender determined how large of a credit line the company might obtain.

As you can imagine, there was quite a bit of room for error in terms of the accuracy of the information disclosed on the application. For example, one customer owned a liquor store and claimed that the total assets equaled their total liquidity. I believe that this applicant was confusing the drinkable liquidity sold in the store with the monetary versions of liquidity. In another example of how early credit scoring algorithms go awry, we had one particular individual who could never quite fill out the entire form. This was surprising given the brevity of the application. In fact, this one particular individual flooded our offices with incomplete applications. It became a running joke in the office how many incomplete applications this one person would submit on a given week. There was no indication of where the application originated. To confound matters, the applicant would often scroll "don't work get check" in the area where the financial disclosure was to occur. After a few months of compiling quite a list of incomplete applications, this individual finally signed on the dotted line, allowing us to pull the personal credit report. Interestingly, this applicant's listed employer on the credit bureau was "don't work get check", and they had a litany of credit cards from multiple issuers. None of them were utilized, but this individual appeared to have a credit card from each major bank. Since I now had the applicant's address, I called the branch nearest to their home and spoke with one of the personal bankers. This individual was known to them, and they were instructed to provide counsel to this person the next time they came into the branch. About a week later, I received a phone call informing me that the credit counseling session had occurred and that all that this individual was looking for was a personal debit card! After this card was received, we never had another application from this individual. This first example contained more of a manual process, with the only real algorithm present being the one which determined the credit score on the credit reports.

Another early credit scoring algorithm was related to my time in small business lending at the start of my banking career. This particular algorithm was built into a credit underwriting tool for small business loan requests. The main objective was to provide a timely indicator of customer loan requests which would not be approved, so the lending department could focus on the rest of the loan request population. The attempt at providing an artificial intelligence approach to the five Cs of credit was apparent. The key ingredients which produced a higher score were known to the credit approver. The first large part of the model was the personal and business credit reports which addressed the character component of our five Cs model. Should any of the credit reports obtained in the evaluation of the credit request contain past due payments, tax liens, bankruptcies, or slow paying trade history, the model would return a final overall application score lower than the minimum where the system would recommend approval. Other criterion in the small business credit algorithm included the industry code for the borrower, the length of time in business, and basic credit metrics such as the debt coverage ratio (i.e., capacity), loan to value (i.e., collateral), and business and guarantor liquidity (i.e., capital). The characteristic conditions were determined by the lender as a result of the analysis of the other four elements just described. Depending upon the overall strength of the borrower, the lender would add financial covenants to the final loan offering.

While this is an example of an elementary algorithm, the idea of subjectivity returns quite prominently. Say for example that you were a small business lender in this credit department, and you were consistently seeing overall application scores below the acceptable minimum but you felt that the customer loan requests should be approved. This actually happened to me when I was placed in the agricultural small loan area. Recalling Shackle's discussion about experience being the key to variability reduction, I always thought that putting a kid from Northern New Jersey in the agriculture lending department was a stretch, but what I continued to notice was that small farmers returned scores less than the desired minimum, and that the low scores were not owing to poor repayment history. What is a lender to do when these small requests continued to be recommended for rejection by the algorithm, but these same customers had been paying their debts annually for about as long as I had been alive at that point? My answer was to approve them. It appeared that the model had a small flaw in that personal credit reports showed the required loan payments for farmers on an annual basis (as is typical in the industry), but the model was annualizing those stated payments, causing their debt coverage ratios to sink way below the break-even point. My non-conformity to the model got the attention of management, and I was called in late on a Friday evening to discuss my large percentage of decisions that reversed the algorithm's suggested declines. I was told to embrace the system and to not make so many decisions contrary to the logic of the model. What I embraced was the door, as I left for the commercial real estate division soon thereafter.

What these short examples help illustrate is that models are only as good as the rules that are programmed into the system, which reinforces the Mises quote that begins this chapter. This early model tracked things that didn't necessary impact the final score. For example, the borrower's industry code was required such that loan repayment performance by industry could be evaluated over time, with the eventual result being that borrowers from certain industries would be penalized for the substandard loan repayment record of their industry as a whole. You might object and say that why would one specific credit underwriting department's loan repayment record matter from a statistical standpoint. Keep in mind that even today there are large third-party vendors who sell basic algorithm models to multiple banks of different sizes and allow some level of customization. But the industry-specific performance data are aggregated for all participating financial institutions. Thus, over time, the model improves on itself and picks up new data points to track and eventually to add to the scoring mechanism of the algorithm.

2.2 Existing models for assuming away variability in valuation

Before we discuss examples of subjectivity in real estate valuation, it is helpful to review some of the existing models that serve to assume away variability. As mentioned in Chapter 1, I do not have any particular problem with these models, but for our purposes they serve as a means to remove the variability in real estate valuation which is present naturally in the market. One of these models consists of a statistical line of reasoning which helps remove variability, while another focuses on software utilized by real estate appraisers and third-party data providers to achieve the same result: the solitary value for a subject property.

Since the future is uncertain, investors contemplating the purchase of commercial real estate will often complete numerous projections of what the future cash flows from a property will be. This is generally called "sensitivity analysis" where key variables in a property's projected income and expense performance can be altered to reflect different future scenarios. An investor might have a property with very short tenant leases whereby the future renewal probability for all of the tenants is cloudy. On the other hand, the investor might be contemplating the purchase of a property where a low percentage of the tenants have expiring leases in the following year or so. Let's take a look at a specific example.

2.2.1 Statistical modeling and variability

Ludwigshafen, LLC is considering the purchase of a multifamily property for $1.5 million. Given the uncertainty in the economy and general tenant lease rollover risk, the owners have projected three possible scenarios for the project as follows:

Pessimistic – Equity cash flow to the investor will be $150,000 in the first year, and will decrease by 2% each year over the five-year holding period. The property would be sold at the end of five years for $1.4 million.

Most likely – Equity cash flow will be $150,000 in the first year, and will remain level over the five-year holding period. The property would be sold at the end of five years for $1.6 million.

Optimistic – Equity cash flow will be $150,000 in the first year, and will increase by 3% each year over the five-year holding period. The property would be sold at the end of five years for $1.9 million.

The investors believe that there is about a 30% probability for the pessimistic scenario, a 40% probability for the most likely scenario, and a 30% probability for the optimistic scenario.

A   Compute the internal rate of return (IRR) for each scenario.
B   Compute the expected IRR and property value after five years.
C   Compute the variance and standard deviation of the IRRs.

So let's tackle part A. The internal rate of return (IRR) utilizes equity cash flows for each year under each predicted scenario. When the projected annual cash flows from operations (net operating income [NOI] for the property minus annual debt service) and reversion (projected sales price of the property minus selling costs and outstanding mortgage balance at the time of projected sale) are taken into account, the pessimistic scenario returns an IRR of 8.51% as shown in Exhibit 2.1.

The investor will project out their most likely scenario as is shown in Exhibit 2.2.

In the most likely scenario, the equity cash flow projected for the first year is expected to continue for the next five years, and the projected sales equity cash flow from the reversion is expected to be $200,000 higher than in the pessimistic scenario. The result is a projected IRR of 11.07%.

Pessimistic Scenario						
Year	0	1	2	3	4	5
Equity CF	(1,500,000)	150,000	147,000	144,060	141,179	138,355
Resale						1,400,000
Total	(1,500,000)	150,000	147,000	144,060	141,179	1,538,355
IRR	8.51%					

Exhibit 2.1 Internal Rate of Return for Pessimistic Scenario.

Most Likely Scenario						
Year	0	1	2	3	4	5
Equity CF	(1,500,000)	150,000	150,000	150,000	150,000	150,000
Resale						1,600,000
Total	(1,500,000)	150,000	150,000	150,000	150,000	1,750,000
IRR	11.07%					

Exhibit 2.2 Internal Rate of Return for the Most Likely Scenario.

Optimistic Scenario						
Year	0	1	2	3	4	5
Equity CF	(1,500,000)	150,000	154,500	159,135	163,909	168,826
Resale						1,900,000
Total	(1,500,000)	150,000	154,500	159,135	163,909	2,068,826
IRR	14.53%					

Exhibit 2.3 Internal Rate of Return for Optimistic Scenario.

In a third investor projection, the investor is feeling very optimistic about the future performance on this property. The resultant IRR is shown in Exhibit 2.3. In this model, year one equity cash flow is expected to increase each year and the reversion is expected to be $300,000 higher than in the most likely case.

The resultant IRR is 14.53% for this most optimistic view of the future. OK great, so now what? We have three different projections of varying degrees of future success. The investor could literally make hundreds of such predictions, offering slight tweaks to various assumptions. For the sake of this discussion, let's assume that three such projections are deemed sufficient for this property given the quality, quantity, and durability of the property's income stream.

Part B provides the next step, as the expected IRR and property value are calculated as shown in Exhibit 2.4.

When the projected internal rate of return for each scenario is multiplied by the investor's perception of the probability that each outcome will occur in the future, the expected IRR is calculated. For our example, this came out to 11.34%. This is basically a weighted average of the three projected outcomes. If we utilize the same probabilities for each scenario multiplied by the expected sales price at the end of five years, the resultant expected property value is $1,630,000. For part C of our problem, we then utilize statistics to craft what an investor might expect in the

	IRR	Prob	IRR x Prob	Value	Value x Prob
	8.51%	30%	2.55%	$ 1,400,000	$ 420,000
	11.07%	40%	4.43%	$ 1,600,000	$ 640,000
	14.53%	30%	4.36%	$ 1,900,000	$ 570,000
	Total	100%	11.34%		$ 1,630,000

Exhibit 2.4 Expected IRR and Property Value.

	Estimated IRR	Expected Return	Deviation	Squared Deviation	Probability Probability	Product
Pessimistic	8.51	11.34	-2.83	8.01	30%	2.40
Most Likely	11.07	11.34	-0.27	0.07	40%	0.03
Optimistic	14.53	11.34	3.19	10.18	30%	3.05
					Variance	5.48
Range of					Std. Dev	2.34
Expected Returns		9.00%	11.34$	13.68%		

Exhibit 2.5 Variance and Standard Deviation of Property Performance.

future in terms of a range of possible returns when assuming a normal statistical distribution.

As shown in Exhibit 2.5, each possible IRR outcome is compared with the expected return to determine each projection's deviation from the expected outcome. When this deviation is squared and then multiplied by the investor's original probability for each possible outcome, the product of the three scenarios is known as the variance (in our example 5.48). From an investor standpoint, the variance from the expected IRR has value in that the larger the variance the more risky is the underlying property.

The square root of the variance is the standard deviation (in our example 2.34). This standard deviation is then added to and subtracted from the expected return in order to achieve the range of expected returns, from 9.00% to 13.68%. Assuming a normal distribution, statistical theory assumes that one standard deviation will on average provide 68% certainty that the actual result will lie somewhere in the range. The probability of accuracy increases to 95%, with three standard deviations increasing the probability that the result will be in the range of up to 99.7%. Of course, the higher your probability of success, the wider the ratio becomes. For our example, assuming three standard deviations from the mean, the low end of the range of expected returns becomes 4.32%, while the upper end of the range becomes 18.36%.

If we utilize the paradigm in Exhibit 2.5 in order to create a range of property values, you wind up with something that looks like Exhibit 2.6.

Since we are dealing with whole numbers, the variance figures look quite large here, but the effect is the same. Once the standard deviation is calculated at $197,484, that figure can be added to and subtracted from the most likely case property value at the end of five years of $1,600,000, to achieve a range of values.

	Estimated Value	Expected Return	Deviation	Squared Deviation	Probability Probability	Product
Pessimistic	1,400,000	1,600,000	(200,000)	40,000,000,000	30%	12,000,000,000
Most Likely	1,600,000	1,600,000	-	-	40%	-
Optimistic	1,900,000	1,600,000	300,000	90,000,000,000	30%	27,000,000,000
					Variance	39,000,000,000
					Std. Dev	197,484
Range of Expected Values		$1,402,516	$1,600,000	$1,797,484		

Exhibit 2.6 Variance and Standard Deviation of Property Value.

At the low end, one standard deviation leads to a lower bound value of $1,400,000, while the upper bound limit is just under $1,800,000. It seems like the optimistic scenario property value estimate of $1.9MM was appropriately named!

The preceding example is illustrative on two fronts. Firstly, it clearly shows how a statistical method assumes away the importance of valuation differences in commercial real estate. Secondly, it helps to confirm that from an investor (i.e., market participant) standpoint, different valuations are possible, otherwise why would they bother with numerous projections with the eventual goal of a range of values of an expected IRR and property values?

2.2.2 Income approach and variability

Before we discuss the various progresses within the real estate industry regarding machine learning and artificial intelligence, I wanted to provide another example of how existing valuation models help to assume away the variability in value. In Chapter 1, we discussed the three forms of value for real estate (namely the sales or market approach, the cost approach, and the income approach). Focusing on the income approach, there are two primary models utilized in the industry: the direct capitalization model and the discounted cash flow model. Rather than focusing on specific types of software, I will address each of these models generally. One thing that I have learned in my career is to not get too dependent on any valuation model because in this regard the only constant is change.

2.2.2.1 Direct capitalization model

The direct capitalization model estimates the gross potential income for a given property, with the primary point of obtaining the NOI for a given period (typically a year). The NOI is then divided by a capitalization rate to obtain an estimate of value. Exhibit 2.6 provides a snapshot for how the layout of this version of the income approach is typically provided.

In our example, we have a four-tenant property which, when fully leased, produces a gross potential income of $200,125. The tenant spaces are of similar sizes, with an average annual rental rate of $10.53 per square foot. The first area of possible subjectivity in this example would occur if one of the spaces were vacant, or if it was known that one of the tenants would soon vacate the property. Typically an appraiser of commercial real estate would stabilize the income stream, in other words would include possible rents for all leasable areas. The question would arise if a market rate should be used or possibly an average of the existing leases already in place. Typically a comparison between the targeted rental rate and the rate for similar space in the property (i.e., comparable space) is made whereby a decision is made on what lease rate to utilize for the direct capitalization projection. If we assume that the last tenant is expected to vacate, Exhibit 2.7 clearly illustrates that this is the highest rental rate for the subject property. Either the existing tenants are paying under market lease rates, or there is something utterly compelling about the fourth space in the subject property, or the appraiser is optimistic. Either way, to emphasize for our purposes in this chapter, a decision must be made, which thereby results in one final value being concluded.

When the NOI of $100,704 is divided by the market capitalization rate of 8.50%, the subject property is valued at $1,180,000 (value is rounded to the nearest $10,000). Should a different number be chosen for any part of the direct capitalization model, then a different final value conclusion could result. Sometimes a small change might not impact the value much. For example, should the tenant four's annual lease rate fall to $11.00, the final value would drop to only $1,150,000.

Some changes can have more material impacts on the final value. Exhibit 2.8 illustrates the impact on the final value conclusion when changing only a few of the assumptions in the direct capitalization model.

While our initial assumptions included a vacancy factor of 10%, and a cap rate of 8.50%, if these two assumptions were tweaked slightly the resultant final value could be anywhere from 5% higher than our original estimate or almost 16% lower. The vacancy rate assumption could vary for numerous reasons: the property currently has a higher or lower vacancy rate as relative to market, the property has a high or low near-term lease rollover risk for the existing tenants, or the location

	Rent psf	Sq Ft	Annual	
Tenant 1	$ 10.00	5,000	$ 50,000	
Tenant 2	$ 10.50	4,500	$ 47,250	
Tenant 3	$ 10.00	5,000	$ 50,000	
Tenant 4	$ 11.75	4,500	$ 52,875	
Total GPI	**$ 10.53**	**19,000**	**$ 200,125**	
Vacancy			$ 20,013	10.00%
Effective Gross Income			**$ 180,113**	
Operating Expenses:				
Taxes			$ 25,000	
Insurance			$ 8,900	
Repairs & Maintenance			$ 12,000	
Utilities			$ 15,000	
Management			$ 9,006	5.00%
Other			$ 5,000	
Replacement Reserves			$ 4,503	2.50%
Total Operating Expenses			**$ 79,408**	
Net Operating Income			**$ 100,704**	
Cap Rate			8.50%	
Estimated Value			**1,180,000**	

Exhibit 2.7 Direct Capitalization Model.

Valuation Subjectivity			
Vacancy %	Cap Rate	Value	% Δ
10.00%	8.50%	$ 1,180,000	0.00%
10.00%	8.00%	$ 1,260,000	-6.35%
5.00%	8.50%	$ 1,290,000	-8.53%
5.00%	9.00%	$ 1,220,000	-3.28%
10.00%	9.00%	$ 1,120,000	5.36%
0.00%	8.50%	$ 1,400,000	-15.71%

Exhibit 2.8 Direct Cap and Valuation Subjectivity.

could necessitate a different vacancy rate when compared with the most similar properties on the market. The cap rate could vary depending on the derivation method utilized by the appraiser. While I have dealt with the varying cap rate derivation models in my first real estate book, we will discuss cap rate issues in detail later in this book.

2.2.2.2 Discounted cash flow model

The second income approach model that we will discuss in this section is the discounted cash flow. Unlike the direct capitalization approach which is concerned with only one operating year, the discounted cash flow is a multiple period projection of income, expenses, and NOI with the goal to arrive at a solitary value conclusion. While this sounds great, most models only vary key assumptions after the first-year NOI is estimated in a method similar to the direct capitalization model.

Let's continue with our same subject property, but this time let's expand our information set. Half of the tenants have two years remaining on their leases, while the other two tenants have three and four years left. Shown another way, see Exhibit 2.9 which outlines the tenant lease rollover risk for the subject property.

Since half of the existing leases have the potential to mature and not be renewed in the second year, a "worst case scenario" is that half of the property becomes vacant and that there is a significant period of time between when the vacancy occurs and when a replacement tenant moves in. Most discounted cash flow (DCF) models require that an estimate for vacancy be made for each year, in other words a solitary selection is required. As noted in our statistical variability example, some investors opt to run numerous scenarios in order to achieve a breadth of possibilities in terms of NOI and final valuation.

Exhibit 2.10 itemizes some key assumptions in the DCF model in terms of the holding period and loan terms.

What is particularly interesting for our discussion on model variability is that the typical assumption is that growth factors for revenues and operating expenses do not change annually but grow at a constant rate. The more the DCF is utilized in a static growth model, the more likely the direct capitalization model is in terms of the chosen valuation model. Exhibit 2.11 shows the result of the DCF valuation model.

We will cover some of the calculations in the DCF in subsequent chapters, but what is important now is that assuming a discount rate of 9.00% annually, the DCF model has estimated the property value at $1,290,000 when assuming the vacancy

Rollover Risk over Holding Period	
Year 1	0%
Year 2	50%
Year 3	26%
Year 4	24%
Year 5	0%

Exhibit 2.9 Lease Rollover Risk.

Holding Period Assumptions		
GPI Growth		3.00%
Op Ex Growth		3.00%
Op Ex % of EGI		35.00%
TI Cost New	$	5.00
TI Cost Renew	$	2.00
LC Cost New		6.00%
LC Cost Renew		2.00%
Avg. Lease Term (yrs)		5
Loan Terms		
Interest Rate		6.00%
Loan Amount	$	750,000
Amortization (yrs)		20
Selling Price	$	1,300,000

Exhibit 2.10 DCF Assumptions.

Period	0	1	2	3	4	5	6
GPI		$ 200,125	$ 206,129	$ 212,313	$ 218,682	$ 225,242	$ 232,000
Vacancy		$ -	$ 103,064	$ 55,872	$ 51,793	$ -	23,200
EGI		200,125	103,064	156,441	166,889	225,242	$ 208,800
Op Ex		70,044	$ 72,145	$ 74,309	$ 76,539	$ 78,835	$ 81,200
TI		-	35,275	19,123	17,727	-	
LC		-	23,189	12,571	11,653	-	
NOI		130,081	(27,545)	50,438	60,970	146,408	127,600
ADS		64,479	64,479	64,479	64,479	64,479	
Reversion							$1,563,098
Equity CF	$ (550,000)	65,602	(92,024)	(14,041)	(3,509)	1,008,280	
Property Value	$ 1,290,000.00						

Exhibit 2.11 Discounted Cash Flow Valuation Model.

factor is equal to the lease rollover risk each year. As shown in Exhibit 2.12, the reversion (or final sales price) is estimated by taking the NOI for year six and dividing by a cap rate of 8.00%, and then deducting for an assumed selling cost of 2% of the sales price.

So the final value is $110,000 higher under the DCF approach than under the direct cap model. By Jove, I believe we have a situation where valuations can be different by the same actor when using different approaches to value! If you return

Reversion Assumptions		
Terminal Cap		8%
Reversion	$	1,594,998
Sales Costs	$	31,900
OB Balance	$	636,747
Equity CF$_5$	$	926,351
Selling Cost		2%

Exhibit 2.12 **Reversion Assumptions.**

quickly to Exhibit 2.11, you will notice that the equity cash flows, under the worst-case scenario depicted (as vacancy is equal to the stated lease rollover risk each year), turn negative in years two through four. Equity cash flow here is defined as the NOI after annual debt service (ADS) is subtracted. The reversionary cash flow is summarized in Exhibit 2.12, and the projected sales price at the end of the fifth year, minus selling costs and the outstanding mortgage balance at the time of sale.

Even the IRR calculation is debatable in this example, as when calculated based solely on the results in the equity cash flow line in Exhibit 2.11, the result is 11.80%, but when a modified IRR is utilized, the result can vary. The modified IRR does not assume that all equity cash flows are reinvested at the calculated IRR of 11.80%. Instead, a finance rate (of say 5.00%) and a reinvestment rate (say of 3.00%) are assumed, with the resulting modified internal rate of return (MIRR) becoming 10.78%.

In the final analysis, an investor or an appraiser will decide on the assumptions which best fit the present scenario and will settle on an offer price. Of course, finding a suitable buyer who agrees with that price will often take time given the sea of other valuation possibilities which may transpire, many of which are defensible by the logic of mathematics and things that Shackle would chalk up to the experience of the market participant.

With all of this possible variability, is there any question why creating an algorithm that will produce the best result has proven difficult to perfect? Later in this chapter, we will discuss whether the purpose of an algorithm should be to incorporate subjectivity, but for now, we will turn to the latest progress in the real estate industry regarding the use of artificial intelligence and machine learning.

2.3 Artificial intelligence in real estate property valuation

The prior discussion on statistical analysis is important as much of the current research interest in utilizing artificial intelligence and machine learning in real estate valuation has focused on creating algorithms that explain the changes in price for properties over time in a given market. Some studies focus on the amenities and the location considerations for a given property relative to others, while other studies attempt to include econometric variables which may also influence property values. While some smaller studies in the literature have achieved a level of success in predictability, no published real estate artificial intelligence or machine learning studies have claimed to have reached the stage where the results and methods of a given study were deemed suitable for all property types in all markets. Some proprietary models exist, but the level of transparency into how these algorithms function is low. Additionally, much of the current literature exhibits a tendency to utilize artificial intelligence and machine learning to arrive at a more robust version of the sales approach to property valuation. Please refer to the bibliography at the end of this chapter for a comprehensive list of sources utilized in this chapter.

2.3.1 Artificial intelligence in residential property valuation

Artificial intelligence in residential property has focused on improving the amenities in a given property as well as increasing the connectedness of properties to smart phones and other electronic devices. An additional avenue of growth of artificial intelligence in residential property has to do with improving the marketing efforts for both sellers and lessors of residential property.

From a property amenities standpoint, artificial intelligence is focused on connecting the homeowner or renter with the internet and smart phone capabilities. In some research examples, wearable technologies were utilized for real-time interface to manage the heating and air conditioning environment of the property. This capability also enhances the ability to track scheduled equipment maintenance for items at home. Additionally, software packages enable the sharing of information about maintenance, security, lease and tenancy, contracts, and work orders among key stakeholders.

Artificial intelligence technology also aids the marketing efforts of property owners and managers. Virtual and augmented realities have enabled things like virtual home tours, walkthroughs, and showrooms, which allow for purchasing and leasing decision time-savings, more targeted marketing for buyers and tenants, and has opened the door to global investors. Drones have been increasingly utilized to create aerial imagery which can provide more information for potential buyers, whereby they can view an entire property and the surrounding neighborhood without physically visiting the property. Property managers increasingly utilize robotics for 3-D renderings of interior spaces, collection of waste materials, and recycling. Artificial intelligence can also help property agents with applicant screening and help investors find more compelling properties for purchase. While nothing can replace a physical site inspection, these technologies allow an investor to determine a short list of properties for purchase and then do a closer inspection of the final properties before making the final purchasing decision.

Finally, when discussing the advances in artificial intelligence in residential properties, there are some standout examples of success. Companies such as Airbnb, Zillow, and WeWork are examples of user-centered, sustainable, and innovative technologies for managing real estate resources efficiently, as key property information is made available to real estate consumers, managers, and agents. Such advances have been termed "smart real estate" whereby digital platforms have opened up sources of revenues to countless homeowners who wish to rent out their properties for profit. While this is not specifically focused on property valuation, the information that is obtained can serve as market information for owners for things like market rental rates, vacancy rates, and other factors which heretofore have been captured in third-party investor reports where a time lag exists between when the information was current and when the report was issued for public consumption.

2.3.2 Artificial intelligence in commercial property valuation

Artificial intelligence in commercial property valuation achieves a similar result to residential property in terms of amenities, monitoring, and control. In addition, big data are utilized in order to provide quicker and more complete market information than was previously available. Third-party data companies like CoStar and REIS have historically provided useful market intelligence primarily focused on major metropolitan markets and on the historical "four food groups" of investment property (multifamily, office, retail, and industrial). Some of the third-party data providers also provide market rental, expense, vacancy, and cap rate information for sub-markets within an existing city. Big data take it to the next level with the generation of safety, transit, and walking scores that aid market participants in understanding the more subjective micro-factors of the property's location.

In terms of property construction, artificial intelligence can allow real estate developers to coordinate multisite projects at the same time. The 3-D scanners can be utilized to produce as-built renderings of the property which can be revised more easily. These scanners can also make the restoration of older properties easier given the ability to quickly adapt the renderings.

Similar to the robo-advisor concept in wealth management, artificial intelligence aggregates property-specific data (i.e., energy consumption, market performance, rent and occupancy rates, space utilization) in combination with key economic indicators. By monitoring the geographic trends in the subject property's geographic area, a property owner or manager has the ability to make real-time changes in property rents (if the lease tenor allows) or reduce the vacancy periods given the current market intelligence.

Not only does real estate technology help the property owner, property manager, and property buyer, but it also has made progress in how real estate loans are funded. Crowdfunding platforms allow an aggregation of funds to come in from a multitude of sources for a specific project. Say, for example, that there is a need for a renovation of a small hotel property in a downtown of a rural community. It is entirely possible that this project would not be funded by a local bank, and in lieu of numerous banks agreeing to fund the project together, crowdfunding could be utilized where investors can contribute to the loan funding and receive interest payments or even a partial ownership share of the net profits.

What should be clear from this section is that there are a myriad uses of artificial intelligence in real estate. While none of the uses offer direct valuation support, they do aid market participants in the aggregation of data which can be used as part of property valuation. A property valuation is only as good as the assumptions which led to the value conclusion, and artificial intelligence provides a needed increase in the timeliness of information which is utilized in making valuation conclusions.

2.4 Machine learning and valuation metrics

While artificial intelligence has not made many inroads in directly influencing real estate property valuation, machine learning has had more success. A review of the current literature reveals algorithms for real estate taxation, land valuation, and even for estimating the usable area of residential buildings. For the most part, however, much of the algorithms appear focused on providing an assumed, more robust version of the sales approach to value.

Some of the articles surveyed on machine learning in real estate offered a blended approach with methods more suited to artificial intelligence. In one study, an algorithm was utilized to assess "news-based sentiment analysis" where an algorithm was created to assess the headlines in commercial real estate articles in order to determine the time lag between when the market actually dropped versus when the headlines turned negative. This article did pique my interest given Shackle's "news from the field" idea that we discussed in Chapter 1. It reminds me of when I taught a class in Germany at the depths of the "great recession". As an introduction to the concept of mortgage securitization, I asked the class to search the internet and provide me with adjectives that were used in articles to describe the various mortgage securitization products. As you can imagine during that time, the descriptors were not too friendly! In the study in question, the authors found a link between the positivity or negativity of commercial real estate headlines and the future movement of the real estate market. The securitization market tended to move more quickly than the direct market, which adds fuel to the fire regarding the subjectivity of mortgage securitization products, which will be discussed in Chapter 9.

Other machine learning algorithms noted in recent published literature include attempts to identify houses listed below the market price, predictions concerning the number of days a published listing will remain online based on how the listed price compares to similar properties, and the prediction of housing list prices prior to listing for sale as well as for real estate auction prices. Some studies combined econometric variables with published real estate data in order to interpret the existing relationship between real estate rental prices and the geographic location of the properties. Other studies focused on how machine learning can be utilized to improve the sensitivity analysis for mass appraisals of real estate. What these models have in common is a focus on the sales approach which combines econometric data with the goal of a more robust version of the sales approach to value.

One machine learning model of note is the Fischer-DiPasquale-Wheaton real estate model. This is a diagrammatic quadrant real estate model which links the space market to the capital market. The four quadrants are typically the market for space, asset valuation, the construction sector, and stock adjustments. The model traces the relationship between the real estate market and asset market variables, as well as the adjustments that take place to establish equilibrium in the supply of and demand for real estate. The primary goal is to determine market equilibrium. The problem with equilibrium models is the lag time for when the point where equilibrium of the supply and demand for space is in relation to when it is reported. It is not like there is a real-time "ringing of the bell" when markets align. The use of machine learning in this regard can only improve the speed to market such that equilibrium models have practical utility.

Another machine learning model of note is the fairly ubiquitous Zillow "*zestimator*" which is a proprietary calculation of the sales approach based on past sales, mortgage records, tax assessments, and building records which include things such as the age and the size of a property. One noted limitation is that the model cannot factor in upgrades or intangibles which are not present in county records. This lack of subjectivity in an algorithm is what we will discuss in the concluding section of this chapter.

2.5 Algorithm subjectivity

In this chapter we have discussed prior versions of credit algorithms used in the banking industry (both entirely conceptual and some that have algorithmic calculations), statistical models to assume away variability, and have elaborated on various methods of the income approach valuation. From there we discussed various technological progresses in the real estate industry, utilizing fields such as artificial intelligence and machine learning. Based on the current review of the literature, the progress being made in the real estate technology space is primarily focused on assumed improvements to the sales approach valuation model.

Some final questions to be asked in this chapter are whether algorithms can or should be subjective. If valuation is inherently a subjective exercise, whereby the market participant doing the valuing has their own predilections and experiences which together form the basis for how they weigh the different attributes of a given property, and if the goal of real estate technology is to reach a more robust and accurate valuation methodology, then algorithms should be subjective. But if the goal of an algorithm is to arrive at the most likely valuation scenario, then the model should be built such that subjectivity (which in mathematical terms can be defined as error) should be removed from the model where possible. Additionally, since the goal of statistical analysis in real estate has heretofore been to remove the variability from valuation, and since an algorithm is essentially an offshoot of statistical analysis, it would seem that the goal of an algorithm would be the removal of subjectivity from the equation.

But since humans are the ones writing the algorithms, and since humans are subjective creatures, it seems unlikely that an algorithm can be written whereby the subjectivity of the writer is somehow removed from the process. Said another way, if the removal of subjectivity of valuation is the goal, it does not seem like a probable endeavor. To quote GLS Shackle,

> If determinism is the truth, we are the deluded slaves of necessity, able perhaps to foreknow what we are obliged to do and what pattern of history those doings will contribute to, but having no claim to call those deeds our own. Men, in that case, are mere tools of fate.

Questions for discussion

1. Which of the "Five Cs" are most important, and which might be the most difficult for an algorithm to provide meaningful prediction?
2. How can statistics be utilized to reduce the importance of the range of property values by instead focusing on a range of investor returns?
3. What are other means of utilizing statistics which can indirectly result in a lack of emphasis on the presence of a range of property values?
4. Describe situations where statistics can be utilized to reinforce the subjectivity of value.
5. Describe the subjectivity of value as it relates to the direct capitalization model. Outline areas in the model where numerous solutions can most prominently impact value.

6. Describe the subjectivity of value as it relates to the discounted cash flow model. Outline areas in the model where numerous solutions can most prominently impact value.

7. Describe current and possible future advances in artificial intelligence in real estate.

8. Describe current and possible future advances in machine learning in real estate.

9. Explain the challenges of making algorithms subjective.

10. Should there be an element of subjectivity in algorithms? Describe the pros and cons of this issue and take a position and defend.

Chapter 2 Market vignette

Cast of characters: Yogi, Boo-Boo, Rachel (Fin-Tech Innovators)
Act: The road to a fully automated commercial real estate valuation model

---

Scene one: innovators innovating

RACHEL: Thank you for coming to the office today. Thanks to our hard work, our Fin-Tech company has been able to sell successful innovations to large financial institutions. If you recall, the last big win for our company was in devising a portfolio management tool that allowed lenders with large portfolios of commercial real estate loans to quickly determine the portfolio impact of various store closings as our retail sector continues to be hard-hit by e-commerce and by the move away from bricks-and-mortar retail locations.

YOGI: Yes that was a big win for us, wasn't it Boo-Boo?

BOO-BOO: It sure was. When the next big box retailer decides to file bankruptcy, the large lenders who have purchased our software will find it much easier to discern portfolio impact.

YOGI: What amazed me was how those banks have been figuring this out over the years. Many of them would rely on email inquiries to various individual employees, asking them to recall the impact of a national retailer closing their doors.

RACHEL: Yes, that was surprising. I think the final selling point for us was to emphasize to our clients that the software was useful not only for tenant bankruptcy situations but also for analysis of the impact of potential national tenant mergers and tenant and industry concentrations in terms of measuring overall portfolio risk.

BOO-BOO: That is for sure! Out with what happened at the properties last year, as now we can focus our attention on what might happen in the future.

YOGI: I know the moss doesn't grow under our feet, so what is our next big adventure, Rachel?

RACHEL: As you know, much of the artificial intelligence and machine learning focus in the real estate industry has been on residential property. What I mean is, technology improvement efforts have almost entirely focused on homes that people occupy as opposed to properties that they own and rent out to a third party. I think we should consider the merits of creating a fully automated commercial real estate valuation and loan underwriting tool.

BOO-BOO: Doesn't the industry already have programs that utilize software to create a discounted cash flow valuation tool? And I believe we have seen credit scoring tools in the marketplace today. So what is our angle, Rachel?

RACHEL: That is correct, Boo-Boo. Most of the models that I have seen regarding discounted cash flow, direct capitalization, and lender underwriting programs require some level of manual input and interpretation. Our big innovation would be in creating a fully automated tool that can be utilized without any human input, at least at the financial institution.

YOGI: I wonder if the large financial institutions would like this lack of human involvement.

RACHEL: I think a big part of our success will be in gaining approval for our software by those that regulate the financial institutions. If the regulators approve of our new model, then the banks will line up. It would have regulatory approval and allow for the continued shrinkage of commercial lending personnel, which would lower the bank's operating expenses.

YOGI: So this is really a two-pronged effort. First, we need to utilize existing software to help us create a fully automated algorithm, while at the same time include members of the regulatory community to guide us as we get closer to the launch of our new product.

BOO-BOO: Let's take a look at what exists today, and what the gaps are that we need to solve for in the near term.

Scene two: focusing on the task

RACHEL: I have spent some time trying to discern the valuation inflection points for commercial real estate which are not present in owner-occupied home valuation. Typically, for homes, the sales approach to value is utilized. For situations where a home is very similar to others recently sold in a given area, the value of the home can be estimated based on a simple sales price per square foot.

YOGI: Yes, I agree. Of course, judgment enters into the picture when the subject property is not as similar to what has been recently sold. In those cases, the existing tax value can serve as a good first estimate of value.

BOO-BOO: I think we are missing something here. For home loans, the bank is typically hiring an appraiser to provide a value, and what the bank is really focused on is the credit history and debt to income of the prospective borrower. So for home loan deals, I think the bank has been agreeing to finance up to a maximum loan-to-value assuming that the personal credit history and debt levels are acceptable.

RACHEL: Exactly. The big difference here is that for commercial real estate, the property itself serves as the primary source of repayment, so a lender will be much more interested in the projected NOI and they want to know this before the appraisal is completed.

YOGI: So if we assume that existing software is sufficient for assessing the personal income and credit history portion of the loan request, our main concern is how to fully automate an income approach valuation model for commercial real estate.

RACHEL: You both are right where I am then, so that is great! I think the valuation inflection points for commercial real estate deal with if a property's current leases are within market averages, what the market vacancy rate and cap rates are, and how high should expenses be relative to income depending on the type and age of the subject property.

BOO-BOO: What would be great is if we could utilize data from either appraisers or lenders to assess the average level of operating expenses based on the age and type of the collateral. I mean, if word gets out that a given bank has a fully automated underwriting model, some borrowers may try to obtain higher loan amounts by showing lower than typical operating expenses.

YOGI: Well, that is always a risk in any lending environment. If a borrower intends to provide faulty financial information, the role of the lender is to utilize comparable properties and common sense to expose those issues to the light of day.

RACHEL: It seems to me that in order to make this work, the software would need to be integrated with a given lender's loan portfolio as well as national third-party data sources such that the market rents, vacancies, and cap rates can be concluded. This might also work for determining the market operating expenses, but as you know, that data have never been as robust when compared to other market data, at least from third-party sources.

BOO-BOO: Yes I agree with that last statement. I think the reason that market property operating expenses are harder to measure is that a given property may have a different expense sharing arrangement than another similar property. For example, assume that you have two similar-sized retail properties. One has a restaurant tenant, and the other has a dollar store. It is probable that the property owner would have the owner of the restaurant pay for their own water as this is a cost driver for that business. In the case of the dollar store, the water may be paid by the property owner as it is not that high of an expense.

YOGI: That is a great point, hey yah Boo-Boo!

RACHEL: Given our success in selling the portfolio management tool to large financial institutions, this new product can attach to that product such that the bank can be provided with real-time estimates of property expense, cap rate, and other variables based on their current portfolios.

YOGI: All that remains is designing the new product!

Scene three: putting pen to paper

RACHEL: Let's draw out a flow chart of how this new product might work. I think we should show the various existing systems and information which would flow into the commercial real estate valuation model. We would have the financial statements, market information from third-party data providers, and loan portfolio information from the lender in question.

YOGI: Yes I have seen some technology that converts financials into digital form, whereby no manual entry is needed. Since it is new, we would need some sort of quality assurance person to review what is transposed from hard copy financials to digital form, but one selling point is that the annual salary of these people would be less than the banks are paying their lending staff currently.

BOO-BOO: I would think that we could design the new platform to have decision criteria related to the market vacancy and rental rates as determined by the third-party data information for a given location, and the portfolio information from the bank, and then to automatically decide on whether to input the actual financials, the market information, or the averages from the bank's loan portfolio.

RACHEL: Yes, that makes sense. For properties with shorter leases, it would seem that the market averages would be dominant, but for longer leases we might go with the value actually being received at the subject property. If we utilize the existing information with decision logic, a fully automated value can then be created.

YOGI: How would the system know if a direct capitalization or a discounted cash flow is most useful for the current situation?

RACHEL: I think the system should produce both. With the inclusion of the discounted cash flow, we will need to obtain discount rates from the third-party sources, and the average holding period could just be estimated at the typical five- or ten-year period.

BOO-BOO: Oh, that brings up a question. What if the third-party data do not have coverage for a specific market? Let's say it is a tertiary market.

RACHEL: I think the best option is to provide decision logic whereby if a market does not have coverage, our model would default to the most proximate market with coverage. While the valuation is fully automated, we can leave certain items changeable by the lender. Our model would utilize the best available resources to estimate a value, but the lender would have discretion to change certain inputs like the overall vacancy rate, cap rate, or discount rate.

YOGI: This sounds like we are really making progress. Now let's take a look at our flow chart and determine our next actionable steps.

(All three review the flow chart as depicted in Exhibit 2.13).

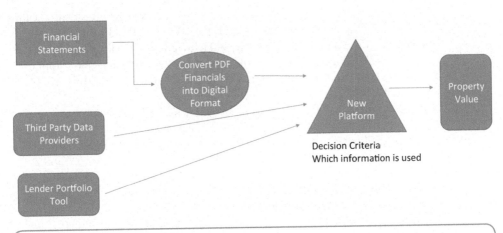

Exhibit 2.13 Flow Chart for Fully Automated Commercial Real Estate Valuation Model.

Questions for discussion

1. Discuss how the subjectivity of value is apparent in this case.
2. Discuss the strengths and weaknesses of the portfolio management tool initially created by this Fin-Tech.
3. Outline the strengths and weaknesses of the plans for a fully automated commercial real estate valuation model.
4. What objections might the financial institutions have for this new product offering?
5. What objections might the regulators have for this new product offering?

Bibliography

Alfaro-Navarro, J.-L., et al. (2020) A Fully Automated Adjustment of Ensemble Methods in Machine Learning for Modeling Complex Real Estate Systems. *Complexity*, 2020, 1–12. doi: 10.1155/2020/5287263.

Baldominos, A., Blanco, I., Moreno, A., Iturrarte, R., Bernárdez, Ó., & Afonso, C. (2018) Identifying Real Estate Opportunities Using Machine Learning. *Applied Sciences*, 8(11), 2321. doi: 10.3390/app8112321

Bodenbender, M., et al. (2019) Broad Application of Artificial Intelligence for Document Classification, Information Extraction and Predictive Analytics in Real Estate. *Journal of General Management*, 44(3), 170–179. doi: 10.1177/0306307018823113.

Bohari, S. N., Saad, S. N. M., Marzukhi, F., Rahim, A., & Darim, A. D. A. (2015) Residential Property Valuation using GIS. *2015 IEEE 11th International Colloquium on Signal Processing & Its Applications (CSPA)*. doi: 10.1109/cspa.2015.7225632

Dawid, L., et al. (2019) Estimation of Usable Area of Flat-Roof Residential Buildings Using Topographic Data with Machine Learning Methods. *Remote Sensing*, 11(20), 2382. doi: 10.3390/rs11202382.

Dimopoulos, T., & Bakas, N. (2019) Sensitivity Analysis of Machine Learning Models for the Mass Appraisal of Real Estate. Case Study of Residential Units in Nicosia, Cyprus. *Remote Sensing*, 11(4), 3047. doi: 10.3390/rs11243047.

Doszyń, M. (2019) Individual Capacities of Hellwig's Information Carriers and the Impact of Attributes in the Szczecin Algorithm of Real Estate Mass Appraisal. *Real Estate Management and Valuation*, 27(1), 15–24. doi: 10.2478/remav-2019-0002

García-Magariño, I., Medrano, C., & Delgado, J. (2019) Estimation of missing prices in real-estate market agent-based simulations with machine learning and dimensionality reduction methods. *Neural Computing and Applications*, 32(7), 2665–2682. doi: 10.1007/s00521-018-3938-7

Giudice, V. D., Paola, P. D., & Forte, F. (2017) Using Genetic Algorithms for Real Estate Appraisals. *Buildings*, 7(4), 31. doi: 10.3390/buildings7020031

Gnat, S. (2019) Measurement of Entropy in the Assessment of Homogeneity of Areas Valued with the Szczecin Algorithm of Real Estate Mass Appraisal. *Journal of Economics and Management*, 38, 89–106. doi: 10.22367/jem.2019.38.05

Goddard, G. J. & Marcum, B. (2012) *Real Estate Investment: A Value Based Approach*. Springer, Heidelberg.

Hausler, J., Ruscheinsky, J., & Lang, M. (2018) News-based Sentiment Analysis in Real Estate: A Machine Learning Approach. *Journal of Property Research*, 35(4), 344–371. doi: 10.1080/09599916.2018.1551923

Hong, J., Choi, H., & Kim, W.-S. (2020) A House Price Valuation Based on the Random Forest Approach: The Mass Appraisal of Residential Property in South Korea. International *Journal of Strategic Property Management*, 24(3), 140–152. doi: 10.3846/ijspm.2020.11544

Hozer, J., Gnat, S., Kokot, S., & Kuźmiński, W. (2019) The Problem of Designating Elementary Terrains for the Purpose of Szczecin Algorithm of Real Estate Mass Appraisal. *Real Estate Management and Valuation*, 27(3), 42–58. doi: 10.2478/remav-2019-0024

Kang, J., et al. (May 2020) Developing a Forecasting Model for Real Estate Auction Prices Using Artificial Intelligence. *Sustainability*, 12(7), 2899. doi: 10.3390/su12072899.

Kokot, S. (2017) Residential Property Price Indices on Small Property Markets. *Real Estate Management and Valuation*, 25(1), 5–18. doi: 10.1515/remav-2017-0001

Kokot, S., & Gnat, S. (2019) Identification and Classification of Real Estate Features for the Purpose of an Algorithm-Based Valuation– Case Study within Szczecin. *Folia Oeconomica Stetinensia*, 19(2), 38–55. doi: 10.2478/foli-2019-0012

Li, M., Zhang, G., Chen, Y., & Zhou, C. (2019) Evaluation of Residential Housing Prices on the Internet: Data Pitfalls. *Complexity*, 2019, 1–15. doi: 10.1155/2019/5370961

Liu, Z., Yan, S., Cao, J., Jin, T., Tang, J., Yang, J., & Wang, Q. (2018) A Bayesian Approach to Residential Property Valuation Based on Built Environment and House Characteristics. *2018 IEEE International Conference on Big Data (Big Data)*. doi: 10.1109/bigdata.2018.8622422

Mason, J., Peoples, B., & Lee, J. (2020) Questioning the Scope of AI Standardization in Learning, Education, and Training. *Journal of ICT Standardization*, 107–122. doi: 10.13052/jicts2245-800X.822.

Metzner, S., & Kindt, A. (2018) Determination of the Parameters of Automated Valuation Models for the Hedonic Property Valuation of Residential Properties. *International Journal of Housing Markets and Analysis*, 11(1), 73–100. doi: 10.1108/ijhma-02-2017-0018

Mises, L. (2006) *The Ultimate Foundation of Economic Science*. Liberty Fund, Indianapolis, IN.

Park, B., & Bae, J. K. (2015) Using Machine Learning Algorithms for Housing Price Prediction: The case of Fairfax County, Virginia Housing Data. *Expert Systems with Applications*, 42(6), 2928–2934. doi: 10.1016/j.eswa.2014.11.040

Pérez Rave, J., González-Echavarría, F., & Correa, J. (2020) Modeling of Apartment Prices in a Colombian Context from a Machine Learning Approach with Stable-Important Attributes. *Dyna (Medellin, Colombia)*, 87, 63–72. doi: 10.15446/dyna.v87n212.80202.

Pupentsova, S., & Livintsova, M. (2018) Qualimetric Assessment of Investment Attractiveness of the Real Estate Property. *Real Estate Management and Valuation*, 26(2), 5–11. doi: 10.2478/remav-2018-0011

Rockel, G., & Barth, L. (2019) IT Requirements in the Real Estate Sector. *International Journal of Innovative Technology and Exploring Engineering*, 9. doi: 10.35940/ijitee.A4029.119119.

Shackle, G. L. S. (1979) *Imagination and the Nature of Choice*. Edinburgh University Press, Edinburgh.

Sun, Y. (2019) Real Estate Evaluation Model Based on Genetic Algorithm Optimized Neural Network. *Data Science Journal*, 18. doi: 10.5334/dsj-2019-036

Tao, F., & Jiao, L. (2019) Coastal and Port Real Estate Forecasting Model Based on Fast-adaptive Algorithm for Large Data Sets. *Journal of Coastal Research*, 97(sp1), 35. doi: 10.2112/si97-006.1

Toit, H., & Cloete, C. (2015) Appraisal of the Fischer-DiPasquale-Wheaton (FDW) Real Estate Model and Development of an Integrated Property and Asset Market Model. *South African Journal of Economic and Management Sciences*, 7, 341. doi: 10.4102/sajems.v7i2.1382.

Tóth, A. (2019) Algorithmic Copyright Enforcement and AI: Issues and Potential Solutions through the Lens of Text and Data Mining. *Masaryk University Journal of Law and Technology*, 13, 361. doi: 10.5817/MUJLT2019-2-9.

Ullah, F., et al. (Mar. 2018) A Systematic Review of Smart Real Estate Technology: Drivers of, and Barriers to, the Use of Digital Disruptive Technologies and Online Platforms. *Sustainability*, 10(9), 3142. doi: 10.3390/su10093142.

Yachim, J.-A., & Boshoff, D. (2018) Impact of Artificial Network Training Algorithms on Accurate Prediction of Property Values. *The Journal of Real Estate Research; Sacramento*, 40(3), 375–418.

Yalpir, S., & Ozkan, G. (2018) Knowledge-Based Fis and Anfis Models Development and Comparison For Residential Real Estate Valuation. *International Journal of Strategic Property Management*, 22(2), 110–118. doi: 10.3846/ijspm.2018.442

Yasar, A., Yalpir, Ş., & Bunyan unel, F. (2014) Using the Fuzzy Logic Approach for the Valuation of Parcels, 361–367. doi: 10.2495/CEEIT140451.

Chapter 3

Overview and pitfalls of home valuation subjectivity

Chapter highlights

- Housing boom revisited
- Looking for that special something – how different people value things differently
- Pitfalls of home valuation

> Reasoning is the result of doing away with the vital distinction which separates subjectivity and objectivity
>
> Søren Kierkegaard

3.1 Housing boom revisited

In this chapter, we will discuss how the subjectivity of value plays into the decision process of owner-occupied residential properties (i.e., homes). We will review primary valuation models utilized when estimating the value of homes and will discuss some of the factors that cause market participants to come to divergent property valuations even when looking at the same market data. Before we delve into these matters, we will first explore theories relating to the underlying causes of housing booms and busts.

A housing boom can be defined as an unsustainable increase in the price of homes which are typically fueled by demand, speculation, and exuberant spending. There are a plethora of opinions and theories as to whether housing bubbles (or housing booms) exist and why indeed they form. Depending on the political persuasion of the economist devising the model, the lion share of the blame can either reside with government intervention or with the speculative nature of the market participant making the valuation choices. Who are the market participants

DOI: 10.4324/9781003083672-3

in question? For starters, we are referring to buyers and sellers of real estate. We are also looking to the financial institutions that lend to the buyers and take a security interest in the property offered as collateral. Additionally, in the context of the housing market, we are also casting a glance at the appraisers that provide the final value on a subject property, and the real estate agents and brokers who lend a hand in the marketing of the properties for sale in the marketplace. Regardless of their place in the story, there is much subjectivity to be found in the home purchase and valuation process.

3.1.1 Classical housing boom models

Some economic schools of thought proffer that housing bubbles should not exist, at least in an economy sans government intervention in markets (Friedman and Malkiel as examples). The theory goes that investors are rational such that with each market participant acting in their own self-interest, the buying and selling of homes (and other assets) will occur when two rational beings agree on a price. Under this scenario, only government intervention in markets would lead to economic calamity. Government interventions, however mild and regardless of intent, tend to create perverse incentives that can lead to market maladies. Specific government interventions in the housing market have occurred in multitudes of markets for many years throughout the world. Some recent examples include mandated targets for what percentage of households should one own versus rent, fiscal policies such as the exemption of housing from capital gains taxation, central banking decisions such as manipulated interest rates to encourage "investment", and a plethora of fiat money stimulus programs injected into the economy which can all encourage the wrong type of investment and spur speculative fervor. If Keynes believed that government deficit spending should occur infrequently and only in the worst of times, modern governments have taken an entirely different route where even the smallest of market wobble begets interventionist policies with the intention of government saving the day for us all.

The Austrian school of economics (Hayek and Mises as examples) prefers the term "malinvestment" to describe poorly allocated investment decisions, which are often attributed to artificially low interest rates and an unsustainable increase in the money supply. Similar to other models from a more classical perspective, these theories also assume the start of the process which eventually leads to a housing boom and bust cycle that originates with government market intervention. The Austrians have coined the "Cantillon effect" to describe the cause and effect relationship that occurs when monetary expansion is targeted at specific industries or individuals. Once omniscient government policymakers have directed money to specific "winners", the asset prices in those targeted industries increase relative to those who did not receive the government induced stimulus. This effect is named after Richard Cantillon, who wrote the first treatise on economics more than four decades before the publication of Adam Smith's heralded *The Wealth of Nations*. When a government targets specific industries for stimulus (whether housing or otherwise), the effect is typically a rise in asset prices in the associated industries, as these market participants have received stimulus money while others have not. For Austrian economists, the central banking authority is typically held culpable for speculative episodes as the low interest rates encourage spending while the money being injected into the economy leads to price increases.

3.1.2 Alternative housing boom models

Housing boom models developed by economists with less classical leanings also include speculation. These models typically reduce, or hold entirely harmless, the role of government in culpability for creating the environment that produces housing bubbles as a direct result. These models (Galbraith and Minsky as examples) tend to focus more on the irrationality of market participants and also seem to imply that this irrationality can spread throughout an existing market based on fear and anxiety once the high asset prices (or in Galbraith's terminology "euphoria") seen during the good economic times start to wane. Others (Keynes for example) have coined the term "animal spirits" to represent how the market as an overall entity can get ahead of itself as the speculative episodes and greed, which led to the unsustainable price level, start to quickly unwind. The term animal spirits is used to describe the instincts and emotions which guide human behavior with the underlying thought that investors can be both rational and irrational and that the cause of irrationality is emotions running amok (rather than the incentives provided in the market) which leads to increases in price.

Hyman Minsky is referenced in the well-known phrase "the Minsky Moment" for when there is a sudden, major collapse of asset values that marks the end of a growth phase in credit markets or business activity. Taken in light of the housing market, the Great Recession of 2009 is an example of such a Minsky moment. On a recent trip to the Zachary Smith Reynolds library at Wake Forest University, I was in search of some examples of Minsky moments as I spent time reviewing various articles and texts that defined business cycles and outlined the reasons for why they might change for the worse. During this visit I came across a book by A.C. Pigou, titled *The Money Veil*. In this book, Pigou utilizes the term veil as money tends to shield the true workings of the economy with the resultant impact on property values, given things like central bank-induced inflation and general price increases. Apparently this is how the Minsky moment can morph into a Pigou pickel! The concept of inflation was famously described earlier by Irving Fisher as "the Money Illusion", whereby all of the goods and services produced in a country were categorized as bread, while the money utilized in the economy was classified as butter. If there is a large central bank stimulus initiative whereby the amount of money in circulation is drastically increased, and if this increase does not lead to an increase in aggregate demand in the economy, the effect is a higher and higher layering of butter onto the existing bread. Regardless of how unappetizing this may sound, the increase in butter in this example signifies the general increase in prices of all goods and services, including the price of homes for sale on the market.

3.1.3 Housing boom participants

A qualified sale of real estate occurs when the buyer and seller, who are not otherwise familiar with each other, reach agreement on the purchase price. The time that a property is on the market can vary from very short to a considerably longer period of time. The more attractive the property and the market, the less time it takes for a listed property to be negotiated successfully for resale. In the next section, we will discuss some of the factors that make potential buyers and sellers arrive at different value conclusions. But before we do this, it is helpful to consider other housing boom participants and the roles that they play.

Real estate agents and brokers can represent either the seller or the buyer in a given transaction. These market participants accumulate information to aid in the estimation of an initial listing sales price, provide backing information in terms of recent sales which are deemed similar to the subject property being sold, and they often accompany the buyer when they visit the subject property prior to deciding on which property is right for them. To categorize these individuals as disinterested third parties would be ignoring the commissions that they receive when a sale is closed. Most agents try to find the property which best matches what their clients are looking to purchase. Some agents may spend a considerable amount of time with the seller prior to arriving at an initial listing price, while some may spend a considerable amount of time with buyers, reviewing multiple properties and providing guidance as to recent comparable property sales in the market. In these instances, real estate agents can directly influence a buyer or a seller, in the same way that an offering memorandum can indirectly influence when it touts the various stellar attributes of the subject property.

Lenders can also provide a helpful nudge to potential buyers of properties. This is especially overt when a potential buyer seeks out a preapproved loan prior to deciding on which property they wish to buy. The lender will review the potential buyer's financial standing and will analyze their current levels of income and indebtedness in order to determine the maximum loan amount for which the potential buyer will qualify. The terms that a lender will offer in terms of interest rates, loan amortization, and cash investment requirements will certainly help form the basis for how much a buyer is willing to offer when they find their chosen property for purchase. Lenders in many jurisdictions are regulated by the government in terms of how they can treat their customers and in how they communicate their financial offerings. In the United States, these regulations are named for letters of the alphabet for easier reference. Currently, there are so many banking regulations that just about every letter of the alphabet is used twice (i.e., Regulation A and Regulation AA). Exhibit 3.1 lists banking regulations that deal with lender interaction with consumers when obtaining a home loan.

While some of the regulations noted in Exhibit 3.1 have been replaced by Dodd-Frank, fear not! These regulations are still in full force but are now included in that ubiquitous legislation. One of the hallmark legislations in the United States is

Housing Regulation Alphabet Soup	
Regulation Title Purpose	
Regulation B	Equal Credit Opportunity Act (ECOA)
Regulation C*	Home Mortgage Disclosure
Regulation M	Consumer Lending
Regulation P*	Privacy of Consumer Information
Regulation V	Fair Credit Reporting
Regulation Z	Truth in Lending
Regulation AA*	Unfair & Deceptive Practices Act
Regulation BB	Community Reinvestment
Regulation DD	Truth in Savings
* denotes replaced by Dodd-Frank	

Exhibit 3.1 Housing Regulation Alphabet Soup.

Regulation B, which disallows discrimination against a borrower for a series of factors such as race, age, and sexual orientation. Many of the laws highlighted in Exhibit 3.1 have at their core the basic idea that a lender should not mislead a borrower about how their interest rate is calculated, what appears on their personal credit reports, and any other facet of the loan terms offered to the potential borrower. If there was any question that lenders have influence over potential buyers, this litany of legislation should quiet those concerns. This section also solidifies the earlier point made about the frequency and breadth of government intervention into financial markets.

Regardless of whether you believe that asset prices are fueled by government intervention, central banking stimulus, the greed and exuberance of market participants, or a combination of factors, there is at least one other area of concern in this regard. Appraisers of real estate have been mandated by governments as the final arbiters of property value whether the asset is being sold, refinanced, or valued for some other purpose. The most common reason for a new appraisal for real estate is when the property is being sold. The role of the appraiser is to serve as an independent third party that will validate or invalidate the agreed-upon sales prices between the buyer and seller. Since classical economics would view both the buyer and seller as rational market participants, you would not expect to find many situations where the appraiser would significantly disagree with the sales price negotiated between the parties to the sale.

In terms of summarizing this section of the chapter in visual form, Exhibit 3.2 attempts to show the ebb and flow of the Minsky moment in housing with possible triggers of economic calamity listed as reference. This concludes our discussion of

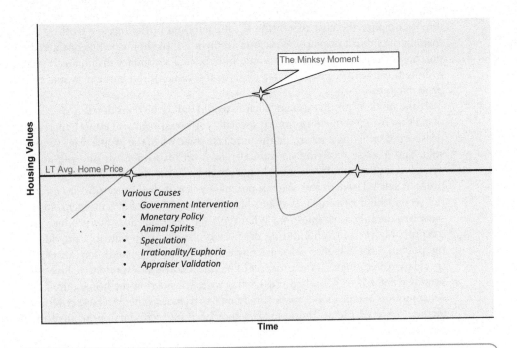

Exhibit 3.2 **The Minksy Moment in Housing.**

possible housing booms and busts. Now we turn our focus to how individual buyers and sellers can value a property differently from each other while looking at the same basic information in order to make their value conclusion.

3.2 Looking for that special something: how different people value things differently

In this section, we will discuss how different market participants can view the same home differently and can reach varying conclusions for property value. One of the first considerations in this process is the discussion about whether a home is an investment or is considered more of a personal consumption choice for the buyer. We will then delve into the specific amenity and location choices that are typically available to the home buyer. Lastly, we will discuss that the stage of life of the buyer can impact the value that they place on certain home amenities and to the general location of the home.

3.2.1 Home as an investment or as consumption

There seems to be differing opinions as to whether the purchase of a home is considered an investment for the buyer or if it is just large ticket consumption. If a home purchase was purely an investment option, then buying a house would always be the right idea for a potential buyer versus the prospect of renting. A home buyer solely concerned with the prospect of a solid return on their home purchase would focus primarily on the numbers involved in the transaction. For example, they might compare the cost of renting a similar home in the market to the cost of owning the subject property. While the aesthetics of the home being considered for purchase would be evaluated, it would only be in a secondary fashion as it relates to how those features would contribute to the value of the home now and in the probable future.

If the home is an investment, then it would surely be considered a speculative one. For most investment options (especially for investment real estate), there is the prospect of receiving a return on the purchase price when the property is eventually sold, and also of receiving an annual return on investment during the holding period of investment. While most home purchases offer the potential to generate a profit at sale relative to the original purchase price of the home, most do not offer the second kind of return. It might help if we step back for a moment and ask ourselves the following question: What type of investment does not produce profit (or probably even income) during the period of ownership but only provides for the potential for a higher sales price when the property is sold? The answer is a speculative investment. If the prospect of buying a house as a speculative investment sounds palatable to you, then great; otherwise, considering the home purchase as consumption may lead to a more satisfying experience as the purchase criteria will include more of the aesthetic factors that become secondary in an investment purchase.

The economist Veblen coined the phrase "conspicuous consumption" which refers to purchasing decisions made largely owing to their potential of boastfulness. In this regard, the "Veblen effect" refers to situations were an increase in the price of an asset leads to an increase in its demand, again owing to the ability to impress your friends, colleagues, or neighbors. In housing terms, conspicuous consumption would involve purchasing the most expensive or largest home in a given neighborhood or town. Veblen also referred to "conspicuous leisure" which relates to housing in terms of the amenities a property provides. Swimming pools, nearby nature trails, tennis courts, or golf courses would fit the bill for conspicuous leisure in housing. A last term from Veblen considered here is "conspicuous waste", which can enter into the home purchase decision in terms of large acreage with only a small home situated at the center, large piles of recycling, yard rubbish, and trash produced by the home owner, or even replacing items in the house owing more to novelty and modernity than utility. Whether speaking of conspicuous consumption, leisure, or waste, all fit the bill in support of speculative purchasing.

We will now turn our attention to the aesthetics of housing and how this might lead to varying valuation conclusions.

3.2.2 Aesthetics of the housing option

When prospective buyers are weighing the various properties offered for sale in the marketplace, there is the potential for different market participants to arrive at very different conclusions for the maximum price that they would pay for a given property. Sometimes, the prospective buyer is immediately sold on a particular housing option as the property and surrounding area have all of the things deemed crucial for the buyer in question. These housing wish list items vary based on different buyers, their tastes and preferences, and where they are in terms of age, family structure, and income levels.

Sometimes married couples with small children prefer a home located on a quiet less-traversed road, or even a cul-de-sac, while single adults may not find these locations as compelling. Sometimes buyers considered city locations as convenient and a key part of their desired housing option. City locations may be preferred given the proximity to employment, schools, and entertainment options. Sometimes home buyers are more interested in suburban or rural locations if they consider peace and quiet and the ability to linger in natural spaces as more important than the urban throng.

The specific layout and construction of the home itself also offers a multitude of options which lead to varying levels of appeal for prospective buyers. Some buyers prefer homes located on one floor, while others enjoy the privacy that numerous floors provide as the primary living space is segmented from the sleeping quarters. The number of bedrooms, bathrooms, and the presence and size of recreation areas also appeal distinctly to different prospective buyers. Some may see a third bedroom as a potential work-from-home office space, while others may see it as a necessity given the size of the family considering the property for purchase. In terms of home construction, some buyers prefer the permanence of brick or stone as the primary façade of the home, while others prefer less permanent and more malleable materials such as wood or vinyl siding. Some buyers desire and are willing to pay for the most modern kitchen cabinets and layouts, while other buyers may prefer the charm and uniqueness of an older home without all of the modern perks.

For some home buyers, having an attached garage is a crucial detail, while for others it is of little consequence. The same goes for things like a patio, screened porch, sun room, or other recreational rooms and spaces either attached or in close proximity to the housing structure. Sometimes a prospective buyer's mind is set on having certain amenities without which the home is not as attractive as a home that checks all of the boxes in terms of desired features. Additionally, the size of the acreage for the subject property can be an important consideration. Sometimes buyers like a larger parcel of land for privacy, gardening, xystus, or the placement of things like a pool, while other buyers are more interested in smaller parcels of land which take less maintenance requirements.

The main point of this section was to emphasize that while beauty lies often in the eyes of the beholder, a prospective buyer's definition of a quality home can vary as well. In a prior book *Customer Relationship Management*, I have termed this the "should versus is" comparison. The various aspects of a home's aesthetics which are important to the particular buyer form what they believe should be there (the "should factor"), while how much the buyer likes the property will often depend on how they perceive which of the features are actually there (the "is factor"). Buyer satisfaction with the home purchase likely comes when the perceived "should factor" is equaled or exceeded by the perceived "is factor". Next we will discuss a few models as pertaining to home selection.

3.2.3 Sociodemographic models of home consumption

Now that we have reviewed how different prospective buyers can come to different value conclusions based on subjective factors of housing aesthetics, it will be instructive to discuss some models which help to determine underlying reasons for why home owners decide to buy a new home in the first place.

One model is known as the housing ladder. The basic idea is to move up the various steps of the ladder, which is defined as more expensive housing options. Buyers move up the housing ladder as they acquire the means to do so. These means are often defined relative to occupation, income, marital status, and age. In this model, it is assumed that the benefits of homeownership and home price appreciation are so great that buyers only want to progress up the ladder steps. The housing ladder model tends to focus on the characteristics of the primary householder, as opposed to the entire family unit. This model also tends to ignore the valuation perception differences that persist in reality and as defined in this chapter. Under housing ladder construction, no buyer would willingly purchase a lower priced home than what they previously owned, and the basic facets of what contributes to home value are not in dispute. As prospective buyers advance through life, the housing ladder model would have them move up the steps of the ladder in a fairly consistent way and to reach specific steps on the ladder at a specific age.

A second model is known as the housing life cycle. According to this model, the changes in size, composition, and housing preferences are correlated to the different stages of nuclear family formation (marriage), expansion (birth of children), contraction (maturation of children), and dissolution (spousal death). Thus, this model tends to focus on the entire family unit as opposed to just the primary householder. As the family transitions into different phases of the family life cycle, new opportunities for purchasing homes are presented. With these new opportunities often come different features of the desired home that cater to the specific circumstances of the prospective buyer. Contrary to the housing ladder model, the housing life cycle approach includes the possibility for a buyer to willingly move down in home value over time. This is typically the case as the buyer's family size declines and as they age. The stages of the housing life cycle are often categorized by marital status and the presence of, and the age of, any children in the household.

A third model is known as housing life course which originates in sociology and developmental psychology. Under this model, the stages of the family as noted in the housing life cycle model are included as well, but this is only one area of concern. There is also relevant movement within other life patterns such as family formation, education, and career choices. Under this model, the movement up or down in the price of housing is associated with this expanded set of events, rather than a focus on simply marriage and children. This model also includes stages related to housing rental as opposed to ownership. Similar to occupation history, the general tendency of this model is skewed toward an increased home price over time as various properties are bought and sold within the household, but there can be downward pressure when income levels or other life pressures dictate. Finally, this model underscores that the age of entry into a particular life stage can be influenced by household savings rates, political factors such as war, and health concerns.

In the prior section, we discussed various attributes of a home that could lead to valuation differences for different buyers in the market. In this section, we discussed some foundational models to help explain how these differences occur over time as family, occupation, and other factors change. In the next section, we will discuss how appraisers handle the subjectivity in home valuation.

3.3 Pitfalls of home valuation

Valuation of real estate is an important part of any purchasing decision. Federal regulations require a current appraised value for loans secured with real estate so that the loan-to-value ratio can be established at origination. The perception of value is important as different appraisers can use the same market data but reach different conclusions as to the appropriate market averages which are relevant for the property being evaluated. What is important is that the federal regulations have helped to elevate the property appraiser's "opinion of value" to the official value utilized by the lender when a loan is established secured by the property. This opinion of value is similar to the agreed purchase price in that this value represents one point across a range of acceptable values for the same property.

During the time when a property is listed for sale, the owner and their agent entertain offers from prospective buyers who are interested in purchasing the property. Offers can be lower than what is desired until such time as an agreeable price is established between the buyer and the seller. Previous offers which were not accepted by the seller may have been lower than what was desired, but those values should have some basis as a rational buyer made a supposed good faith offer of purchase. In the words of F. A. Hayek, "*A (price) solution is produced by the interactions of people each of whom possesses only partial knowledge*". Sometimes appraisers have the knowledge of a market agreed sales price when they are completing their valuation, but in other situations there has not been a recently agreed sales price. Thus, appraisers can theoretically have a wider range of possible values as there is not necessarily a cap on the value that is present when there is a pending sale on the given property.

3.3.1 Sales approach subjectivity

While there are three forms of value (income, sales, and cost), the home appraisal usually focuses on the sales approach as there is typically not an income component with an owner-occupied home. Superficially, the sales approach would appear to be a rather objective form of valuation as the primary method of the approach is based on the historical sales prices of properties which are deemed similar to the subject property of the appraisal. The appraiser terms these similar properties "comparable", and if there is no material differences between these historical sales and the subject property, then the valuation exercise is easy and primarily objective. In cases where the subjectivity comes in, it involves the determination of how the historical sales differ from the subject and the impact on the historical sales prices as a result.

When estimating the final value of a residential property, the punch line in the valuation is the final adjusted sales price per square foot. As to the subject property, it is easy to determine what the proposed sales price would translate into on a per square foot dollar basis (divide asking price by total home square footage), but the basic question of any real estate valuation is the following: Is the price being contemplated for sale reasonable when compared with market averages?

In order to answer that important question, the appraiser must select recent sales in the market that are deemed comparable to the subject property. While in some commercial property valuation instances the local market is not as important (for example, a national credit tenant with a long lease where the investor is purchasing the property based on the investment grade of the tenant versus the specific market demographics), it is crucial for home sales. The subdivision within a given city can even be considered such that sales of the closest in nature to the subject can be obtained. A couple of things should be noted about the comparable property selections. First, the sales should be recent. Depending on the stability of the local market, what is considered reasonably recent can vary, but one rule of thumb is that sales should be within the last six months to a year, depending on the vibrancy of the market in question. If the market has steeply declined in recent months (or conversely steeply increased), the time frame for reasonableness will condense. The second thing to be noted here is that the appraiser should not include pending sales in the list of comparable properties. Pending sales are just that, pending. They are not final sales, so utilizing them in the sales approach appears misguided.

Exhibit 3.3 provides a subject property and comparable properties for consideration.

The subject property is smaller than two of the three comparable properties, but bigger than one of them. The average square footage for the three comparable properties is roughly the same size as the subject property itself. If we consider the date of the appraisal as September 1, 2021, each final sale occurred within the last few months.

As we have discussed various aesthetic factors for home valuation subjectivity in this chapter, Exhibit 3.4 shows how an appraiser might reconcile the differences between the subject property and the comparable properties when arriving at the adjusted sales price per square foot.

As Exhibit 3.4 illustrates, a multitude of characteristics that are considered by the appraiser in order to adjust the sales prices of the comparable property to more closely resemble the subject property. If a comparable property is deemed superior

Subjectivity of Sales Approach for Residential Property					
Property	Subject	Comparable 1	Comparable 2	Comparable 3	Comp Avg.
Sales Date	NA	08-08-21	25-07-21	25-06-21	
Sales Price	NA	$ 209,000	$ 235,000	$ 235,000	$226,333.33
Gross Living Area (sq ft)	2,148	1,884	2,232	2,301	2,139
Sales price psf		$ 110.93	$ 105.29	$ 102.13	$ 106.12

Exhibit 3.3 Subject Property and Comparables for Residential Home Sale.

Property	Subject	Comparable 1		Comparable 2		Comparable 3		Comp Avg.
Value Adjustments	Subject	Description	Adjust $	Description	Adjust $	Description	Adjust $	
Sales/Financing Concessions	None	FHA $5,000	$ (5,000.00)	None	$ -	None	$ -	Avg.
Location	Avg.	Avg.		Avg.		Avg.		Avg.
Leasehold/Fee Simple	Fee Simple	Fee Simple		Fee Simple		Fee Simple		Fee Simple
Site (acres)	0.50	0.90	$ (1,200.00)	0.45	$ -	0.50	$ -	0.62
View	Avg.	Avg.	$ -	Avg.	$ -	Avg.	$ -	Avg.
Design (Style)	Ranch	Ranch	$ -	Ranch	$ -	Ranch	$ -	Ranch
Quality of Construction	Avg.	Avg.	$ -	Avg.	$ -	Avg.	$ -	Avg.
Actual Age (years)	35	40	$ -	38	$ -	36	$ -	38
Condition	Avg.	Avg.		Avg.		Avg.		Avg.
Total Rooms	9	7		7		9		8
Total Bedrooms	4	3		3		4		3
Total Baths	2	2		2		2	$ (2,500.00)	2
Gross Living Area (sq ft)	2,456	2,765	$ 6,600.00	2,550	$ (2,100.00)	2,845	$ (3,800.00)	2,720
Basement & Finished	Partial	Full	$ (4,000.00)					
Rooms Below Grade	Part Fin	Part Fin/Bath	$ (5,000.00)	Finish Bath	$ (7,500.00)	Finish Bath	$ (7,500.00)	
Functional Utility	Avg.	Avg.	$ -	Avg.	$ -	Avg.	$ -	Avg.
Heating & Cooling	HVAC	HVAC	$ -	HVAC	$ -	HVAC	$ -	HVAC
Energy Efficiency	Avg.	Avg.	$ -	Avg.	$ -	Avg.	$ -	Avg.
Garage/Carport	2 Car Gar	Carport	$ 11,000.00	2 Car Gar	$ 1,000.00	2 Car Gar	$ 1,000.00	
Porch/Patio/Deck	Patio	Deck/Porch	$ (2,000.00)	Patio	$ -	Pat/DeckPorch	$ (4,000.00)	2
Fireplace	2	2	$ -	2	$ -	2		
Pool	Inground	Inground	$ -	None	$ 5,000.00	None	$ 5,000.00	
Sunroom	Yes	None	$ 4,000.00	None	$ 4,000.00	Yes	$ -	
Net adjustment Total			$ 4,400.00		$ 400.00		$ (11,800.00)	
Adjusted Sales Price	$ 226,068		$213,400.00		$235,400.00		$223,200.00	$224,000.00
Adj Sales Price psf	$ 105.25		$ 113.27		$ 105.47		$ 97.00	$ 105.25

Exhibit 3.4 Sales Approach Valuation Subjectivity.

to the subject property for any of the characteristics shown, the appraiser would adjust downward the historical sales price of the comparable sale. For example, if you review the line item for basement finishing, the first comparable was fully finished while the subject property was only partially finished. The sales price of the first comparable was reduced to account for this difference. If the subject property is deemed superior to the comparable property in a specific category, the appraiser would increase the value of the historical sales price of the comparable property. For example, if you review the pool category toward the bottom of Exhibit 3.4, comparable properties two and three did not have a pool, so the historical prices were increased by $5,000 in each case.

Once all the adjustments have been made, the historical sales price per square foot for each comparable becomes an adjusted sales price per square foot for the sole purposes of valuing the subject property. Obviously, the owners of the comparable properties do not know this process is going on and are not impacted by the analysis. This is solely an exercise that utilizes historical (and final) sales prices and adjusts them upward or downward to arrive at the adjusted sales price required to value the subject property. In the example of Exhibit 3.4, the final adjusted sales price per square foot is $105.25 for a final sales approach valuation of the subject property of $224,000.

This all seems reasonable and tidy, but now we can address some subjectivity issues with this process. One issue that should immediately come to mind is how does the appraiser purport to know whether a difference between a comparable property and the subject is something inferior or superior? In some cases this question is not hard to ascertain. Typically the more bathrooms and bedrooms, the higher the value. If this is in question, try adding a bathroom and see if you can get away without your local government coming to review the finished product (for safety regulation purposes but also to increase your tax value!).

Some of the areas for difference are not as easy to determine whether a positive or negative impact should be the result. Take for example the pool. The appraiser in our example appeared to consider the pool an additive feature to value as the two comparable properties that did not have a pool received positive adjustments to their historical sales prices. But is the pool always desired? What if the buyer does not know how to swim or does not have children? Admittedly this example is done with tongue-in-cheek, but the main point here is that the up or down valuation conclusion is up for interpretation.

You might take an issue with the prior statement about the subjectivity for whether a particular feature of a property deserves an upward or downward valuation movement. But this next point should be a much easier sell. How does the appraiser determine the specific dollar adjustments for each specific value adjustment? Why, for example, was the adjustment for not having a pool $5,000 for each comparable property that did not have a pool? Might the appraiser have combed sales properties to determine the average price differential between homes that sold with pools and homes that sold without? Or might some more robust statistical method have been utilized nationally to determine this same differential?

Given that the appraiser if often provided with the negotiated sales price for the subject property, some of the machinations in the sales approach, while subjective, may be targeted toward arriving at the desired value conclusion. In any event, what this section illustrates is that the same level of subjectivity which exists at the buyer level for arriving at different valuation conclusions is also present at the appraiser level. While the sales approach seems like a largely objective valuation approach, once adjustments to the historical sales prices of the properties deemed comparable to the subject enter into the valuation process, subjectivity surely exists.

3.3.2 Gross income multiplier subjectivity

As mentioned at the start of the prior section, the sales approach is the most common primary valuation method for home appraisals. Since the cost approach is often not included (might be included if the property is newly constructed), and since a second approach to value is needed to claim academic distance, the income approach is typically chosen as the secondary verification of value. Since home sales do not typically have an income component (except for an example where you are leasing out a spare room!), the more robust income approach valuation models (direct capitalization, discounted cash flow) are seldom utilized for home appraisals. What is left is the most simplistic income approach method: the gross income multiplier.

The gross income multiplier, as its name implies, only considers the gross income that a property could produce as opposed to subtracting out vacancy and collection loss (to arrive at effective gross income) or property operating expenses (to arrive at NOI). Since this approach is often used when assessing the value of a rental residential home, it can also be utilized as a secondary value estimate for home appraisals (after the sales approach method). In order to calculate the gross income multiplier, two primary things are needed. One is the market rental rate for local area houses, and the second is what the multiplier is by which homes have sold relative to the gross income produced.

Let's return to Exhibit 3.4 and assume that we are trying to utilize the gross income multiplier to arrive at an income approach value for the subject property of $225,000. If we assume that the market rental rate for the subject property would be $2,500 per month ($30,000 annually), then in order to arrive at the final value of $225,000, the gross income multiplier would need to be 7.5. In other words, in order to validate the value of the subject property at $225,000, the appraiser would need to show that sales prices for properties with gross income in the market have sold at an average of 7.5 times higher than the gross rent received annually at the subject property. Since most of the time the appraiser simply shares the gross income multiplier without much backing information, it does tend to feel like this approach is a plug process to arrive at the desired result (recall our Kierkegaard quote at the beginning of the chapter), rather than a strong, independent valuation measure.

The subjectivity in the gross income multiplier approach consists of the often sparse data on market rental rates for rental properties, and how strong is the data utilized to support the multiplier of which this method gets its name.

3.3.3 Cost approach subjectivity

Since we have discussed the elements of subjectivity in home price valuation in terms of the sales approach and the income approach, the final valuation method to cover is the cost approach. The cost approach is typically utilized for new construction or when determining the replacement cost of a property for insurance coverage calculations. The cost approach considers the value of the site (or land where the property is situated) plus the replacement cost for the property when new, and then subtracts out the effects of depreciation. The following formula is often referenced for the cost approach: $MV = S + RCN - D$, where MV stands for market value, S stands for site, RCN stands for replacement cost-new, and D stands for depreciation.

Returning to the home valuation exercise depicted in Exhibit 3.4, the goal of the cost approach would be to determine the estimated value for the home if it were reconstructed today. The cost approach would start with the valuation of the site as vacant land as of the date of the evaluation. The next step would be to estimate the replacement cost (new) of the structural improvements as of the date of the evaluation. For existing (i.e., non-new) properties, the final step would be to estimate the accumulated depreciation for the improvements on the site. This last piece of the valuation is what typically renders the cost approach applicable primarily for new properties. The thought is that if time erodes the value of the construction, then the older the property, the less value for the owner. This may or may not be accurate, as the impairments to a property owing to the passage of time can either be curable or not. For those things seen as being incurable, a straight line depreciation is assumed whereby a 35-year-old property with an economic life of 50 years would be considered 70% depreciated for those things considered to be incurable. For curable items, the typical response in the valuation is to subtract the short-term curable deficiencies from the final value. The element of depreciation certainly renders any attempt to make the cost approach a purely objective exercise obsolete.

Sometimes the incurable deficiencies can be labeled as either functional or external obsolescence. Functional obsolescence are features associated with the existing property that make it less palatable when compared to the competition where the ability to improve these issues cannot be done without considerable expense. An example of functional obsolescence in homes would be a very small home (say 900 square feet) that has three bedrooms, whereby the size of the home relegates the small bedrooms as insufficient. Another example would be having a five-bedroom home with only one full bathroom. External obsolescence considers factors outside of the home itself that contribute to a negative value perception when compared to competing properties. These could be changes in zoning whereby undesirable properties are adjacent to the subject property, or things in the surrounding neighborhood that negatively impact value.

Exhibit 3.5 provides an example of how the subject property outlined in Exhibit 3.4 would be valued under the cost approach methodology. As you review this exhibit, consider factors that could be subjective under this valuation approach.

	Unit Cost	Cost New
Base Building Costs		
Building (Sq ft)	2,456 $ 56.25	$ 138,141
Total Base Building Costs	**2,456**	**$ 138,141**
Additions/Site Improvements Units/Size Unit Cost		**Cost New**
Swimming Pool & Decking		$ 20,000
Curb & Gutter		$ 5,500
Landscaping		$ 6,500
Total Site Improvements		**$ 32,000**
Furniture, Fixtures, and Equipment		
Description	Units/Size Unit Cost	Cost New
Kitchen Appliances	1 $ 6,465	$6,465
Total FF&E		**$ 6,465**
Building Improvements		$ 138,141
Site Improvements		$ 32,000
Appliances/FF&E		$ 6,465
Subtotal		$ 176,606
Entrep Profit and Soft Costs		
Entrep Profit (% of hard costs)	10%	$ 17,014
Soft Costs (% of hard costs)	5%	$ 8,507
Replacement Cost New		**$ 202,127**
Depreciated Cost		**$ 202,127**
Estimated Land Value		$ 20,000
Estimated Value by Cost Approach		$ 222,127
Estimated Value (Rounded)		**$ 222,000**

Exhibit 3.5 Cost Approach Valuation Subjectivity.

When assessing the base building costs, an appraiser might utilize knowledge of the actual costs of recently completed buildings in order to obtain an estimate for the cost per square foot. Similar to the subjective elements in the sales approach as depicted in Exhibit 3.4, the cost approach also utilized market information whereby similar, but not exactly the same, properties are utilized when compiling market estimates. The type of construction of the comparable properties does introduce an element of subjectivity into the valuation process. Another method of determining the estimated building cost involves the preparation of an inventory of the quantity of each material and the time of its placement in the structure. While this might sound like a fairly objective process, the costs for components and raw materials vary among sources, and so which records are used provides an element of subjectivity in valuation.

This same element of cost subjectivity is present in the estimated cost of the pool, landscaping work, and furniture, fixtures, and equipment (FF&E), as shown in Exhibit 3.5. Chapter 1 highlighted that the French physiocrats created the basic cost approach as they considered value to be equal to the cost of production. One modern twist to the cost approach is the inclusion of entrepreneurial profit. Without the profit mechanism included, the cost approach would tacitly assume that a property builder would sell the structure once completed for the cost that it took to build, which is rarely, if ever, the case. In Exhibit 3.5, we assume a profit for the builder at 10% of the hard costs of the project. Hard costs are explicit costs associated with the construction of the property, while soft costs appear as a contingency in the construction budget to account for unforeseen expenses associated with financing or other things other than specific building costs. Typically, market surveys or rules of thumb are referenced in determining the percentage allocation for property and soft costs in the construction budget. When the cost of land is included in the valuation, the cost approach estimates the property value at $222,000, which is similar to (but not exactly the same as) the sales approach property value estimate of $226,000 as shown in Exhibit 3.4. As a reminder, the gross income multiplier approach valued the property at $225,000. Since the three approaches to value have provided similar but divergent valuation conclusions, what remains is for the appraiser to conclude the final market value for the subject property. This decision is fraught with subjectivity as well, as one appraiser may just average the three values to arrive at a value of $224,000 (which incidentally no valuation method actually exactly estimated), while another might just utilize the sales approach value of $226,000 as it is the most common method for home price valuation (thereby relegating the efforts to estimate value from the income and cost approach moot), and a third appraiser might offer some other variant to these approaches. What is clear is that each element of property valuation has subjectivity at its heart, and the final value conclusion will depend on the experience, risk tolerance, and motivations of the market participant performing the valuation.

In this chapter, we have discussed the nature of various housing boom models, some historical theories on how to classify home buyers based on where they are in the life cycle, and have highlighted subjective valuation elements in all three forms of property value. Our next chapter helps to further the case for a range of acceptable values for commercial real estate proper, given that the remainder of this book will be focused on more complicated examples of the income valuation approach for commercial properties.

Questions for discussion

1. Differentiate between classical and alternative housing boom models and provide examples of each of the components in those models witnessed in the real world.
2. Which of the government regulations noted in the chapter might be most likely to contribute to a run-up in housing prices?
3. Should an owner-occupied home be considered an investment or consumption? Take a position and defend.
4. Provide examples of conspicuous consumption, leisure, and waste as related to residential properties.
5. Describe the differences and similarities among the housing ladder, housing life cycle, and housing life course models of home consumption.
6. Is an update to the housing consumption models needed in the 21st century? If so, elaborate on the suggested improvements, and if not, describe why these models are still accurate.
7. Describe how the selection of comparable properties for the sales approach can be fraught with subjectivity.
8. Describe the subjectivity related to the adjusted sales price per square foot in the sales approach.
9. Describe the subjectivity related to the gross income multiplier approach.
10. Describe the subjectivity related to the cost approach valuation method.

Chapter 3 Market vignette

Cast of characters: Fred (home buyer), Barney (friend of Fred), Chad (Mountain realtor)
Act: Small mountain town in high demand

Scene one: the car ride to the mountains

BARNEY: So as we are driving up to the mountains today, what are we going to be seeing Fred?

FRED: We are heading up to Brevard again and I hope we can see some white squirrels this time! I have also contacted a real estate agent and told him what we are looking for in terms of investment property.

BARNEY: Oh nice, what did he say?

FRED: Well I explained that we are looking for a small cabin in the woods to possibly lease out and for us to occupy when we have the time with friends and family. I was looking at some of the prices for homes in the area on the realtor's website and the prices looked pretty high to me. So I told him that we would for now be interested in looking at some land for sale.

BARNEY: Did he give you some good leads?

FRED: Yes, I think so. I noticed that the good flat land available in town was listed for around $100,000 per half acre, so I wanted to keep the cost down to around $25,000. I told him that if we needed to go higher in price in order to get closer to town, I would be fine with that, but wasn't interested in getting ripped off.

BARNEY: Ha, what did he say to that?

FRED: He said he would try to stay below $35,000 and so hopefully we can see some decent properties that aren't too far out in the middle of nowhere.

BARNEY: Right like when you stayed at that rental place a few months ago with no phone or cell coverage.

FRED: Exactly. I told him that mountain isolation was good but I didn't want to feel like I was surrounded by America's Most Wanted for neighbors.

BARNEY: I hope the weather holds as it looks like it's starting to rain. When are we meeting this guy?

FRED: I saw the weather forecast and thought that it might keep the elusive white squirrels inside their tree homes but that it was otherwise a decent day for viewing some dirt. We have an appointment with him this morning, so I think we can just drive straight to his office and get started.

Scene two: realtor interaction

CHAD: Welcome to Mountain Realty! Thanks for contacting me earlier this week. I have gathered a few listings for land acreage for sale that meet the specifications that we discussed.

FRED: Hi Chad, that is great. I hope that you don't mind that I brought my friend Barney along. I have not purchased land before, and since he grew up in the mountains I thought he could add much to our discussion.

CHAD: That's fine, nice to meet you both. If you follow me in my car, I will take you to the first of three properties that we will view today.

FRED AND BARNEY: Sounds good.

CHAD: Well it is starting to rain a good bit out here, so I am glad you both brought your rain coats! As you saw as we drove up to this property, this land is located within a very popular residential community just minutes from downtown. I remember Fred that you didn't like having to drive a half an hour to the grocery store when you stayed in a rental property here last month.

FRED: That is so true. This is a great neighborhood, and I was surprised that land was available here at a price within my desired range.

BARNEY: This is a great spot and looks like there has been much recent construction. Fred took me by the rental home that he stayed at last month and there are three houses under construction just near that house. We were surprised that there was so much rental market activity for such a small town.

CHAD: Well, Brevard is located in the Pisgah National Forest as you both know. We have the famous white squirrels, and a classical music festival that lasts much of the summer, so those factors have contributed to the high demand for homes. I am sure you noticed that recently an 800 square foot home situated on less than a half an acre sold for $350,000.

BARNEY: Wow that seems really, really high Chad. What do you think?

CHAD: Well people are willing to pay that price. And people are willing to buy land and construct new homes on the few parcels left in the area. Did you know that current construction costs are $300 per square foot?

FRED: Wait, so people are spending $600,000 to construct a 2,000 square foot home?

CHAD: Yes they are. It seems like a high price to pay, but many people are desiring moving away from cities to more rural areas, and Brevard certainly has its charm.

BARNEY: It sure does. This is the second time that I have come up here in recent months, and I know Fred has fallen in love with the area.

FRED: Its sure is a nice place. I might fall out of love with it just a bit at those prices though! Haha!

CHAD: So as you can see, this property would need some significant work to support a home, but if you look across the street you can see a similar lot and the end result.

FRED: Barney, what do you think of this land? As a city slicker, I am having trouble envisioning the finished product on this lot. All I see are trees, and land that drops off pretty quickly to depths far below.

BARNEY: While the lot does drop off a bit, I could see a home being built on this, but it would probably cost you more than you are willing to spend.

CHAD: Well the next property is just down the road, let's go see that one. Here is a copy of the listing for the property we just saw as well as the next two.

Both cars drive to the next property location.

CHAD: Well, this second property is a bit larger in terms of acreage and a bit more expensive. I really think the first property is nicer and probably more of what you are desiring. The benefit of this property is that a potential driveway has already been created, although it would need to be made more permanent with rocks or asphalt once a house is constructed.

FRED: Speaking of home construction, are there any building requirements in these communities?

CHAD: Based on our prior conversation, you had mentioned wanting to build a home of at least 1,500 to 2,000 square feet, so the only real restrictions for these properties is that they have minimum home size requirements that restrict tiny home construction.

BARNEY: I seriously doubt Fred would want a tiny home as he is a bit claustrophobic.

FRED: You can say that again! My idea of creature comfort typically includes the ability to stretch out.

CHAD: The tiny homes have taken the rental market by storm. This is why many communities have begun to require minimum home sizes. Since this property is so similar to the first, I would like to take you both to our final property. It is located just a few minutes' drive from here.

Both cars drive to the final property of the day.

CHAD: Hi Fred, sorry for calling you on your phone while we are driving but I think you will need to pull off to the side of the road and let me drive you to this property. I am not sure if your car will be able to navigate the rough road on the way.

FRED: Ok thanks, we are happy to do that. (Fred and Barney join Chad in his car and ride to last property.)

CHAD: The first thing that you notice here is the street noise when you get out. The property is nice, but there are also some power lines along the boundary of the property that could prove problematic.

FRED: I was thinking the same thing. While the road was rough going, the land itself seems more realistic for constructing a home given the lack of steep drop-offs in elevation.

BARNEY: I would agree but am curious about how busy you are selling properties like this?

CHAD: Most of the remaining land has sat on the market for a while, to be honest. There is very limited home inventory on the market, and when someone does offer a property for sale it does not last long. What we are seeing is that the first bid on a property offered for sale comes in higher than the asking price.

FRED: Wow, so people are actually offering more than what the seller wants?

CHAD: Right, they are expecting to get into a price war, so are trying to avoid that. With interest rates being kept so low for so long, people are willing to spend more to get what they truly desire.

BARNEY: Fred it seems like this is a great place to buy a property, but we are not the first ones to figure this out.

FRED: I was thinking the same thing Barney! Chad, thank you for showing us these properties today.

Barney and I will review the materials that you have provided and will get back with you in the next few days.

Questions for discussion

1. Does this small mountain town exhibit any signs of a possible housing bubble?
2. Which symptoms highlighted in this chapter are most prevalent in this case?
3. Which sociodemographic housing model can best be utilized in describing the buyer in this case?
4. Is now the time to buy? What would you tell Fred and Barney?
5. How might you critique the sales approach of Chad in this case?

Bibliography

Affuso, E., Cummings, J. R., & Le, H. (2017) Wireless Towers and Home Values: An Alternative Valuation Approach Using a Spatial Econometric Analysis. *The Journal of Real Estate Finance and Economics*, 56(4), 653–676. doi: 10.1007/s11146-017-9600-9

Arribas, I., García, F., Guijarro, F., Oliver, J., & Tamošiūnienė, R. (n.d.). (2016) Mass Appraisal of Residential Real Estate Using Multilevel Modelling. *International Journal of Strategic Property Management*, 20(1), 77–87. doi: 10.3846/1648715x.2015.1134702

Benefield, J. D., Sirmans, C. S., & Sirmans, G. S. (2019) Observable Agent Effort and Limits to Innovation in Residential Real Estate. *The Journal of Real Estate Research; Sacramento*, 41(1), 1–36.

Bhutta, N., & Keys, B. J. (2016) Interest Rates and Equity Extraction during the Housing Boom. *The American Economic Review*, 106(7), 1742–1774.

Cerutti, E., Dagher, J., & Dellariccia, G. (2017) Housing Finance and Real-estate Booms: A Cross-country perspective. *Journal of Housing Economics*, 38, 1–13. doi: 10.1016/j.jhe.2017.02.001

Chan, S., Dastrup, S., & Ellen, I. G. (2015) Do Homeowners Mark to Market? A Comparison of Self-Reported and Estimated Market Home Values during the Housing Boom and Bust. *Real Estate Economics*, 44(3), 627–657. doi: 10.1111/1540-6229.12103

Chen, K., & Wen, Y. (2017) The Great Housing Boom of China. *American Economic Journal: Macroeconomics*, 9(2), 73–114.

Chinloy, P., Hardin, W., & Wu, Z. (2016) Foreclosure, REO, and Market Sales in Residential Real Estate. *The Journal of Real Estate Finance and Economics*, 54(2), 188–215. doi: 10.1007/s11146-015-9544-x

Cox, J., & Ludvigson, S. (2018) Drivers of the Great Housing Boom-Bust: Credit Conditions, Beliefs, or Both? doi: 10.3386/w25285

Defusco, A., Ding, W., Ferreira, F., & Gyourko, J. (2018) The Role of Price Spillovers in the American Housing Boom. *Journal of Urban Economics*, 108, 72–84. doi: 10.1016/j.jue.2018.10.001

Dieci, R., & Westerhoff, F. (2016) Heterogeneous Expectations, Boom-bust Housing Cycles, and Supply Conditions: A nonlinear Economic Dynamics Approach. *Journal of Economic Dynamics and Control*, 71, 21–44. doi: 10.1016/j.jedc.2016.07.011

Edvinsson, R., Eriksson, K., & Ingman, G. (2020) A Real Estate Price Index for Stockholm, Sweden 1818–2018: Putting the Last Decades Housing Price Boom in a Historical Perspective. *Scandinavian Economic History Review*, 1–19. doi: 10.1080/03585522.2020.1759681

Federal Reserve System Board of Governors, List of Regulations. https://www.federalreserve.gov/supervisionreg/reglisting.htm, accessed September 5, 2020.

Fisher, I. (1928) *The Money Illusion*. Adelphi Company, New York.

Fonseca, M. B. C. B. F., Ferreira, F. A. F., Fang, W., & Jalali, M. S. (2018) Classification and Selection of Tenants in Residential Real Estate: A Constructivist Approach. *International Journal of Strategic Property Management*, 24(1), 1–11. doi: 10.3846/ijspm.2018.317

Friedman, M. (1962) *Capitalism and Freedom*. The University of Chicago Press, Chicago, IL.

Galbraith, J. K. (1993) *A Short History of Financial Euphoria*. Penguin Books, New York.

Goddard, G. J. (2010) Global Housing Boom: Local Dimensions. In *The Psychology of Marketing: Cross-Cultural Perspectives*, edited by G. Raab, G. J. Goddard, R. A. Ajami, & A. Unger, pp. 337–345. Gower Publishing Company, Surrey, Burlington, VA.

Hayek, F. A. (1972) *Individualism and Economic Order*, Gateway Edition. Henry Regnery Company, Chicago, IL.

Hayek, F. A. (2012) *Monetary Theory and the Trade Cycle*. Martino Publishing, Mansfield Centre, CT.

Hoen, B., & Atkinson-Palombo, C. (October–December 2016) Wind Turbines, Amenities, and Disamenities: A Study of Home Value Impacts in Densely Populated Massachusetts. *The Journal of Real Estate Research; Sacramento*, 38(4), 473–504.

Huang, J., & Rong, Z. (2017) Housing Boom, Real Estate Diversification, and Capital Structure: Evidence from China. *Emerging Markets Review*, 32, 74–95. doi: 10.1016/j.ememar.2017.05.008

Ihlanfeldt, K., & Mayock, T. (2014) The Impact of REO Sales on Neighborhoods and Their Residents. *The Journal of Real Estate Finance and Economics*, 53(3), 282–324. doi: 10.1007/s11146-014-9465-0

Keynes, J. M. (1936) *The General Theory of Employment, Interest, and Money.* London: Palgrave Macmillan.

Kierkegaard, S. (1962) *The Present Age*, 1st ed. Harper Row Publishers, New York, USA.

Laeven, L., & Popov, A. (2017) Waking Up from the American Dream: On the Experience of Young Americans during the Housing Boom of the 2000s. *Journal of Money, Credit and Banking*, 49(5), 861–895. doi: 10.1111/jmcb.12408

Li, H., Wei, Y. D., Wu, Y., & Tian, G. (2019) Analyzing Housing Prices in Shanghai with Open Data: Amenity, Accessibility and Urban Structure. *Cities*, 91, 165–179. doi: 10.1016/j.cities.2018.11.016

Ma, X., Zhang, Z., Han, Y., & Yue, X.-G. (2019) Sustainable Policy Dynamics—A Study on the Recent "Bust" of Foreign Residential Real Estate Investment in Sydney. *Sustainability*, 11(20), 5856. doi: 10.3390/su11205856

Malkiel, B. G. (1973) *A Random Walk Down Wall Street: Time Tested Strategy for Successful Investing.* W.W. Norton & Company, New York.

Manitoba Real Estate Association, Unit Six on the Cost Approach, Real Estate as a Professional Career, Module 1 – Unit 6 (realestatemanitoba.com), accessed February 15, 2021.

Matthews, R. C. O. (1959) *The Business Cycle.* The University of Chicago Press, Chicago, IL.

McMillan, A., & Chakraborty, A. (2016) Who Buys Foreclosed Homes? How Neighbourhood Characteristics Influence Real Estate-Owned Home Sales to Investors and Households. *Housing Policy Debate*, 26(4–5), 766–784. doi: 10.1080/10511482.2016.1163277

Minsky, H. P. (1986) *Stabilizing an Unstable Economy.* Yale University Press, New Haven, CT & London.

Mises, L. (1912) *Theorie des Geldes und der Umlaufsmittel.* Duncker & Humblot Verlag, München und Leipzig.

Mises, L. (1980) *The Theory of Money and Credit.* Liberty Classics, Indianapolis, IN.

Morrow-Jones, H. A., & Wenning, M. V. (2005) The Housing Ladder, the Housing Life-Cycle, and the Housing Life Course: Upward and Downward Movement among Repeat Home-Buyers in a US Metropolitan Housing Market. *Urban Studies*, 42(10), 1739–1754.

Oliveira, I. A., Carayannis, E. G., Ferreira, F. A., Jalali, M. S., Carlucci, D., & Ferreira, J. J. (2018) Constructing Home Safety Indices for Strategic Planning in Residential Real Estate: A Socio-Technical Approach. *Technological Forecasting and Social Change*, 131, 67–77. doi: 10.1016/j.techfore. 2017.10.012

Pfeiffer, D., & Morris, E. A. (2017) Are Homeowners Better Neighbors During Housing Booms? Understanding Civic and Social Engagement by Tenure during the Housing Market Cycle. *Cityscape*, 19(2), 215–238. www.jstor.org/stable/26328337.

Pigou, A. C. (1949) *The Money Veil.* MacMillan & Co. Ltd., London.

Raab, G., Ajami, R. A., Gargeya, V. B., & Goddard, G. J. (2008) *Customer Relationship Management: A Global Perspective.* Gower Publishing Limited, Aldershot.

Ribeiro, M. I. F., Ferreira, F. A. F., Jalali, M. S., & Meidutė-Kavaliauskienė, I. (2017) A Fuzzy Knowledge-Based Framework for Risk Assessment of Residential Real Estate Investments. *Technological and Economic Development of Economy,* 23(1), 140–156. doi: 10.3846/20294913.2016.1212742

Sevka, V. G., Panchenko, V. V., & Kilimnik, E. A. (2018) The Residential Real Estate Market Influence on the Reconstruction and Housing Restoration Potential in the Region. *Materials Science Forum,* 931, 1204–1209. doi: 10.4028/www.scientific.net/msf.931.1204

Thornton, M. (2018) *The Skyscraper Curse: and How Austrian Economists Predicted Every Major Economic Crisis of the Last Century.* Mises Institute, Auburn, AL.

Veblen T. (1899) *The Theory of the Leisure Class.* Penguin Books, New York, London.

Voronina, E. V., Yarosh, O. B., Bereza, N. V., & Zakieva, N. I. (2018) Mathematical Model of Forecasting the Residential Real Estate Market Prices Level. *Materials Science Forum,* 931, 1101–1106. doi: 10.4028/www.scientific.net/msf.931.1101

Wang, A.-M. (2016) Agglomeration and Simplified Housing Boom. *Urban Studies,* 53(5), 936–956. https://doi.org/10.1177/0042098015572975

Wright, D., & Yanotti, M. B. (2019) Home Advantage: The Preference for Local Residential Real Estate Investment. *Pacific-Basin Finance Journal,* 57, 101167. doi: 10.1016/j.pacfin.2019.06.014

Xia, Z., Li, H., & Chen, Y. (2018) Assessing Neighbourhood Walkability Based on Usage Characteristics of Amenities under Chinese Metropolises Context. *Sustainability,* 10(11), 3879. doi: 10.3390/su10113879

Chapter 4

Subjectivity of commercial real estate valuation

Chapter highlights

- Imagination and the nature of choice
- Range of acceptable values study
- Range of value survey components
- Range of value survey results

> Choice is a business of the whole psyche. It involves intellection of sense-impressions and their assimilation to a scheme or geometry (coherent account) of a supposed field outside the thinking being's thought; the origination of imagined paths of history out of the abstract permanent elements which compose the scheme of the field, paths unrealized and unreported, but deemed possible in their freedom from discerned obstruction; the location of these paths as rival suggestions of the content of time-to-come, the time which is the inferred, invented consequence of the transience of thought, the transience of the present, the time which is a space accommodating succession.
>
> GLS Shackle

4.1 Imagination and the Nature of Choice

The Shackle quote that begins this chapter is quite the mouthful. Once you read it a few times, you will begin to understand why this quote was chosen to head up this chapter. I always thought that this quote would have made a great T-shirt or bumper sticker saying. Seriously though, this quote represents the basis for the survey that was conducted in that each survey respondent brings to the table a different set of experiences, expertise, and predilections that impact how they might

DOI: 10.4324/9781003083672-4

answer a survey that asks them to consider market data and to respond with their answers as to what are the most reasonable assumptions for the market rental rates, cap rates, and discount rates, among other queries.

In G.L.S. Shackle's *Imagination and the Nature of Choice*, the academic framework for a range of values was most completely explained. The Shackle Possibility Curve introduced in Chapter 1 was highlighted in an attempt to explain how different individuals can reach very different choices of action. Choice involves valuation, as by making a decision, an individual is exhibiting preferences for one option over a multitude. Shackle believed that there were three basic themes that guided the chooser's thought and eventual action (or choice). The first was the news or reports from the field that helped to sway the individual's actions. Sometimes the news can be overly optimistic, which influences the risk tolerance of the market participant. At other times, news can be overly pessimistic, which can cause a higher probability of caution in the action undertaken. The second theme was what he termed a gradually integrated scheme. This is a plan that describes what the field is like in its general principles. This includes the range of possible options for action, some of which equate well with the market participants experience, and others which do not. The further away an action resides from the experience of the individual, the higher the possibility for error. Error is more likely in situations where the gap between the individual's experience and the action at hand is wide. Shackle termed this concept "un-knowledge" and believed that "*un-knowledge liberates the imagination which seizes and occupies the void of time-to-come*". The third theme was referred to as the imagined-deemed possible. Based on the experience of the individual in question, along with news from the external environment, the chosen action is what is considered the most reasonable conclusion based on the market participant's current understanding of the perceived risks, facts, and rewards.

The book for which this section is named served as the starting point for the survey which is summarized in this chapter. The initial hypothesis was that if different market participants are presented with the same basic market information, each person's perception of that information could differ and those divergences could help to provide evidence that there can be a range of property values at any given moment in time. When I was presented with a situation where the same appraiser utilized the same market data on multiple properties concurrently, it seemed like a good basis for an experiment. The appraiser did arrive at slightly different conclusions for market rental rates and vacancy rates relative to the multiple properties being valued, but for the purposes of this survey, I chose to compare the appraiser's final value conclusion for one property to the assumptions made by each survey respondent.

4.2 Range of acceptable values study

In order to test the hypothesis that market participants viewing the same market data can and should reach differing conclusions of value, a survey was conducted in four MBA courses, as well as one expert sample of appraisers at a large financial institution. The first survey was conducted as part of the summer 2013 Real Estate Investments MBA course at the University of North Carolina at Greensboro, and the second was conducted as part of the spring 2014 Real Estate Investments MBA course at Wake Forest University. The appraisal expert survey was conducted in the summer of 2014, while the fourth survey was conducted as part of the fall 2014 Globalization at the Crossroads MBA course at the University of Applied Sciences in Ludwigshafen, Germany. The final survey was conducted as part of the Financial Markets and Institutions MBA course at UNC-Greensboro in the summer of 2016. The U.S. MBA students surveyed were asked to complete a survey toward the end of the course such that the students had covered the relevant course material concerning the meaning and dissemination of market information in commercial real estate. German MBA students surveyed were asked to complete the survey during the end of the course, although many of the students did not have familiarity with commercial real estate.

All 122 respondents completed the same three-page survey. All student surveys were conducted outside of class, while the expert sample was disseminated via email. Survey respondents were asked to review the market information concerning rental rates, cap rates, discount rates, and equity yield rates, and to then supply their best estimate for final market averages for these data points. Survey respondents essentially completed blanks on the back of the third page in order to document what they assumed would be the final market rates for a commercial real estate property. The rent roll information revealed that the subject properties consisted of four grocery store-anchored retail properties. The comparable sales information revealed that these properties were likely located in the eastern part of North Carolina, U.S.A. It was left up to the survey respondent to conclude value based on their own perception of the factors supplied. Since the remainder of this book concerns commercial real estate value subjectivity, I wanted to provide this explicit example of how different market participants can reach very different value conclusions at this point in our journey.

The 2013 UNC-G MBA class consisted of 32 students, with 31 completed surveys submitted. The 2014 Wake Forest MBA class consisted of 20 students, with 16 completed surveys submitted, while all 24 German students completed the survey. The expert sample consisted of 24 completed surveys, while the 2016 UNC-G MBA class consisted of 27 respondents. The total survey response rate was 92% for the student sample, 50% for the expert sample, with an overall response rate of 79% for the 122 surveys completed. The samples included survey respondents from across the United States as well as an international component in the U.S. classes along with the German sample. The implication was that no U.S. sample consisted of a majority of respondents who were from North Carolina specifically. Geographic dispersion was desired such that the survey could be representative of a larger population.

Once the completed surveys were obtained, the estimates of market values provided in the surveys were summarized so as to compile survey averages. These market estimates were then utilized to value the first property on the list, and the final value as estimated by each student was then compared with the final appraised value for the property.

4.3 Range of value survey components

What follows is a reproduction of the survey that respondents were asked to review and complete. In order to provide as accurate an example of what was provided, this section will essentially reproduce this information. In the following section of this chapter, we will discuss the results.

Assume that you are considering a grocery-anchored retail property as an investment alternative. You have obtained recent appraisals for four similar properties that are all within 20 miles of the subject property. Your task is to review the following charts and then fill out the survey questions at the end. Just utilize these charts to make your best guess at what constitutes market value. The purpose of this exercise is to assess the range of possible answers for market value for an investment property.

You have also been provided cap rate and discount rate information as is shown below:

Tenants	SF	Annual Rent/SF	Lease Remaining	Total
Grocery	29,284	$ 7.80	2 Years	$ 228,415
Pharmacy	6,400	$ 13.48	1 Year	$ 86,272
Pizza	1,600	$ 11.20	2 Years	$ 17,920
Clinic	1,600	$ 7.88	5 Years	$ 12,608
Sub Shop	1,600	$ 11.63	2 Years	$ 18,608
Nail Salon	800	$ 7.58	2 Years	$ 6,064
Hair Salon	800	$ 7.58	2 Years	$ 6,064
Asian Food	1,600	$ 10.49	2 Years	$ 16,784

Survey Exhibit A Rent Roll # 1

Tenants	SF	Annual Rent/SF	Lease Remaining	Total
Grocery	42,206	$ 5.17	7 Years	$ 218,205
Gym	9,600	$ 2.75	3 Years	$ 26,400
Sub Shop	1,200	$ 14.00	4 Years	$ 16,800
Vacant	1,260			$ -
Asian Food	1,680	$ 8.21	3 Years	$ 13,793
Vacant	1,260			$ -
ATM			1 Year	$ 3,500

Survey Exhibit B Rent Roll # 2

Tenants	SF	Annual Rent/SF	Lease Remaining	Total
Grocery	32,040	$ 4.33	6 Years	$138,733
Pharmacy	5,500	$ 3.27	1 Year	$ 17,985
Vision Center	1,300	$ 6.23	2 Years	$ 8,099
Hair Salon	1,300	$ 5.77	1 Year	$ 7,501
Farm Bureau	1,300	$ 6.46	3 Years	$ 8,398
Burgers	2,600	$ 7.38	4 Years	$ 19,188
Pizza	1,300	$ 6.69	4 Years	$ 8,697
Internet Café	2,250	$ 7.33	1 Year	$ 16,493
Asian Food	1,300	$ 10.53	2 Years	$ 13,689

Survey Exhibit C Rent Roll # 3

Tenants	SF	Annual Rent/SF	Lease Remaining	Total
Grocery	30,280	$ 7.80	3 Years	$236,184
PC Store	7,020	$ 2.52	5 Years	$ 17,690
Tax Preparation	1,468	$ 9.40	3 Years	$ 13,799
Nail Salon	1,298	$ 7.53	2 Years	$ 9,774
Vacant	**1,609**			$ -
US Cellular	2,050	$ 10.68	2 Years	$ 21,894
Vacant	**1,609**			$ -

Survey Exhibit D Rent Roll # 4

Y	=	Annual Rate of Yield of Equity on Cash	=	10.5%
M	=	Loan to Value Percent Ratio	=	70%
MTG	=	Maximum Available Mortgage Length (Years)	=	20
RATE	=	Mortgage Interest Rate	=	5.75%
Rm	=	Annual Loan Constant	=	0.0842500
CR	=	(M*Rm)+ ((1-M)*Y)	=	0.0904750
CR	=		=	**9.05%**

Survey Exhibit E Band of Investment Method

DCR	1.05	2.00
LTV	70%	70%
Mortgage Constant	0.0842500	0.0842500
OAR	6.19%	11.80%

Survey Exhibit F Lender's Yield Analysis for Cap Rate Derivation

Reputable Source	Range	Avg
Most Recent QTR National Retail Anchored	5.29%-13.09%	10.24% Cap
Most Recent QTR Regional Retail Anchored	8.26%-17.20%	12.28% Equity
Most Recent QTR State Regional Anchored	5.81%-12.70%	10.29% Discount

Survey Exhibit G Third-Party Data References

Sale Property	Sale Date	NRA	Built	Cap Rate
Strickland Bridge	Listing	50,148	1987	9.59%
Wrightsboro Plaza	Listing	44,180	1993	8.48%
Andrews Commons	Pending	53,280	1990	8.75%
Tyrell Village	Pending	28,853	2004	8.82%
College Lakes Plaza	Pending	43,041	1987	9.20%
Northview Plaza	This year	39,362	1988	9.50%
Pender Landing	This year	58,872	1985	11.44%
Moores Chapel Village	This year	52,445	2008	7.85%
Mountain View	This year	43,555	1988	8.54%
Ram's Plaza	Last year	113,000	1980	7.58%
Wakefield Crossing	Last year	75,927	2001	9.40%
Moyock Commons	Last year	33,019	1999	8.83%
Ayden Crossing	Last year	50,788	2000	9.07%
Forestdale Plaza	Last year	53,239	2001	9.12%
Liberty Square	Last year	45,300	1991	9.07%
Eden Centre	Last year	57,590	1990	9.83%
Shoppes at Battle Bridge	Two years	56,615	2007	8.32%
			Min	7.85%
			Max	11.44%
			Mean	9.02%

Survey Exhibit H Market Abstraction Method

Survey questions

Based on the information shown above, please fill in your estimates of market value for the following:

Rent per square foot for average size local tenant: _____

Rent per square foot for larger size local tenant: _____

Rent per square foot for restaurant space: _____

Rent per square foot for anchor space: _____

Capitalization Rate: _____

Terminal Cap Rate: _____

Discount Rate: _____

Equity Rate: _____

4.4 The survey results

The average value for the commercial property was 9% lower for the 2013 UNCG MBA class relative to the appraised value, 10% lower for the 2014 Wake Forest MBA class relative to the appraised value, 14% lower for the expert sample, 7% higher for the German sample, and 8% lower for the 2016 UNCG MBA class sample.

4.4.1 Sample 1: 2013 UNC-Greensboro MBA survey

Exhibit 4.1 summarizes the comparison of the average response for the 2013 UNCG class relative to the appraisal.

While the 2013 UNCG MBA class on average valued the property nine percentage points lower than the actual appraised value, individual respondents varied from a valuation which was 21% higher than the appraisal to one which was 50% lower than the appraisal. Most respondents were within 15 percentage points of the appraiser (either higher or lower). Specifically, 13% of the survey respondents were within 5% of the value, 39% were within 10% of the value, 81% were within 15% of the value, and 90% were within 21% of the value.

Exhibit 4.2 shows the range of individual survey respondent values from the 2013 UNCG MBA class.

Relative to the appraised value of $2,890,000, most of the estimated values were similar to this result, but none of the estimated values equaled the appraisal exactly, and only four of the survey respondents' estimated values were less than 5% higher or lower than the appraisal.

	Sq Ft/%		Class		Appraiser
Anchor	29,284	$	188,235	$	197,667
Large Tenant	6,400	$	35,658	$	40,768
Avg Tenant	3,200	$	26,281	$	27,200
Restaurant	4,800	$	46,995	$	52,800
GPI	43,684	$	297,169	$	318,435
Vacancy Factor	10%	$	10,893	$	12,077
EGI		$	286,275	$	306,358
Op ex	15%	$	42,941	$	45,954
NOI		$	243,334	$	260,404
Cap Rate			9.27%		9.00%
Value		$	2,620,000	$	2,890,000
% Difference			-9%		

Exhibit 4.1 2013 UNCG MBA Class vs. Appraiser.

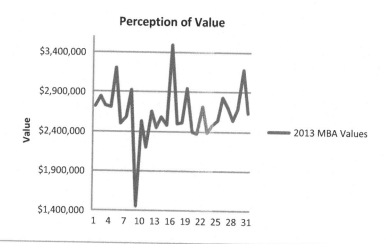

Exhibit 4.2 Range of Value for 2013 UNCG MBA Sample.

4.4.2 Sample 2: 2014 Wake Forest MBA survey

Exhibit 4.3 summarizes the results of the 2014 Wake Forest MBA surveys relative to the same appraised value of the grocery-anchored retail shopping property in Eastern North Carolina.

While the 2014 Wake Forest MBA class on average valued the property 10 percentage points lower than the actual appraised value, individual respondents varied from a valuation which was 27% higher than the appraisal to one which was 21% lower than the appraisal. Most respondents were within 15 percentage points of the appraiser (either higher or lower). Specifically, 13% of the survey

	Sq Ft/%		Class		Appraiser
Anchor	29,284	$	187,811	$	197,667
Large Tenant	6,400	$	38,202	$	40,768
Avg Tenant	3,200	$	25,271	$	27,200
Restaurant	4,800	$	46,314	$	52,800
GPI	43,684	$	297,598	$	318,435
Vacancy Factor	10%	$	10,979	$	12,077
EGI		$	286,619	$	306,358
Op ex	15%	$	42,993	$	45,954
NOI		$	243,626	$	260,404
Cap Rate			9.41%		9.00%
Value		$	2,590,000	$	2,890,000
% Difference			-10%		

Exhibit 4.3 2014 Wake Forest MBA Class vs. Appraiser.

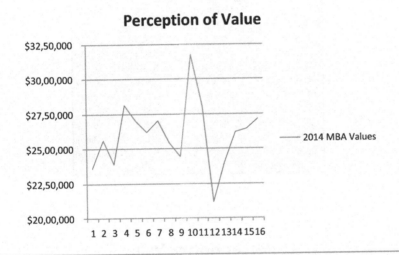

Exhibit 4.4 Range of Value for 2014 Wake Forest MBA Sample.

respondents were within 5% of the value, 56% were within 10% of the value, 69% were within 15% of the value, and 94% were within 20% of the value.

Exhibit 4.4 shows the range of individual survey respondent values from the 2014 Wake Forest MBA class.

Relative to the appraised value of $2,890,000, most of the estimated values were similar to this result, but none of the estimated values equaled the appraisal exactly, and only two of the survey respondents' estimated value was less than 5% higher or lower than the appraisal.

4.4.3 Sample 3: 2014 appraisal expert survey

Exhibit 4.5 summarizes the comparison of the average response for the expert sample relative to the appraisal.

The 2014 expert sample came in lower than the students samples, as the average value for the property was 14% lower than the appraiser's estimate of value. Individual respondents varied from a valuation which was 21% higher than the appraisal to one which was 33% lower than the appraisal. Most respondents were within 15 percentage points of the appraiser (either higher or lower). Specifically, 4% of the survey respondents were within 5% of the value, 29% were within 10% of the value, 75% were within 15% of the value, and 75% were within 20% of the value. Among them, 94% of survey respondents were under the value provided by the appraiser.

Exhibit 4.6 shows the range of individual survey respondent values from the expert sample.

	Sq Ft/%	Experts	Appraiser
Anchor	29,284	$ 177,339	$ 197,667
Large Tenant	6,400	$ 27,927	$ 40,768
Avg Tenant	3,200	$ 24,513	$ 27,200
Restaurant	4,800	$ 45,970	$ 52,800
GPI	43,684	$ 275,749	$ 318,435
Vacancy Factor	10%	$ 9,841	$ 12,077
EGI		$ 265,908	$ 306,358
Op ex	15%	$ 39,886	$ 45,954
NOI		$ 226,022	$ 260,404
Cap Rate		9.10%	9.00%
Value		$ 2,480,000	$ 2,890,000
% Difference		-14%	

Exhibit 4.5 2014 Expert Sample vs. Appraiser.

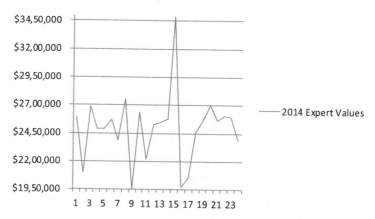

Exhibit 4.6 Range of Value for Expert Sample.

Relative to the appraised value of $2,890,000, a few of the estimated values were similar to this result, but none of the estimated values equaled the appraisal exactly, and only one of the survey respondents estimated value was less than 5% higher or lower than the appraisal. Interestingly, the expert sample valuations were consistently lower than the student valuations, and on average the expert sample showed a wider value range than did the student samples relative to the appraised value.

4.4.4 Sample 4: 2014 German MBA survey

Exhibit 4.7 summarizes the comparison of the average response for the German MBA class relative to the appraisal.

While the 2014 German MBA class on average valued the property seven percentage points higher than the actual appraised value, and individual respondents varied from a valuation which was 179% higher than the appraisal to one which was 21% lower than the appraisal. Most respondents were within 15 percentage points of the appraiser (either higher or lower). Specifically, 21% of the survey respondents were within 5% of the value, 42% were within 10% of the value, 63% were within 15% of the value, and 75% were within 20% of the value. If the three German survey respondent results where the final value was over 100% higher than the appraised value are removed from the analysis, the remaining German respondents would have had an average valuation 6% below the appraiser. The reason for the three outlier responses is related to the German students' lack of prior knowledge of commercial real estate terms. The school does not offer a course in real estate investment, so this survey was probably the first opportunity that those students had to assess market intelligence from a commercial real estate perspective.

Exhibit 4.8 shows the range of individual survey respondent values from the 2014 German MBA class.

Relative to the appraised value of $2,890,000, most of the estimated values were slightly lower than this result, with one estimated value equaling the appraisal

	Sq Ft/%	German	Appraiser
Anchor	29,284	$ 241,318	$ 197,667
Large Tenant	6,400	$ 37,424	$ 40,768
Avg Tenant	3,200	$ 25,246	$ 27,200
Restaurant	4,800	$ 44,294	$ 52,800
GPI	43,684	$ 348,282	$ 318,435
Vacancy Factor	10%	$ 10,696	$ 12,077
EGI		$ 337,585	$ 306,358
Op ex	15%	$ 50,638	$ 45,954
NOI		$ 286,947	$ 260,404
Cap Rate		9.26%	9.00%
Value		$ 3,100,000	$ 2,890,000
% Difference		7%	

Exhibit 4.7 German MBA Sample vs. Appraiser.

Perception of Value

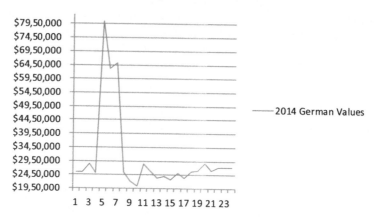

Exhibit 4.8 Range of Value for German Sample.

exactly, and only four additional survey respondents achieving an estimated value less than 5% higher or lower than the appraisal.

4.4.5 Survey 5: 2016 UNC-G MBA survey

The fifth and final survey results are summarized in Exhibit 4.9.

While the 2016 UNC-G MBA class on average valued the property eight percentage points lower than the actual appraised value, individual respondents varied from a valuation which was 11% higher than the appraisal to one which was 17% lower than the appraisal. Most respondents were within 15 percentage points of the appraiser (either higher or lower). Specifically, 11% of the survey respondents were within 5% of the value, 56% were within 10% of the value, 93% were within 15% of the value, and 100% were within 20% of the value.

Exhibit 4.10 shows the range of individual survey respondent values from the 2016 UNC-G MBA class.

Relative to the appraised value of $2,890,000, most of the estimated values were slightly lower than this result, with only three survey respondents achieving an estimated value less than 5% higher or lower than the appraisal.

4.4.6 Perception of value: home on the range

Now that we have discussed the surveys separately, it is helpful to view the combined results relative to the appraisal. This will help illustrate that, based on the surveys conducted, there is a wide range of acceptable values for commercial real estate based on reviewing the same market data. Exhibit 4.11 summarizes the values for all survey respondents relative to the "official" appraised value.

Obviously, the outlier values should be discarded as not being credible. But when the 122 surveys are seen relative to the constant of the appraisal, a case can be made

	Sq Ft/%	Class	Appraiser
Anchor	29,284	$ 190,026	$ 197,667
Large Tenant	6,400	$ 36,587	$ 40,768
Avg Tenant	3,200	$ 26,301	$ 27,200
Restaurant	4,800	$ 47,201	$ 52,800
GPI	43,684	$ 300,115	$ 318,435
Vacancy Factor	10%	$ 11,009	$ 12,077
EGI		$ 289,106	$ 306,358
Op ex	15%	$ 43,366	$ 45,954
NOI		$ 245,740	$ 260,404
Cap Rate		9.29%	9.00%
Value		$ 2,650,000	$ 2,890,000
% Difference		-8%	

Exhibit 4.9 2016 UNC-G MBA Sample vs. Appraiser.

Perception of Value

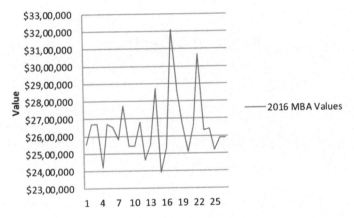

Exhibit 4.10 Range of Value for UNC-G 2016 MBA Sample.

that various market participants can look at the same market data and arrive at different estimates of a reasonable value for the same commercial property. Exhibit 4.12 summarizes the difference in values for the surveys relative to the appraisal.

As Exhibit 4.12 shows, based on our survey results, the bulk of the respondents obtained estimated property values within 25 percentage points (higher or lower) than the appraisal. These findings help validate the point that an appraisal is an "opinion of value" and that there is a fairly wide range of values that could reasonably be assumed for a subject property. It is only when the opinions of the buyer and seller coincide that a transfer of the property from one to the other is possible.

Exhibit 4.13 summarizes how all of the surveys compared to the appraisal. The percentages compare the survey results with the appraisal on an absolute basis (i.e., "within 5%" refers to plus or minus 5%).

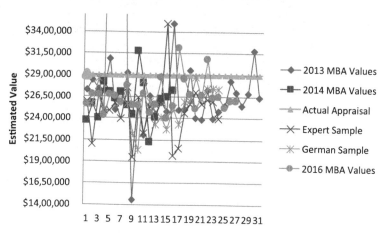

Perception of Value

Exhibit 4.11 Home on the Range Combined Results ($).

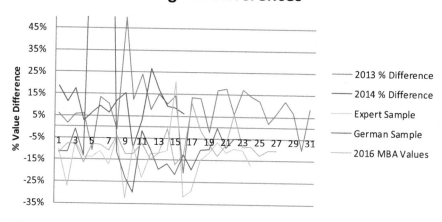

Exhibit 4.12 Home on the Range Combined Results (%).

The data shown in Exhibit 4.13 indicate that the majority of respondents provided results that were within plus or minus 15% of the appraisal. What is also clear is that the survey respondents provided results lower than the appraiser's value 89% of the time. Exhibit 4.14 provides a summary of how each survey group compared with the appraisal.

Based on the data provided in Exhibits 4.13 and 4.14, it would appear that a reasonable estimate for the range of values based on the 122 surveys evaluated in this study is from 10% to 15%. The differences in valuation in this survey have

All Surveys	
Within 5%	12%
Within 10%	43%
Within 15%	77%
Within 20%	87%
Under Value	89%
Exact	1%

Exhibit 4.13 Range of Survey Values Relative to Appraisal.

Overall Averages	
2013 % Difference	-10%
2014 % Difference	-10%
Expert Sample	-13%
German Sample	7%
2016 % Difference	-8%
Exact Total	1%

Exhibit 4.14 Average Survey Response Relative to Appraisal.

been limited to subjective factors, as all survey respondents were asked to consider the same market data in order to reach their conclusions. The wide variety of answers and estimated values helps shed some light on why real estate is considered an illiquid asset, and why it sometimes takes quite a long time to sell a property once it is listed on the market.

4.5 Chapter conclusion

The purpose of this chapter was to illustrate that the value of a commercial property is truly based on the eyes of the beholder. Government regulations require an official opinion of value, but it is just that: an opinion of value. Granted appraisers have quality credentials which make their opinions more telling than the layman, but the simple fact remains that the trained eye can provide slightly differing opinions as to the current value of commercial real estate. Just a slight tweak in an assumed cap rate, vacancy rate, or rental rate could lead to different final value conclusions. This does not mean that there is an inherent flaw in the market or in the appraisal process. It just means that there can be differing opinions as to the "true value" of a commercial property, and that these differing views can lead to a range of acceptable values for a specific property at a certain period of time. Investors and lenders should periodically update their appraised values, so the opinion of value from a few years ago does not continue to remain the "official opinion" of today.

Areas of future research include expanding the model to include data collection by the survey respondents in an attempt to include more factors of perception in valuation. Other future studies might expand the number of properties in the survey to assess whether the range of appropriate values implied in this survey carries over to multiple properties. Another possible avenue for future research could be to expand the type of investment from commercial real estate to other asset classes, namely, stocks and bonds. The key to those studies being conducted accurately would be in the determination of the "correct valuation", something that in this survey was represented by the appraised value.

Two quotations from Ludwig von Mises help us to summarize this chapter. "*All the desperate efforts to reduce thinking and valuing to mechanical principles have failed*". This quote is appropriate for this study as the machinations employed to arrive at value still provide divergent conclusions. Mises also said that

> *We know nothing about the process that produces within the body of a living man thoughts and ideas. Almost identical external events that impinge on the human mind result, with different people and with the same people at different moments, in different thoughts and ideas. Individuality- the product of all that a person has inherited at birth from their ancestors and all that they have experienced up to the critical moment-determines the final resolution.*

This survey attempted to provide evidence that the valuation of real estate is highly subjective, and that a range of acceptable values is the result at any given point in time.

In our next chapter, we delve deeper into how specific market participants can resolve their value differences in the marketplace.

Questions for discussion

1. Summarize the Shackle quote at the beginning of the chapter and provide an example of how it can pertain to property valuation or really any other thought or action of the human mind.
2. What are some of the weaknesses of the survey method employed?
3. What are some strengths of the survey method employed?
4. How could this survey approach be expanded in the future?
5. What does the range of values discussed in this survey imply for appraisal theory?
6. Is there an underlying reason why the expert sample shows lower values than the student samples?
7. How might artificial intelligence or machine learning discussed in Chapter 1 deal with the range of values for real estate?
8. How might a similar study of owner-occupied real estate be conducted?
9. Provide examples of when news from the field swayed your actions (both positively and negatively).

10. How might Shackle's un-knowledge be related to entrepreneurial risk taking?

Chapter 4 Market vignette

Cast of characters: Mickey (Student/Survey Respondent), Minnie (Student/Survey Respondent)
   Act: Campus Study Lab

Scene one: initial range of acceptable values survey discussion

MICKEY: Hi Minnie! Fancy meeting you here in the study lab. I guess you are working on Professor Goddard's Perception of Value study too?

MINNIE: Hi Mickey! Yes since this is due tomorrow, I thought I would spend some time filling it out today. I am glad that he said that we didn't need to research anything as it would really take more time to fill out.

MICKEY: Right, I remember him saying that we should just review the market data in the survey and then simply try to answer the questions at the bottom of the survey. I wonder what he is going to do with these results.

MINNIE: To me it seems like he wants to see how many people choose a certain answer over another. He mentioned in class something about a frequency distribution, so maybe that's it.

MICKEY: Yeah maybe so. Let's take a look and see if we can fill it out together. It looks like the survey starts out with four rent rolls for a grocery-anchored retail shopping center. I like how property three has an internet café. Do those things still really exist?

MINNIE: Ha I know, I saw that too. Otherwise it looks like a bunch of restaurants and nail salons as the support tenants. I see he wants us to essentially look at the four rent rolls and provide our thoughts on the rent per square foot for local tenants, restaurants, and the anchor. I wonder what he means by "average size vs. larger sized tenants".

MICKEY: I am not sure about that either. Let's start with the easier ones to figure out first, like the anchor and restaurant space. For the four anchor tenants, two of them have annual rents of $7.80 per square foot, while the other two are lower.

MINNIE: What is interesting with the anchor space is that the two lower rent spaces have longer lease terms. I wonder if this means that those leases were signed more recently.

MICKEY: Oh wow, good point. I didn't notice that. I was planning on calculating the weighted average for each, but now you have introduced another element of subjectivity.

MINNIE: Well Professor Goddard talks about subjectivity all the time, so I bet he is trying to trick us a bit here! I bet what most people do is come up with the weighted average for each type of tenant based on the square footage and current rental rates per square foot, but the remaining lease term must be provided for a reason.

MICKEY: Maybe we can weigh the longer leases more heavily than the ones with shorter lease tenors?

MINNIE: Lease tenors, I like that. It sounds like an opera or something. What I will probably do is come up with some mathematical formula to account for rent, size, and remaining lease term to answer the first four questions.

MICKEY: Yes, same here. Once we do that we will be halfway through with the survey questions. I can see how you can really get varied answers just with the rents, given what we just discussed.

MINNIE: For sure. Some will just take an average, others might take a weighted average, and some might just put their finger in the air to see which way the wind blows.

Mickey and Minnie spend time working on their excel calculations to answer the first four survey questions concerning rental rates.

Scene two: completion of the survey

MICKEY: Ok, so let's focus on the second part of the survey now. Seems like he has given us a series of charts based on the cap rate derivation models that we went over in class.

MINNIE: Yes, I agree. Seems like all we need to do is average the results for each of the cap rate models to answer that question.

MICKEY: That's true, but for the third-party data references we have both ranges and a final average cap rate. I think I will just use the average cap rate for those and average them all together. What is a terminal cap rate? It sounds serious.

MINNIE: I remember we talked about this in class. This is the cap rate at the end of the investment period, like when you sell the property. Typically, the terminal cap rate is higher than the current cap rate, which I think is also called the going in cap rate. The terminal cap rate is higher as it is further in the future and the property will have aged as well.

MICKEY: Wow, you were really paying attention Minnie! I wonder how much higher the terminal cap rate should be? Now that you mention it, I remember Professor Goddard saying that the terminal cap rate is often between 25 and 50 basis points higher than the going in cap rate. I will go with 50 points higher for my estimate.

MINNIE: OK, that sounds good, I will go with 25 basis points higher for my terminal cap rate, just for fun.

MICKEY: Just to make this easy, I am going to choose the average equity rate and discount rate per the third-party data references section.

MINNIE: Me too. I have two tests this week, and I am so far behind on studying.

MICKEY: Same here. Did he say this survey was for a grade or just for class contribution?

MINNIE: This is not for a grade, so I think we are fine and can move on to other assignments.

Questions for discussion

1. Discuss the elements of subjectivity in the estimation of market rates for the four properties included in the survey.
2. Discuss the elements of subjectivity in the estimation of the market cap rates, terminal cap rates, equity rates, and discount rates.
3. Discuss how other methods could be utilized for estimating market rates for this survey.
4. If research was required for this survey, would the range of values provided been narrower? Elaborate how this might or might not have been the case.
5. Focus on the market abstraction portion of the survey and highlight methods for ascertaining the suitability for which sales to include and which not to include in the final analysis.

Bibliography

Bellman, L., & Öhman, P. (2016) Authorised property appraisers' perceptions of commercial property valuation. *Journal of Property Investment & Finance*, 34(3), 225–248. doi: 10.1108/jpif-08-2015-0061

Goddard, G. J. (2014) Kierkegaard and Valuation in a Business Context. *Business and Economics Journal*, 5(2).

Hayek, F. A. (2014) *The Sensory Order*. Martino Publishing, Mansfield Centre, CT.

Kierkegaard, S. (1962) *The Present Age*, 1st ed. Harper and Row Publishers, New York.

Lachmann, L. (1986) *The Market as an Economic Process*. Basil Blackwell Ltd., Oxford & New York.

La Voie (1994) *Expectations and the Meaning of Institutions: Essays in economics by Ludwig Lachmann*, edited by Don La Voie. Routledge, London.

Menger, C. (1971) *Principles of Economics*. English Translation of original German "Grundsatze der Volkswirthschaftslehre" (1871). New York University Press, New York and London.

Mises, L. (2006) *The Ultimate Foundation of Economic Science*. Liberty Fund, Inc., Indianapolis, IN.

Mises, L. (2007) *Bureaucracy*. Liberty Fund, Inc., Indianapolis, IN.

Radetskiy, E. L., Spahr, R. W., Sunderman, M. A. (2015) Gated Community Premiums and Amenity Differentials in Residential Subdivisions. *The Journal of Real Estate Research; Sacramento*, 37(3), 405–438.

Shackle, G. L. S. (1979) *Imagination and the Nature of Choice*. Edinburgh University Press, Edinburgh.

Shackle, G. L. S. (1969) *Decision, Order and Time in Human Affairs*, 2nd ed., pp. 277–296. Cambridge University Press, London and New York.

Shackle, G. L. S. (1966) *The Nature of Economic Thought*, pp. 162–186. Cambridge University Press, London and New York.

Shackle, G. L. S. (1970) *Expectation, Enterprise, and Profit*, pp. 122–169. Aldine Publishing Co., Chicago, IL.

Chapter 5

Market participant value perceptions

Chapter highlights

- Divergent expectations
- Seller perceptions of value
- Buyer perceptions of value
- Third-party perceptions of value
  - Commercial real estate brokers
  - Commercial real estate appraisers
  - Commercial real estate lenders

> Different actors will typically hold divergent expectations about the same future events.
>
> Ludwig Lachmann

5.1 Divergent expectations

In this chapter, we will utilize the Ludwig Lachmann quote above to discuss how different actors in the commercial real estate market can have different expectations about the future. Those divergent pathways often lead to different value conclusions, which creates a range of possible values for real estate property value which is the central theme of this book. We will first start with the sellers of commercial property and how they can utilize various models to increase their asking price as high as is possible. Then we will turn to how buyers utilize these same models to beget a lower asking price relative to that of the seller. While eventually a buyer and seller will agree on a price, this process takes quite a bit of time typically for real estate sales.

DOI: 10.4324/9781003083672-5

This implies that there can be a legion of possible buyers for one particular commercial property. Once we have discussed the buyer–seller narrative, we will turn our focus to other market participants in the commercial real estate world, namely, brokers, lenders, and appraisers. Each of these indirect participants in the sale of a property comes to the valuation process with their own inherent motivations, which may lead to different opinions for the final value.

G.L.S. Shackle elaborated on the bargaining process in his book *Expectations in Economics*. While the range of property values as discussed in Chapter 4 is still at play, two market participants must finally agree on a price in order for the sale of a commercial property to occur. How the final price is determined opens up the door to uncertainty in the bargaining process. A seller will determine what their absolute minimum price (m) is for a prospective sale, and will state their gambit price at the outset (g), which is the price a property is offered for sale. The agreed price (v) should result in a gain, which is calculated as v - m. The descent (s) is equal to g - v, where the gambit (or offering) price will decline overtime. As the offering price declines, the prospective gain from sale also declines.

In order to more clearly illustrate the concept of different opinions of value for the same property among numerous market participants, we will utilize a hypothetical example of a property where the current situation is different from both the past performance of the property and its expected future performance. While this example can lead to wide valuation swings depending on the motivation of the person who is doing the evaluation, all properties for sale on the market have the potential for similar, if not as wide, valuation spectrums.

5.2 Seller perceptions of value

Assume that five years ago, a seller (call him Mr. Slick) purchased a multifamily residential property for $2 million. The property consists of 28 two-bed, one-bath units within three buildings on the same parcel of land. The land is located in an urban area where there are many competing units. Over the last few years, there has been significant urban renewal and gentrification whereby numerous properties in the market have been improved to the point where the target demographic of the tenant has switched from working-class families to young urban professionals.

When reviewing the current rents for competing properties in the area, some of the properties have achieved a significant increase in rents after the improvements have been made, while other properties have either not yet attempted such improvement or are in the process of doing. Mr. Slick perceives that once property improvements have been made, the rents in the subject property can be increased from the current rate of $500 per month to $900 per month. Exhibit 5.1 illustrates the impact of the potential rent increase on the properties' gross potential income.

Seen from an annual perspective, gross potential income would increase from $168,000 to $302,400 once the improvements are made and the property is fully leased. The seller has been contemplating making the necessary improvements in order to raise rents, but given the large movements in the market, occupancy rates are currently lower than they have been since he has owned the property. Based on an annual projection of current rents, the estimated property value using the direct capitalization approach is shown in Exhibit 5.2.

	# Units	Sq Ft	Current Rent	Monthly Income	Pro-Forma Rents	Monthly Income
Apartment Rent Roll	28	828	$ 500	$ 14,000	$ 900	$ 25,200
Total	28	23,184	$ 500	$ 14,000	$ 900	$ 25,200
						$ 1.09

Exhibit 5.1 Apartment Rent Increases in an Improving Market.

	Current	%	Pro-Forma	%
Gross Potential Rent	$ 168,000		$ 302,400	
Other Income	$ -		$ 8,400	
Gross Potental Income	$ 168,000		$ 310,800	
Vacancy/Collection	$ 8,400	5.00%	$ 9,072	3.00%
Effective Gross Income	$ 159,600		$ 301,728	
Operating Expenses		Per Unit		Per Unit
Real Estate Taxes	$ 24,870	$ 888	$ 24,870	$ 888
Insurance	$ 7,952	$ 284	$ 7,964	$ 284
General & Admin	$ -	$ -	$ 1,500	$ 54
Repairs & Maintenance	$ 16,800	$ 600	$ 22,400	$ 800
Water & Sanitation	$ 14,449	$ 516	$ 14,449	$ 516
Gas & Electric	$ 25,411	$ 908	$ 25,411	$ 908
Management Fee	$ 7,980	$ 285	$ 15,086	$ 539
Replacement Reserves	$ 7,000	$ 250	$ 7,000	$ 250
Total Op Ex	$ 104,462	$ 3,731	$ 118,680	$ 4,239
Net Operating Income	$ 55,138		$ 183,048	
Sales Price	$2,600,000		$ 2,600,000	
Implied Cap Rate	2.12%		7.04%	
Sales Price/GPI	15.48 GRM		8.37 GRM	

Exhibit 5.2 Tale of Two Perspectives: Seller's Eyes.

5.2.1 Seller tenders an offer

Mr. Slick is set on a selling price of $2.6 million and, based on the current and pro-forma operating statements shown in Exhibit 5.2, the NOI and cap rates are vastly different depending on which perspective an investor utilizes. Should an investor decide that the best approach is to value the property based on an annual projection of the current occupancy and rental situation? If he chooses that option, it might be very difficult to find other recent property sales that justify someone paying a cap rate that is near 2%. On the other hand, if Mr. Slick utilizes the pro-forma operating case situation, the resultant cap rate is a much more normalized 7%. There would most certainly be other properties on offer in the market at a cap rate close to this amount. Additionally, Mr. Slick would note that the rental rates being considered for the pro-forma operating scenario have been vetted in the market today. In other words, there are properties that are successfully charging this rental amount to their tenants.

Another metric shown in Exhibit 5.2 is the gross rent multiplier (GRM). The GRM for the current rents scenario is almost double the pro-forma scenario. Finding comparable sales at this higher level of GRM might prove difficult, further showing that the asking price based on current rents may be considered outside of the norms seen in the market.

Why is Mr. Slick stuck on the property value of $2.6 million? Certainly a case could be made for a range of values in this case or at least a range of cap rates producing different values relative to the NOI estimated by the seller for the next 12 months. Exhibit 5.3 shows how the final property value might change based on the two NOI scenarios depicted in Exhibit 5.2 as the cap rates change.

Our seller appears to be stuck on the $2.6 million asking price for his property as this represents the most favorable NOI situation at a cap rate that is supportable in the market. What the seller may be missing is that in order to achieve the rental rate increases necessary to achieve the higher NOI in Exhibit 5.3, there is a significant cost and time investment required.

Of course looking at the direct capitalization value is not the end of the story. In order for the investor to determine a reasonable selling price, they should also review what their returns have been while owning the property since it was purchased five years ago.

5.2.2 Seller's return calculations

When any seller originally contemplates a new purchase, the price that they decide upon should consider what other investors are paying in the market at the time of sale, whether they can make a profit during the holding period of the investment, and if can they resell the property after a certain period of time at a profit relative to the purchase price. In our example, Mr. Slick purchased the property five years ago for $2 million and is now ready to sell. He feels that given the large market movements regarding property improvements and rental rate increases, now is a good time to make a profit.

One way he might look at things is how a homeowner might view their return. In this way, he might compare the sales price at present, relative to the purchase price and all of the costs associated with holding the property over time. Unless the homeowner has a renter in the property, there really is no annual income to consider. For commercial property, since there typically is rental income during the investment holding period, a good way to assess whether an investment has been profitable is to view what the equity cash flows to the investor have been since the inception of the investment. Exhibit 5.4 illustrates how the internal rate of return for Mr. Slick could be calculated assuming his desired asking price of $2.6 million.

If Mr. Slick considers his initial equity investment of $500,000 (he received a loan of $1.5 million when he purchased the property for $2 million five years ago),

NOI	4.00%	5.00%	6.00%	7.00%	8.00%
$55,138	$1,378,450	$1,102,760	$918,967	$787,686	$689,225
$183,048	$4,576,200	$3,660,960	$3,050,800	$2,614,971	$2,288,100

Exhibit 5.3 Range of Values as Cap Rates Change.

	0	1	2	3	4	5	6
Net Operating Income		$ 125,322	$ 130,100	$ 116,783	$ 119,767	$ 108,118	$ 183,048
Annual Debt Service		$113,877	$113,877	$113,877	$113,877	$113,877	
Reversionary CF						$ 1,229,608	
Equity Cash Flow	$ (500,000)	$ 11,445	$ 16,223	$ 2,906	$ 5,890	$ 1,223,849	
						20.84% IRR	
Property Value	$ 2,075,171						
Discount Rate	9.00%						

Reversion	$ 2,600,114
Selling Costs (5%)	$ 130,006
Outstanding Loan Balance	$ 1,240,500
Equity from Reversion	$ 1,229,608

Exhibit 5.4 Seller's Calculation of Internal Rate of Return.

his actual equity cash flows received over the holding period (periods one through five), and his current sales price of $2.6MM, the IRR for his investment over the five-year period is 20.84%. Equity cash flows are defined as the annual NOI of the property minus the annual debt service paid. Mr. Slick obtained a loan of $1.5MM (75% of purchase price) at a rate of 4.50% with monthly compounding over a loan amortization of 240 months. After five years assuming a traditional mortgage-style loan amortization, the balance on Mr. Slick's loan (if assuming no prepayments) is $1,240,608. When calculating the equity cash flow for year five, there are two components to be considered. The first is the cash flow from operations (year five NOI minus annual debt service), and the second is the reversion (i.e., sale) of the subject property.

Since Mr. Slick is contemplating selling the property, the relevant cash flow in Exhibit 5.4 for the next buyer is the year six NOI (which as mentioned earlier is certainly up for discussion!). The reversionary cash flow is calculated by taking the projected year six NOI of $183,048 (also known as year one cash flow for the buyer) and dividing by a terminal cap rate of 7.04% as shown in Exhibit 5.2. This leads to the estimated property value of $2,600,114, or simply $2.6 million. Since the IRR considers equity cash flows, the sales price is subtracted by any selling costs paid by the owner and the outstanding mortgage balance at the time of sale.

If the seller can obtain a buyer at his price of $2.6 million, his IRR looks pretty good at over 20%. The estimated property value via the discounted cash flow model does not support this amount, coming in at just over $2.075 million when using a discount rate of 9.00%. While the property valuation based on the direct capitalization model and the discounted cash flow model is divergent, there is one more analytical tool as shown in Exhibit 5.5 which might shed light on why Mr. Slick is fixated on a sales price of $2.6 million.

As shown in Exhibit 5.5, the net present value for the project at the 9% discount rate employed is just above break-even. In fact, when holding all other variables constant, if the sales price is less than $2.5MM (actually the break-even value is $2,494,000, but what's $6,000, among friends?), the investment does not lead to profitability using the net present value model. From a terminal cap rate perspective, the net present value (NPV) break point is achieved as cap rates increase from 7.04% to 7.34% relative to the projected year six NOI (i.e., the first year for the new buyer).

Period	Equity CF	PV of Equity CF
0	$ (500,000)	$ (500,000)
1	$ 11,445	$ 10,500
2	$ 16,223	$ 13,655
3	$ 2,906	$ 2,244
4	$ 5,890	$ 4,173
5	$ 1,223,849	$ 795,418
		$ 42,782 NPV @ 9%

Exhibit 5.5 Seller's Calculation of Net Present Value.

	Not PV of CF				PV of CF @ 9.00%	
IRR Partition	Operating CF	Reversion CF		IRR Partition	Operating CF	Reversion CF
Period 1	$ 11,445			Period 1	$ 10,500	
Period 2	$ 16,223			Period 2	$ 13,655	
Period 3	$ 2,906			Period 3	$ 2,244	
Period 4	$ 5,890			Period 4	$ 4,173	
Period 5	$ (5,759)	$ 1,229,608		Period 5	$ (3,743)	$ 799,161
Total	$ 30,706	$ 1,229,608		Total	$ 26,829	$ 799,161
% of Total	2%	98%		% of Total	3%	97%

Exhibit 5.6 Seller's Partition of the Internal Rate of Return (IRR).

What we have discussed so far is that from the seller's perspective, there can be many competing motivations for why they desire a certain sales price. Sometimes the profitability of an investment will be largely determined by the sales price at the end of the holding period. In Mr. Slick's apartment building case, where such a large portion of the equity cash flows is dependent on the final sales price (since many of the years exhibit break-even operating cash flow which is defined as annual debt service subtracted from the annual NOI), the sales price achieved could literally make or break the investment from a profitability standpoint. This is made clear by reviewing the partitioning of the IRR of the investment as shown in Exhibit 5.6. Since almost all of the cash flows come from the sale of the property, this investment can actually be considered to be speculative.

Next we turn to the motivations of a potential buyer for this transaction.

5.3 Buyer perceptions of value

For every seller of commercial real estate there exist numerous (hopefully!) potential buyers. Some of these buyers may lose interest early on in the evaluation process. Some may drop out of the competitive bidding owing to the condition or location of the property, and may not even offer a bid price for the property. Other potential buyers may engage a real estate agent and inspect the property either in person or virtually. What should be clear from the prior chapters is that each potential buyer must evaluate their specific situation relative to the asking price and if they think the price on offer by the seller is reasonable.

From the buyer's perspective, it looks as if Mr. Slick is desiring to have his cake and eat it too. On the one hand, there apparently has been some success in the market in changing the demographics of existing apartment projects, whereby once property improvements have been made, significant rental rate increases have been achieved. On the other hand, our subject property has not yet achieved those rent increases, and the necessary improvements required to help facilitate the increase in rents have not yet transpired. A potential buyer might very well ask the following question: *Why would I pay an asking price today which assumes that the property has been successfully converted to a higher-income property when this has yet to occur?*

5.3.1 Buyer considers an offer

Let's relook at Exhibit 5.2, but this time with the eyes of a potential buyer (let's call her Ms. Slack). When comparing the tale of two perspectives, the current situation is starkly different when compared to the pro-forma case. The gross potential income is currently based on rents of $500 per month per unit, while the pro-forma case assumes a rent of $900 per month per unit. That subtle but substantial difference leads to the widely divergent NOI and cap rate results. While the pro-forma case cap rate of 7.04% should be easily confirmed as being in the range of acceptable cap rates for recent transactions in the market, the current case cap rate of 2.12% appears unrealistic. Ms. Slack may rather prefer to calculate what the asking price should be based on the current NOI and an assumed market cap rate of 7.00%. Please refer to Exhibit 5.7 for the calculation.

Ms. Slack might prefer to counter Mr. Slick's very optimistic valuation with an equally pessimistic version of her own. If the current NOI of the subject property is capitalized into property value at a market rate of 7.00%, the property might only be worth just under $800,000. Ms. Slack may decide to stop right there, and given the large gap between her valuation and the asking price of $2.6 million, just call it a day. In fact, plenty of potential buyers made this same calculation and may have decided not to offer a counter proposal. But Ms. Slack is an experienced real estate investor, and she sees value here. She will certainly not get to the buyer's current sales price of $2.6 million, but she will concede that the property is fully leased, sits in an improving market, and that there is some wiggle room in her final counter-offer amount.

Since Mr. Slick would certainly not accept an offer as low as $800,000 for the subject property, Ms. Slack needs to sharpen her pencil a bit to see if she can strike a deal. Ms. Slack may be attracted to the property for its general location. Let's assume that she owns three other properties in the same town, and since she is fully leased at those properties, she feels confident that if the subject property can be purchased at a reasonable price, she can make a good return on her investment.

Net Operating Income	$	55,138
Market Cap Rate		7.00%
Implied Price	$	787,686

Exhibit 5.7 Buyer's Rebuttal.

	# Units	Unit Type	Sq Ft	Current Rent		Monthly Income	Pro-Forma Rents		Monthly Income
Rent Roll	28	2 Bed 1 Bath	828	$	500	$ 14,000	$ 750	$	21,000
Total	28		23,184	$	500	$ 14,000	$ 750	$	21,000
			Rent pfs	$	0.60	$ 0.60	$ 0.91	$	0.91

Exhibit 5.8 Buyer's Projected Rent Increase.

Ms. Slack decides to visit the subject property in order to ascertain the current condition of the units. She is looking to project an average "turnover cost" that it would take to release the units should the current tenants vacate their units. She will be paying special attention to things like the age and condition of appliances, roof, parking lot, and any other expensive items requiring immediate replacement. It is one thing to consider a complete renovation such that rents can be increased from $500 per month to $900 per month per unit, but maybe there is a deal here with less of a significant investment.

It is in this moment where G.L.S. Shackle's *news from the field* is so helpful. Ms. Slack owns three similar properties in the same market, and based on her tenant history, she feels that Mr. Slick was leaving some rent on the table even before the improvements were made. At the current rent of $500 per unit per month, and with each unit being the same size of 828 square feet, the current rent per square foot is $0.60. Ms. Slack is currently charging her tenants' rents of between $0.85 and $0.95, and based on the age, condition, and location of the units, she has estimated that she could increase rents to just over $0.90 per square foot once she takes ownership of the subject property. This calculation is shown in Exhibit 5.8.

Ms. Slack has determined that she can raise rents from the current rate of $500 per unit per month to $750 per unit per month, without a significant investment. Since the subject property is only 28 units, even if the current tenants balk at this increase, Ms. Slack feels that she can find suitable replacement tenants quickly. While moving from $0.60 per square foot in monthly rent to $0.91 per square foot monthly seems like a large increase, keep in mind that the market is currently supporting closer to $1.10 per square foot per month, so the more cosmetic (and low-cost) investments that Ms. Slack can make, the closer she can get to that rental level in the near term. For now, Ms. Slack is confident that she can achieve the rental increases shown in Exhibit 5.8.

So what does this rental rate increase mean in terms of Ms. Slack's potential counter-offer purchase price? Exhibit 5.9 compares Ms. Slack's counter-offer case with the current valuation provided by Mr. Slick.

As shown in Exhibit 5.9, the estimated value of the property when considering changes to the revenue stream as projected by the potential buyer is $2 million. Ms. Slack has had success in obtaining ancillary fees for pets, on-site laundry, and other items, which allow for the additional $14,000 in "other income". While this is not the $2.6 million that Mr. Slick is desiring, depending on how long he has had the property listed for sale, this may be a counter-proposal that could be accepted by the seller. If Mr. Slick and Ms. Slack were to have a conversation to further the negotiation, Ms. Slack might offer that any more of an increase in rents (which would lead to a higher purchase price offer) would have to come with increased expenses in order to improve the property relative to others in the market, which are now charging monthly rents per square foot over $1.00.

	Current	%	Pro-Forma	%
Gross Potential Rent	$ 168,000		$ 252,000	
Other Income	$ -		$ 14,000	
Gross Potental Income	$ 168,000		$ 266,000	
Vacancy/Collection	$ 8,400	5.00%	$ 7,560	3.00%
Effective Gross Income	$ 159,600		$ 258,440	
Operating Expenses		**Per Unit**		**Per Unit**
Real Estate Taxes	$ 24,870 $	888	$ 24,870 $	888
Insurance	$ 7,952 $	284	$ 7,964 $	284
General & Admin	$ - $	-	$ 1,500 $	54
Repairs & Maintenance	$ 16,800 $	600	$ 22,400 $	800
Water & Sanitation	$ 14,449 $	516	$ 14,449 $	516
Gas & Electric	$ 25,411 $	908	$ 25,411 $	908
Management Fee	$ 7,980 $	285	$ 15,086 $	539
Replacement Reserves	$ 7,000 $	250	$ 7,000 $	250
Total Op Ex	$ 104,462 $	3,731	$ 118,680 $	4,239
Net Operating Income	$ 55,138		$ 139,760	
Sales Price	$ 2,600,000		$ 1,996,571	
Implied Cap Rate	2.12%		7.00%	
Sales Price/GPI	15.48 GRM		7.51 GRM	

Exhibit 5.9 Tale of Two Perspectives: Buyer's Eyes.

While this hypothetical conversation would be interesting for illustrative purposes, neither party would likely reveal their exact intentions regarding their pricing strategy. While Mr. Slick's offering memorandum as prepared by the commercial broker provides a current and pro-forma case, how to get from point A to point B is not clearly elucidated. The movement up in rents is the issue for the next owner of the property. Ms. Slack would also not likely share that the rents that she is able to obtain for her three comparable properties located in the same market are much higher than those of Mr. Slick.

5.3.2 Buyer's return calculations

Before Ms. Slack makes a formal offer of $2 million for the subject property, she runs calculations for the IRR for this project assuming that she holds the investment for five years. This calculation is summarized in Exhibit 5.10.

When viewing Exhibit 5.10, the first year for the investment is the "current" situation as depicted by Mr. Slick in the offering memorandum. The second-year NOI assumes the rental rate increases projected by Ms. Slack. Annual debt service is calculated on the same terms as for Mr. Slick (loan of 75% of purchase price of $2 million at an annual interest rate of 4.50% over a 240-month amortization). Interestingly, Ms. Slack is also keying on a value of roughly $2.6 million, but in her projections this is the assumed sales price after she has owned the property for five years, while the $2.6 million represents what Mr. Slick desires to obtain at present. In order to achieve these positive results, Ms. Slack had to assume a terminal cap rate of 6.25% (which leads to a reversion of $2,640,000 when the year six NOI of $165,000 is divided by the terminal cap rate of 6.25%). Utilizing a discount rate

	0	1	2	3	4	5	6
Net Operating Income		$ 55,138	$ 120,000	$ 130,000	$ 140,000	$ 150,000	$ 165,000
Annual Debt Service		$113,877	$113,877	$113,877	$113,877	$113,877	
Reversionary CF						$ 1,267,500	
Equity Cash Flow	$ (500,000)	$ (58,739)	$ 6,123	$ 16,123	$ 26,123	$ 1,303,623	
						20.05%	IRR
Property Value	$ 2,078,668						
Discount Rate	9.00%						

Reversion	$ 2,640,000
Selling Costs (5%)	$ 132,000
Outstanding Loan Balance	$ 1,240,500
Equity from Reversion	$ 1,267,500

Exhibit 5.10 Buyer's Calculation of Internal Rate of Return.

Period	Equity CF	PV of Equity CF
0	$ (500,000)	$ (500,000)
1	$ (58,739)	$ (53,889)
2	$ 6,123	$ 5,154
3	$ 16,123	$ 12,450
4	$ 26,123	$ 18,506
5	$ 1,303,623	$ 847,266
		$ 28,287 NPV @ 9%

Exhibit 5.11 Buyer's Calculation of Net Present Value.

	Not PV of CF			PV of CF @ 9.00%		
IRR Partition	Operating CF	Reversion CF		IRR Partition	Operating CF	Reversion CF
Period 1	$ (58,739)			Period 1	$ (53,889)	
Period 2	$ 6,123			Period 2	$ 5,154	
Period 3	$ 16,123			Period 3	$ 12,450	
Period 4	$ 26,123			Period 4	$ 18,506	
Period 5	$ 36,123	$ 1,267,500		Period 5	$ 23,478	$ 823,788
Total	$ 25,754	$ 1,267,500		Total	$ 5,699	$ 823,788
% of Total	2%	98%		% of Total	1%	99%

Exhibit 5.12 Buyer's Partition of the Internal Rate of Return.

of 9.00%, the present value of the property per Ms. Slack's projections is just under $2.1 million. Similar to Mr. Slick, Ms. Slack goes a bit further to calculate the project's net present value and IRR partition. These will be discussed separately in Exhibits 5.11 and 5.12.

Based on the information presented in Exhibits 5.11 and 5.12, at a $2 million purchase price, Ms. Slack will experience a positive net present value at a discount rate of 9%, and similar to Mr. Slick, almost all of the equity cash flows from investment over the holding period (defined as NOI minus annual debt service) will come from the eventual sale of the property. Given the positive NPV, the projected current property value of just under $2.1 million, and based on her knowledge of the market, Ms. Slack decides to formally propose a counter-offer for the subject property at $2 million.

Should Mr. Slick accept Ms. Slack's offer of $2 million for the subject property? This will depend on a few factors. One is the length of time that the property has been listed for sale. If this is relatively early in the listing process, Mr. Slick may not be agreeable to Ms. Slack's counter-proposal. Mr. Slick may still feel that there is some novice investor out there who would be willing to pay top dollar for a property that has yet to make the necessary improvements in order to get revenues above $1.00 per square foot per month. Another factor would be if Mr. Slick is truly a motivated seller. If he really needs the money, Mr. Slick may be willing to accept the counter-offer in order to move the property from his possession. Another factor would be the input from the commercial broker. They may tell Mr. Slick that this is the best deal that he is going to get right now, especially as his pro-forma cap rate is so far out of line in terms of what the market will bear. A final factor might deal with the activity of the listing. If Mr. Slick is getting a lot of investor interest in this deal, he may decide to hold off accepting Ms. Slack's counter-offer. Since we are all fans of happy endings, let's assume that Mr. Slick and Ms. Slack agree on a purchase price of $2 million.

5.4 Third-party perceptions of value

Now that we have outlined the thought process of the property seller and buyer in this case, we need to expand the focus to include other relevant players in the transaction process. The three players that I have in mind are the commercial real estate broker, appraiser, and lender. The broker comes into the picture early in the process, while the property appraiser and the commercial lender come into view once an offer price for sale has been agreed upon. One other important player in the sale process is the real estate closing attorney. They are not typically part of the valuation discussion, as they serve more to facilitate the legal transfer of ownership between the seller and buyer regardless of what value is being conveyed. For that reason, this final section of the chapter will focus on the broker, appraiser, and lender and how they may directly or indirectly influence the property value.

5.4.1 Commercial real estate brokers

The role of the commercial broker is to provide assistance to the seller in listing their commercial property for sale. The commercial broker prepares an offering memorandum (also called a broker package) which lists the sales price of the property, salient attributes, and specifics of the property's historical operating performance which supports the sales price. The broker has access to information concerning recent sales and also has access to other market information such as rental rates and operating expenses for competing investments. The broker is paid a percentage of the final sales price, and often the buyer will also enlist a real estate agent who will make them aware of properties for sale in the market and provide access to market information to aid in the buyer's decision. Brokers can also serve as leasing agents for commercial property owners. In that scenario, brokers are paid upfront for the value of the lease that they obtain for tenancy in a property. In both the sale and lease scenarios, brokers are paid once they serve their function (find a tenant for lease or find a property where an offer is made for sale). Since the broker commission is based on a percentage of the total sales price, they are motivated to get as high a sales price as possible. Of course if they shoot too high, the property will not sell quickly, causing delays and leading to offering price reductions.

Regarding the subject property, the commercial real estate broker should have realized that Mr. Slick was trying to sell the property at a price which assumed that all of the necessary improvements were made to justify the higher rents and sales price. The broker, while motivated to sell at as high a price as is feasible, would more than likely have provided Mr. Slick with information on comparable properties in the market. The broker would have likely searched his database to find the most similar properties in proximity to the subject property in order to ascertain if Mr. Slick's offering price was reasonable per market averages. Exhibit 5.13 provides summary of the five most comparable properties per the broker's market data.

Based on the five properties deemed most comparable to the subject property in terms of age, condition, and proximity, the broker can assist Mr. Slick in determining that his asking price seems too high. Firstly, his current rents are the lowest of the comparable set (something that Ms. Slack also noticed), and this is causing the cap rate at the original offering price of $2.6 million to be very low relative to the market averages. The price per unit is also comparable to two of the properties shown in Exhibit 5.13, and these have rents more similar to Mr. Slick's property. It should be noted, however, that comparable number three and number five have higher rents and a higher cap rate than the subject property.

Since the final broker package contained two income scenarios (current and pro-forma), it can be assumed that Mr. Slick understood from the broker that his asking price was high, but they decided to see if they could cast a net to obtain a willing buyer at $2.6 million. More than likely, the idea to show both income scenarios was a compromise between a seller wanting as high a price as possible, and a broker wanting to maintain a rational perspective on the asking price relative to the competitive set. It could be the case that Mr. Slick and the broker agreed to list the property for sale initially without the "current case", but buyers typically want to see something relative to the current leasing scenario when making a purchase decision on an investment property.

While we do not know how long our subject property sat on the market until Ms. Slack came along, it can be assumed that the broker was glad that someone with both financial wherewithal and market intelligence was able to realize that Mr. Slick's rents were low and that with limited improvements, the investment could be profitable at the counter-offer price of $2 million. While the broker does not

Comparable Listings	Rent psf	Cap Rate	Price/Unit
Subject Property	$ 0.60	2.12%	$ 92,857
Comparable #1	$ 1.02	6.15%	$ 116,389
Comparable #2	$ 1.10	5.06%	$ 106,667
Comparable #3	$ 0.70	8.06%	$ 93,000
Comparable #4	$ 1.05	5.85%	$ 110,000
Comparable #5	$ 0.88	7.00%	$ 93,548

Exhibit 5.13 Broker's Market Data.

have much to say about the final property valuation, they are motivated to obtain the highest price possible to aid their client and to improve their commission.

5.4.2 Commercial real estate appraisers

Commercial real estate appraisers will often enter the timeline of a real estate transaction toward the end. Assuming that the new owner will obtain financing at a bank, an appraisal is required to provide the official opinion of value for the subject property. In the United States, recent years have seen a large increase in regulations that impact banks generally, and the appraisal process specifically. One such regulation specifies that the bank must order an appraisal rather than utilizing one that was ordered by the buyer or seller. If one of the parties to the transaction was to order the appraisal, there is the assumption that the appraiser might be influenced as to the value conclusion. That an appraiser could be so easily led to the value conclusion is, for some, hard to fathom. An early part of the valuation process does entail inquiring about the contracted sales price. This fact has always brought up the following Kierkegaard quote to my mind, "*in case he who should act was to judge himself according to the result, he would never get to the point of beginning*". In other words, the appraiser knows the desired answer before they get started with their valuation.

Even without knowing the desired answer (i.e., the purchase price agreed between the buyer and seller), the appraiser still comes to the valuation exercise with their own experience, predilections, and market data. Thus, the appraiser's perception of the value drivers will influence the methods that they utilize or at least in how they interpret the market and property data. Recalling Shackle's *news from the field* concept again, if an appraiser has a range of values to consider for things such as the market vacancy rate, cap rate, or discount rate, if they hear overly positive or negative opinions about what the future may reveal, this could influence their final selections for key variables that lead to the valuation conclusion.

One segment of existent literature that relates to the subject of this section is that of objectivity and error in real estate valuation. The most relevant articles in the literature relate to the concept of "accuracy", which is defined as when the appraised property value equals the purchase price, or an assessment of the factors influencing inaccuracy in valuation. These articles discuss what factors can lead to faulty valuations (primarily by appraisers), underlying the thought that valuation is an art rather than a science. Some noted factors in the literature affecting valuation concern visible factors such as the age and condition of the property, while others note that uncertainty in valuation is inherent as market-based determinants can lead to a range of acceptable property values and that final sale represents just one point in the accepted range of property values.

Going back to the example of the multifamily property being sold by Mr. Slick, the appraiser would need to validate that whatever valuation metrics are utilized, they are within reasonable market averages. Since the leases for the subject property can be assumed to be rather short (i.e., a year or less), just utilizing the current leasing rates (called a leased fee income property valuation) may not make sense in a changing or rising rent environment. Utilizing the current market lease rates (called a fee simple income property valuation) may also not be a perfect match, given that it appears that Mr. Slick is charging rental rates that appear below the market averages.

The appraiser might utilize both the current and pro-forma direct capitalization models to estimate NOI for the first year. A blended approach might be to consider a five-year holding period and to utilize a discounted cash flow to show how value is influenced by the time it takes to get the rents in the subject property up to the market levels. Exhibit 5.14 outlines how the five-year discounted cash flow valuation might look.

Rents per Square Foot	23,184 $	0.60 $	0.75 $	0.85 $	0.95 $	1.00		$	1.05	
	Year 0	Year 1	Year 2	Year 3	Year 4	Year 5	Reversion		Year 6	Comments
Gross Potential Income		168,000	208,656	236,477	264,298	278,208			292,118	
Other Income	-		7,000	14,000	15,000	16,000			170,000	
Vacancy Factor	10.00%	8,400	20,866	23,648	26,430	27,821			29,212	
Efffective Gross Income		159,600	194,790	226,829	252,868	266,387			432,907	
Taxes	5.00%	24,870	26,114	27,419	28,790	30,230			31,741	
Insurance	5.00%	7,952	8,350	8,767	9,205	9,666			9,956	
Repairs & Maintenance	5.00%	16,800	17,640	18,522	19,448	20,421			21,033	
Management	5.00%	7,980	8,379	8,798	9,238	9,700			9,991	
Utilities	5.00%	39,860	41,853	43,946	46,143	48,450			49,904	
Other	5.00%	-	3,000	3,150	3,308	3,473			3,577	
Replacement Reserves	10.00%	7,000	7,700	8,470	9,317	10,249			11,274	
Total Expenses		104,462	113,035	119,072	125,449	132,187			137,475	
Net Operating Income		55,138	81,755	107,757	127,419	134,200	3,216,923		295,432	
Annual Debt Service		113,877	113,877	113,877	113,877	113,877				
Tenant Improvements		-	-	-	-	-				
Leasing Commissions		-	-	-	-	-				
Debt Coverage Ratio		0.48	0.72	0.95	1.12	1.18				
Net Cash Flows	(500,000)	(58,739)	(32,122)	(6,120)	13,542	1,996,746				
BTIRR On Equity	28.82%									
Property Value		$ 2,370,000.00								

Exhibit 5.14 Appraiser's Compromise.

	NOI	Cap Rate	Value
Current	$ 55,138	6.50%	$ 848,277
Pro-Forma	$ 183,048	6.50%	$ 2,816,123
DCF			$ 2,370,000
Average			$ 2,011,467

Exhibit 5.15 Appraiser's Value Conclusion.

As shown in Exhibit 5.14, the appraiser used both the current and pro-forma scenarios to essentially "split the difference" to arrive at a five-year projection for NOI, along with the year six estimate for NOI for the reversion. The sales price at the end of five years is determined by dividing the year six NOI by a terminal capitalization rate of 9.00% (for a value of $3,282,578 in five years, theoretically once all of the renovations have been made to entirely convert the property to the higher rent market). If you discount the NOI and reversion by a rate of 10%, the estimated property value will be $2,370,000.

The appraiser might show this scenario to prove that the current NOI of $55,138 is not the best method to value this property, and would more than likely eventually settle at a market value of $2,000,000, which is the purchase price negotiated between Mr. Slick and Ms. Slack. This can be arrived at by taking an average of the estimated values that the appraiser determined given the current property performance, the projected future operating performance, and the discounted cash flow value. This is summarized in Exhibit 5.15.

5.4.3 Commercial real estate lenders

The last market participant that we will discuss is the commercial lender. The lender comes into the transaction timeline typically just before the appraiser, but will utilize the appraiser's work to help ascertain the market value of the property as well as to better understand the condition of the market and subject property. Similar to an investor, the lender is interested in assessing what I have called elsewhere the "QQD Framework": the quantity, quality, and durability of the income stream. The quantity of the income stream considers the amount of income relative to debt and in relation to the market rents for the subject property. The quality of the income stream considers the strength of market and, where applicable, the quality of the tenants in place. The durability of the income stream deals with the market vacancy factor and the ability to find a suitable replacement tenant, the length of the leases relative to the term of the loan, and the strength of sponsorship. As discussed in Chapter 2, the five Cs of credit are also utilized by the lender to render a verdict on whether the loan request should be approved. The QQD fits into the five Cs in terms of capacity to repay, the conditions present in the market, the collateral offered, and the capital present for the sponsors. The final of the five Cs, character, is a part of each and every loan decision, from the smallest opportunity to the largest request for credit.

From a commercial real estate standpoint, the lender is primarily concerned with three main metrics: loan to value, debt service coverage ratio, and debt yield. The loan to value requires the complete appraisal in order to evaluate, so this is where the lender's and appraiser's interest intertwine. The higher the loan to value, the higher the risk for the lender as it implies that the borrower has less equity invested into the deal. The debt service coverage ratio compares the annual NOI of the property to the annual debt service, where higher ratio means that there is a cushion between the properties net income and debt service. The debt yield compares the NOI to the loan amount, and this ratio will be discussed at length in the next chapter.

When looking at the subject transaction from the eyes of the lender, a few things stand out. First, when viewing Exhibit 5.14, it is apparent that there is not sufficient NOI to service the annual debt service for each of the first three years, and the debt service coverage ratios for years four and five are less than what is typically considered desirable (i.e., at least a 1.25x coverage). Also if we assume a loan amount equal to 75% of the $2 million purchase price, this equates to a loan of $1.5 million. Again looking at Exhibit 5.14, the debt yield for the first year (NOI of $55,138 divided by $1.5 million) is only 3.6%, which is a far cry from the 10% or so typically desired by lenders. While the loan to value is right where lenders would desire it to be (at 75%), the debt service coverage and debt yield are much lower than required such that unless Ms. Slack has additional collateral to pledge to the loan until the property "stabilizes", the deal is unlikely to be approved by a cash flow lender. Some smaller financial institutions solely focus on the loan to value, so if Ms. Slack is dealing with one of those, she might get a favorable response.

In this chapter we have discussed the divergent expectations for various market participants and how those can contribute to both the subjectivity of commercial property valuation and lead to a possible range of acceptable property values. This chapter followed on the heels of Chapter 4 where we discussed a survey of various market participants and how they can interpret the same market data differently when valuing a commercial property. In Chapter 6, we will discuss a few salient points from Chapter 5 that may have left you wanting: the subjectivity of capitalization rates, discount rates, and the lender's debt yield. These subtle yet important numbers can make all the difference in determining success and failure for investors and lenders alike.

Questions for discussion

1. Elaborate on how divergent expectations of market participants are good and bad for economic growth.
2. Explain how the interests of the real estate property broker and seller are often aligned.
3. Explain how the interests of the real estate property lender and buyer are often aligned.
4. Provide examples of situations when the interests of the real estate broker and lender are aligned.
5. Provide examples of situations when the interests of the real estate broker and lender are in opposition.
6. Describe situations where the interests of the real estate broker and the seller are in opposition.
7. Describe situations where the interests of the real estate lender and the buyer are in opposition.
8. How might government intervention in markets affect the market participants involved in the sale of a real estate property?
9. Discuss how an appraiser can help bridge the valuation gap between the "eyes of the buyer" and the "eyes of the seller" of a real estate property.
10. Discus how a lender can help bridge the valuation gap between the "eyes of the buyer" and the "eyes of the seller" of a real estate property.

Chapter 5 Market vignette

Cast of characters: Garfield, Heathcliff, Belvedere (investors)
Act: Low-income housing as an investment option discussion

Scene one: difference of opinion

GARFIELD: Hello Heathcliff, what do you think of low-income housing as an investment option?

HEATHCLIFF: Hi Garfield, well that is an interesting question. I have not invested in those before. Why do you ask?

GARFIELD: I saw a report on television about all of the new government programs that were targeted toward lower-income people. I am thinking about looking for some properties that rent to these individuals as a new growth strategy for my firm.

HEATHCLIFF: Well, as you know, I like the residential market for investment properties. What I don't really like about many of the properties that focus on lower-income renters is that the government restricts the amount of rent that you can charge, but doesn't seem as concerned about restricting the increases in operating expenses associated with those same rental properties. Additionally, I have heard that the tenants do not take care of the properties.

GARFIELD: Those are good points Heathcliff! I guess these properties are similar to investing in rent-controlled housing markets like in New York City. But still, I think these investments are really worth consideration for us investing in a few properties together. I am thinking that we would stay away from apartments that focus on lower-income properties, and focus mainly on the single-family market.

HEATHCLIFF: I would think the single-family market would be an easier entry point. If we hypothetically purchased a large apartment complex focused on the lower-income renter, it would seem that the government would be more involved in our business model. Plus with the single-family home market, we would have less tenants and could be a bit more selective.

GARFIELD: I think the government would be involved regardless of the property size, Heathcliff. What also really attracts me to this asset class is that there is a long waiting list for tenants to obtain housing where the government provides subsidies for their rent and expenses depending on their income situation.

HEATHCLIFF: Wait, so the government subsidizes the rent and the expenses for tenants in these properties? I think they are called Section Eight apartments if I am not mistaken.

GARFIELD: Yes, that is correct. Maybe we should call our friend Belvedere as he is really an expert in this type of investment property.

HEATHCLIFF: Yes, that is great idea. Maybe he can set us straight on whether to invest or not, and offer guidance on how big our first foray should be. I am not as excited about this investment option as you are, but I am willing to listen.

(Garfield and Heathcliff agree to call Belvedere jointly)

Scene two: expert opinion

GARFIELD: Hello Belvedere, long time no speak. How are you? I have my friend Heathcliff on the line as we would like to ask you a few questions about your experiences with lower-income housing investments.

BELVEDERE: Hi guys! It's really prescient that you called, as I was just reviewing an offering memorandum for a lower-income housing deal in the Bronx.

HEATHCLIFF: That is great. How is it looking?

BELVEDERE: Well, it is an older apartment complex that is in poor condition, but the occupancy is high and it complies with all of the various conditions whereby tenants get a portion of their rent and expenses paid each month.

GARFIELD: Can you explain how these deals work, Belvedere?

BELVEDERE: Certainly. The low-income housing program was enacted by Congress to encourage new construction and rehabilitation of existing rental housing for low-income households and to increase the amount of affordable rental housing for households whose income is at or below specified income levels. The U.S. Congress recognized that a private sector developer may not receive enough rental income from a low-income housing project to cover the costs of developing and operating the project, in addition to providing a sufficient return to investors. To spur investment, Congress authorized the states, within specified limits, to allocate tax credits to qualifying housing projects.

HEATHCLIFF: Oh, so there are tax credits for these deals. This is starting to make more sense to me.

BELVEDERE: Yes, these are great investment opportunities. How it works is that each state is annually allocated tax credits in an amount equal to a statutory dollar amount per state resident. The state agencies are responsible for determining which housing projects should receive tax credits and the dollar amount of tax credits each should receive. The IRS allocates provides the tax credits to each state housing credit agencies based on state population. The tax credits are awarded via a competitive process based on the total points for the type of construction, desirability of the location (i.e., amount of poverty in the area), and ownership experience in this type of project.

GARFIELD: So if we are new investors, we might not get the tax credits if we purchase an existing deal?

BELVEDERE: Well the owners would be eligible as long as the tax credits apply. Tax credits are calculated as a percentage of costs incurred in developing affordable housing property and are typically claimed annually over 10 years. Tax credits are indirect federal subsidies claimed by investors on their federal tax returns. In order to qualify, at least 40% of units should be occupied by renters earning no more than 60% of the area's median income (40/60 test) or at least 20% of the units should be leased to renters earning no more than 50% of the area's median income (20/50 test). Rent for these units must be less (including utilities) than 30% of imputed income based on the area's median income.

GARFIELD: Wow, you really know your stuff Belvedere. How does the tenant qualification process for subsidies work?

BELVEDERE: Typically the subsidizing entity pays 70% of gross rents and utilities. The gross rents charged must conform to median household income levels for the given area. In order to raise rents, the property owner must submit a request to the subsidizing entity verifying that the proposed rental increase is affordable for that area based on demographic information. For tenants approved in the program, as their personal income increases, the amount of subsidy provided will often decrease. Essentially as an owner of a property like this, you would be getting paid by both the tenants and the relevant government entity providing the subsidy.

HEATHCLIFF: This is really helpful Belvedere. Thank you for this information.

(Call ends with talk of how close the Bronx property is to Yankee stadium)

Scene three: final decision

GARFIELD: Well, that was an interesting conversation. It does seem like there could be much paperwork associated with these investments, but on the other hand, there would appear to be more tenants wishing to qualify than the available housing market could support.

HEATHCLIFF: I was thinking the same thing. To me, the only way that I would want to get involved in this sector is if we could find a property being sold at a low price that did not need a lot of immediate repairs.

GARFIELD: Right, and with the tax credits really making the deals attractive, I would imagine that any current owner who is receiving a tax credit for a property of this sort would not be willing to part with it at a low price.

HEATHCLIFF: Maybe we should keep looking for deals in this asset class and maybe we will find something worth pursuing!

Questions for discussion

1. Describe how the subjectivity of value might impact the viability of this investment alternative.
2. Does this seem like a good investment option? Discuss the pros and cons and take a clear position.
3. Does the idea of focusing on single-family homes in this space versus larger apartment complexes make sense? Discuss the pros and cons and take a clear position.
4. Elaborate on the risk and probability of government funding in this asset class going away. How might the loss of subsidies impact the risk profile of this property type?
5. How easy or difficult would it be to remove a property from the government subsidy program in an effort to increase rents and change the tenant profile for the property that was the primary focus of this chapter?

Bibliography

Aluko, B. T. (2007) Examining Valuer's Judgment in Residential Property Valuations in Metropolitan Lagos, Nigeria. *Property Management*, 25(1), 98–107.

Babawale, G. (2013) Valuation Accuracy – The Myth, Expectation and Reality! *African Journal of Economic and Management Studies*, 4(3), 387–406.

Babawale, G. K. & Omirin, M. (2012) An Assessment of the Relative Impact of Factors Influencing Inaccuracy in Valuation. *International Journal of Housing Markets and Analysis*, 5(2), 145–160.

Barańska, A. & Nowak, D. (2015) Function Modelling of the Market and Assessing the Degree of Similarity Between Real Properties – Dependent Or Independent Procedures in the Process of Office Property Valuation. *Real Estate Management and Valuation*, 23(3), 36–46. doi: 10.1515/remav-2015-0023

Bonazzi, G. & Iotti, M. (2016) Evaluation of Investment in Renovation to Increase the Quality of Buildings: A Specific Discounted Cash Flow (DCF) Approach of Appraisal. *Sustainability*, 8(3), 268. doi: 10.3390/su8030268

Brown, R. & Klingenberg, B. (2015) Real Estate Risk: Heavy Tail Modelling using Excel. *Journal of Property Investment & Finance*, 33(4), 393–407. doi: 10.1108/jpif-05-2014-0033

Burada, C. O. & Demetrescu, T. C. (2018) Historical Real Estate Valuation by Cost Approach. *Applied Mechanics and Materials*, 880, 371–376. doi: 10.4028/www.scientific.net/amm.880.371

Canas, S. R. D., Ferreira, F. A. F., & Meidutė-Kavaliauskienė, I. (2015) Setting Rents in Residential Real Estate: A Methodological Proposal Using Multiple Criteria Decision Analysis. *International Journal of Strategic Property Management*, 19(4), 368–380. doi: 10.3846/1648715x.2015.1093562

Chen, F. Y. & Yu, S. M. (2009) Client Influence on Valuation: Does Language Matter? *Journal of Property Investment & Finance*, 27(1), 25–41.

Christersson, M., Vimpari, J., & Junnila, S. (2015) Assessment of Financial Potential of Real Estate Energy Efficiency Investments–A Discounted Cash Flow Approach. *Sustainable Cities and Society*, 18, 66–73. doi: 10.1016/j.scs.2015.06.002

Crosby, N., Devaney, S., & Wyatt, P. (2018) The Implied Internal Rate of Return in Conventional Residual Valuations of Development Sites. *Journal of Property Research*, 35(3), 234–251. doi: 10.1080/09599916.2018.1457070

de La Paz, P. T. & McGreal, S. (2006) Assessing Subjectivity in the Valuation of Retail Properties in Spain. *Journal of Property Research*, 23(1), 53–74, doi: 10.1080/09599910600748667.

Ding, L., & Nakamura, L. I. (2015) The Impact of the Home Valuation Code of Conduct on Appraisal and Mortgage Outcomes. *SSRN Electronic Journal*. doi: 10.2139/ssrn.2635461

Fisher, J. D. (2002) Real Time Valuation. *Journal of Property Investment & Finance*, 20(3), 213–221.

French, N. & Gabrielli, L. (2004) The Uncertainty of Valuation. *Journal of Property Investment & Finance*, 22(6), 484–500.

Goddard, G. J. & Marcum, B. (2012) Real Estate Investment: A Value Based Approach, Springer, Heidelberg.

Kebeck, G. (1994) *Perception: Theories, Methods, and Research Results of Perception Psychology*. Springer Verlag, Weinheim.

Kierkegaard, S. (1994) *Fear and Trembling*. Alfred A. Knopf, New York, London, Toronto.

Lachmann, L. & LaVoie, D. (ed.) (1994) *Expectations and the Meaning of Institutions: Essays in Economics*. Routledge, London.

Mintah, K., Higgins, D., & Callanan, J. (2018) A Real Option Approach for the Valuation of Switching Output Flexibility in Residential Property Investment. *Journal of Financial Management of Property and Construction*, 23(2), 133–151. doi: 10.1108/jfmpc-05-2017-0017

Palm, P. (2018) Outsourced Property Management: The Regulations of the Property Manager. *Property Management*, 36(5), 620–632. doi: 10.1108/pm-03-2017-0015

Payne, T. H. & Redman, A. L. (2003) The Pitfalls of Property Valuation for Commercial Real Estate Lenders: Using a Comparative Income Approach to Improve Accuracy. *Briefings in Real Estate Finance*, 3(1), 50–61.

Shackle, G. L. S. (1949) *Expectation in Economics*. Cambridge University Press, London.

Shi, S., Yang, Z., Tripe, D., & Zhang, H. (2015) Uncertainty and New Apartment Price Setting: A Real Options Approach. *Pacific-Basin Finance Journal*, 35, 574–591. doi: 10.1016/j.pacfin.2015.10.004

Sipan, I. & Rahman, R. A. (1996) Objectivity in Valuation Techniques. *Bulletin Ukur*, 7, 190–197.

Wong, S. K. & Cheung, K. S. (2017) Renewing a Lease at a Discount or a Premium? *The Journal of Real Estate Research; Sacramento*, 39(2), 215–234.

Źróbek-Różańska, A. (2016) Compensation in Residential Real Estate Purchasers' Decisions. *Real Estate Management and Valuation*, 24(4), 70–78. doi: 10.1515/remav-2016-0031

Subjectivity of cap rates, discount rates, and debt yields

Chapter highlights

- Just a few little numbers
- Cap rate universe
- Discount rates mysteries revealed
- Riddle of the debt yield

> If you shut your door to all errors, truth will be shut out.
>
> Rabindranath Tagore

6.1 Just a few little numbers

Now that we have discussed how the valuation of a real estate property can be influenced by the subjective perceptions of various market participants, the next step in our journey is to discuss how the selection process of seemingly minor classifications can also provide the same level of impact. This chapter will discuss the various methods for selecting capitalization rates, discount rates, and debt yield, and by so doing will attempt to live up to the Rabindranath Tagore's quote which starts this chapter.

While capitalization rates and discount rates are key components of valuation, most appraisals only shed light on the process for selection (amidst the myriad of alternatives) for a few pages in the appraisal. In fact for the direct capitalization income approach valuation methodology, value is determined by dividing the NOI by the desired capitalization rate. The large majority of the appraisal narrative concerns elucidation of the machinations involved in projecting the NOI.

DOI: 10.4324/9781003083672-6

This process has much support data in the form of market information concerning the specific location's amenities relative to similar properties, market rental, vacancy, and expense information relative to similar properties, and how this market information can be utilized in determining the projected NOI of the subject property. By comparison, the cap rate selection process is often limited to one or two pages in total. While I have written extensively on the universe of cap rate models as denoted in the chapter resources, in this chapter I will discuss these models in light of the subjectivity of valuation.

Discount rates appear in valuation when the discounted cash flow model is employed. Once the appraiser moves to a multiple period view of the income stream, a discount rate is required in order to account for future uncertainty and to obtain the net present value of the future cash flows today. If the cap rate is limited in scope for the average commercial appraisal to only a few pages, the discount rate takes up even less space. Sometimes an appraiser will utilize the discount rate in the discounted cash flow but will provide little to no discussion as to how the rate was selected. In many university-level finance texts, the discount rate is often provided, so there is much left to the imagination as to how this important risk metric is estimated. This section of the chapter will shed light on this lightly explored ideal.

Finally, we will discuss "the Riddle of the Debt Yield", the majority of which was published in the referenced *RMA Journal* article in early 2016. I call that piece the article that saved my banking career, as on two occasions, reference to that small paper was cited for improving my continued career prospects after banking restructures left me without a chair once the music had stopped. The debt yield is not an appraisal tool but rather an underwriting metric utilized by commercial lenders to assess the quality of a given property for a commercial loan. In previous chapters, we have discussed other lender underwriting metrics such as the debt coverage ratio and the loan to value. The debt yield, which owes its origin to mortgage-backed securities (which are the subject of Chapter 9), was introduced in commercial banking at a time when cap rates were at unsustainably low levels whereby the loan to value was coming in lower than previously seen, given higher projected property values (which concurrently signaled low risk of default), while the debt coverage ratio (NOI relative to annual debt service) was not as rosy. It was thought that the debt yield would provide a third lender measure which did not rely on things seen to be subjective: interest rates, amortizations, and cap rates. As discussed in this section of our chapter, that thought was erroneous. As Tagore says, errors are fine just as long as we learn from them.

6.2 Cap rate universe

A capitalization rate is any rate that converts an income stream to a value. Capitalization (or "cap") rates are also measure of risk. Cap rates measure the percentage of NOI relative to its value. The value could be either at purchase price or at any time during the holding period of the investment, but it is typically an annual measurement. In the discounted cash flow model, the terminal cap rate is associated with the end of the investment. If an investor expects to hold an investment for ten years, the terminal cap rate is often depicted as the NOI for the eleventh year (also known as the first year's NOI for the buyer) divided by the expected sales price at that time. The higher the return, the higher the cap rate.

To ensure that the relationship between cap rates and risk is clear, an example might be helpful. Assume that an investor is contemplating the purchase of two equally sized single-tenant drug stores located in the same town. Both have the same projected NOI (say $150,000 for the first year). The difference is that one property is a locally owned and operated store, while the second is a nationally known tenant with a strong debt rating. For fun, let's assume that the name of the locally owned store is Marley Drugs, and the nationally known company is Walgreens. Since investors can look up Walgreens' debt rating, assuming that this is currently a good rating (anything BBB or better is considered investment grade), the location in your neighborhood will attract much more potential buyer interest relative to Marley Drugs. Additionally, people may associate the name Marley with Bob from reggae music or Jacob from the Christmas Carol, neither of which leads to a mass volume of willing investors when compared to a nationally known tenant.

What might be the impact on the cap rate in this situation? Since the Walgreens is attracting national (and perhaps international) interest in terms of potential buyers, there will be more demand for the Walgreens which will push up the purchase price of the investment. Since the NOI remains constant, the effect of a higher price is a lower cap rate. As NOI remains at a constant of $150,000, the property value will change as cap rates change, as is shown in Exhibit 6.1.

When Exhibit 6.1 is considered alternatively, the possible investors for the Marley Drug would not want to pay as high a price as they would for the Walgreens, given the perceived higher relative risk. As the purchase price declines, the resultant cap rate increases.

While this theoretical underpinning is important, keep in mind that the role of the market participants, highlighted in Chapter 5 (investor, broker, appraiser, lender), is to assess the subject property's cap rate in light of the competition. By so doing, the problem of unsustainable cap rates is less likely to reoccur, as the 2% case cap rate for Mr. Slick's apartment property in Chapter 5 would never see the light of day once that very low rate is compared to the market averages. What follows is a discussion of each of the known cap rate derivation models in our current universe, with a discussion of strengths, weaknesses, and area of subjectivity noted in each model.

6.2.1 Market-based cap rate derivation

The appraiser's attempt to build a comparable cap rate typically falls into two distinct categories. First, there are "market-based cap rates" which are sales observed in the market. This category can also include survey results from

NOI	$ 150,000	$ 150,000	$ 150,000
Value	$ 3,000,000	$ 3,500,000	$ 4,000,000
Cap Rate	5.00%	4.29%	3.75%

Exhibit 6.1 Impact Value Change on Cap Rate.

third-party data providers who offer, for a fee, market demographic information to include focused commercial real estate information such as leasing rates, vacancy rates, cap rates, and discount rates. In vibrant markets, these approaches are more favored as the appraiser (or broker) has numerous observable sales at their disposable which they can use to compare the current property. The second category of cap rate derivation is academic models, which will be discussed shortly.

6.2.1.1 Market abstraction

Market abstraction (also known as market extraction) is the most common form of market-based cap rate derivation. The appraiser will show comparable sales in the market in an effort to find the properties which most closely resemble the subject property. Proximity is often included as a means of settling on the best "competitive set" of recent sales, but not always. In the case of a nationally known single tenant, it is common to review like sales of properties occupied by the same (or similar) tenant irrespective of where the properties are located.

Let's return to the example of Mr. Slick's apartment complex, described in Chapter 5. Exhibit 6.2 updates Exhibit 6.13 to complete a market abstraction analysis for properties deemed similar to the subject property.

When choosing from a list of recent sales which could serve as comparable properties for a market abstraction analysis, proximity is important since this is an apartment. Also important would be obtaining recent sales as opposed to sales from the distant past. Even this has an element of subjectivity to it, as the longer a given market has been relatively stable, the longer in the past a historical sale would be considered acceptable for this exercise. Conversely, if the market has recently contracted or gone through considerable expansion, sales from prior to that event date might not be considered truly comparable to today's market conditions. For apartments, the square footage, age, condition, and number of units would also be relevant information for deciding if a sale is acceptable for this analysis. For other property types, the types of tenants, the quality of tenants, and the durability of the leases would also be valid inclusion reasons for comparable sales.

What is not acceptable is the inclusion of pending sales. This happens all too often in appraisals. By definition, a pending sale is not yet final, so including it in a list of historical sales seems like a non-starter. If a market has only pending sales to

Comparable Listings	Rent psf	Cap Rate	Price/Unit
Subject Property	$ 0.60	2.12%	$ 92,857
Comparable #1	$ 1.02	6.15%	$ 116,389
Comparable #2	$ 1.10	5.06%	$ 106,667
Comparable #3	$ 0.70	8.06%	$ 93,000
Comparable #4	$ 1.05	5.85%	$ 110,000
Comparable #5	$ 0.88	7.00%	$ 93,548
	Min	2.12%	
	Max	8.06%	
	Mean	5.71%	
	Alt	6.42%	

Exhibit 6.2 Market Abstraction for Slick Apartments.

consider, other cap rate derivation approaches would seem better suited for market conditions. The strength of the market abstraction is its ease of use. The weakness of this model is the lack of relevance if there are no market sales. The subjectivity involved has to do with which sales are considered reasonable for inclusion and on what basis.

6.2.1.2 Third-party data providers

Another means of market-based cap rate derivation is via published data sources. There are a myriad of companies that provide metro-level market information (sometimes also at the sub-market level) by property type. These data are usually compiled via confidential surveys to investors and is organized by property and market. For example, the Boston metro market would typically have numerous third-party data providers serving the multifamily, retail, office, and warehouse markets. Each report is issued at least quarterly and is available for a fee.

While this seems like a fairly objective method to obtain comparable cap rates, it is also awash with subjectivity. First, what is the orientation of the survey questions utilized to collect this information? Are the questions typically future-oriented (i.e., what do you expect to see?) or past-oriented (i.e., what have you seen?). This subtlety is more important during markets in transition or when there are significant market movements. If a market is relatively stable, the orientation of the question is not as important. When I was doing research for my first real estate book, I saw a number at the end of a report for questions. I decided to call and inquire about the time orientation of the questions. The person on the other end of the line seemed perplexed by my question and, after a significant hold time, instructed me to contact the company's legal department for explanation. What I received hardly instilled confidence in this method as it resembled the Wizard of Oz in paying no attention to the man behind the curtain, or more curtly, "how dare you question where we get our information but please feel free to cite it blindly ad nauseam".

Sometimes appraisers will utilize "market participant interviews" along with providing data from third-party market providers to derive cap rates. This seems a bit redundant since we are in effect asking the opinion of certain unnamed (but undoubtedly fabulous) sources plus citing a publication that provides survey-level data for the market to render two distinct opinions of cap rate rationale.

The strength of third-party data providers is the ease of obtaining the information. The weakness is that these studies are primarily concerned with major metro markets. If your property is not located there, you have to do a bit of line drawing to determine how high or low your tertiary market would be relative to the most proximate surrounding major markets. Another weakness is that these surveys often only include institutional quality-type properties, such that if you are investing in a smaller property, the implication is that your cap rate should be higher, but by how much is up for interpretation. Herein lies the subjectivity of these approaches, in that all markets are not surveyed, all properties are not surveyed, and how to assess impact on the final cap rate is up for interpretation.

6.2.2 Academic cap rate derivation

The weaknesses of the market-based cap rate derivation models beget the more academic models. Each of these models has at its heart the concept of weighted average cost of capital. In other words, the cap rate can be built based on some proxy for the investor's equity return and the cost of debt. While many of the inputs for these various models are quite objective (i.e., loan amortization, interest rate, lender's required debt service coverage ratio), some are quite subjective, as will be discussed in this section.

6.2.2.1 Band of investments

The band of investments model was developed independently by Thurston Ross in 1937 and was further improved by S. Edward Kazdin in 1944. While this is quite an old model, it is still well utilized in appraisals today. The basic premise of the band of investments is to break up the cap rate derivation into an equity component and a debt component. The debt component is much easier for investors and lenders to understand, as it focuses on the loan constant, the loan interest rate, and the loan amortization. Subjectivity enters into the equity calculation.

If we recall Mr. Slick's apartment property from Chapter 5, the appraiser settled on a cap rate of 6.50%. Exhibit 6.3 highlights the band of investments model. Since the loan to value is equal to 75%, this is the weighting for the debt portion of the cost of capital. The loan constant is calculated as the fractional annual amount that it takes to pay down the entire mortgage to zero based on an annual interest rate of 4.50% and a loan amortization of 240 months. Assuming a $1 (or $100 million as it does not matter) loan at an annual interest rate of 4.50% for 240 months, the annual payment would be 0.76 (rounded from what is shown in Exhibit 6.3). The first column of Exhibit 6.3 represents what an appraiser might input in order to devise a resultant cap rate of 6.50%. The problem here is that the annual rate of yield on equity required to make this calculation is quite low at 3.50%. The second column shows how things would look if the loan amortization was increased to 300 months, with the result based on a required annual rate of return on equity of 6.00%.

You might be asking what exactly an annual yield of equity on cash is. This is an equity cash flow to the investor on an annual basis divided by the total equity invested. Equity cash flow is calculated as taking the NOI and subtracting the annual debt service. While this can be done for any property being purchased, the total equity invested component is a little less concrete when the property has been held by the same owner for quite some time. The appraiser and lender may have a situation where the current owner wishes to increase their indebtedness rather than a new purchase where the equity being invested is much clearer. In the case of the purchase, the appraiser would quickly determine what the subject property's NOI

				Actual	Sensitize
Y	=	Annual Rate of Yield of Equity on Cash	=	3.5%	6.0%
M	=	Loan to Value Percent Ratio	=	75%	75%
MTG	=	Maximum Available Mortgage Length (Years)	=	20	25
RATE	=	Mortgage Interest Rate	=	4.50%	4.50%
Rm	=	Annual Loan Constant	=	0.0759179	0.0666999
CR	=	(M*Rm)+ ((1-M)*Y)	=	0.0656884	0.0650249
CR	=		=	6.57%	6.50%

Exhibit 6.3 Band of Investments Method.

is projected to be, and then subtract that by the annual debt service. That equity cash flow is then divided by the amount of equity invested (in the case of Mr. Slick that would be 25% of the purchase price) to arrive at the property's specific return on equity. Then that rate can be compared to third-party data provider market estimates.

Regarding the cost of debt parameters, appraisers can utilize their banker friends or various websites that share the latest annual interest rates and loan amortizations relative to the age and condition of the property. The newer and nicest properties would generally have the lowest interest rates and the longest loan amortizations, ceteris paribus. There is also a case where a borrower could be debt averse and want a quicker amortization of their loan principal, but generally the idea holds. Older, less-quality properties would be on offer at a higher annual interest rate and a shorter loan amortization period.

The strength of the band of investments model is that most of the inputs are known to the market participants (loan to value, loan amortization, and interest rate). The weakness of the model is that the equity yield rate must be estimated from outside sources. The subjectivity of this approach lies in how to obtain the equity yield rate.

6.2.2.2 Lender's yield analysis

The lender's yield analysis is so good that it has four names! Other than the lender's yield, I have also seen it invariably called the debt service coverage analysis, the underwriter's formula, and the Gettel equation (in honor of Ronald Gettel, who created this model in 1978). To contrast with the band of investments, the lender's yield model removes the subjective equity yield rate from consideration and replaces it with the desired debt service coverage ratio. Exhibit 6.4 summarizes the inputs for the lender's yield model.

The two columns in Exhibit 6.4 have the same assumptions for the annual loan constant which were discussed in Section 6.2.2.1. The good news here is that all of the inputs in the lender's yield model are known to the investor and lender. The bad news is that utilizing this approach can provide wide disparity in the calculated cap rates. By simply changing the annual loan constant in column two from 240 months to 300 months, the cap rate dropped by 87 basis points. Theoretically it makes sense that as the annual debt service has declined (given the extension of the loan amortization period), the principal is still being paid back slower. This could cause a higher default risk relative to a scenario where the loan amortization is shorter.

The strength of the lender's yield model lies in its simplicity, as all terms are known by the market participants. The weakness of the model is that there is a wide variety of cap rates as the model changes slightly, for example, if we change column one in Exhibit 6.4 to a 1.40× debt service coverage ratio (i.e., more equity), the resultant cap rate balloons to 8.48%. The subjectivity of this model involves which

Desired Debt Service Coverage Ratio (DSCR)	1.49	1.25
Loan to Value (LTV)	75%	75%
Annual Loan Constant	0.0759179	0.0666999
Overall Rate (OAR)	8.48%	6.25%

Exhibit 6.4 **Lender's Yield Model.**

inputs to consider as lenders have differing standards for their loan terms, and much of the data provided are varied in terms of "most likely", "most arduous", and "most liberal" lending terms and it is up to the market participant as to which category their property most likely resembles.

6.2.2.3 Ellwood and Akerson

The last two cap rate derivation models in our known universe are named after those who created them. L.W. "Pete" Ellwood was the chief appraiser at NY Life Insurance Company and created the model that bears his name in 1957. His model takes the band of investments model and time limits it (to say a period of five years). Then it considers the impact of loan repayment over this time period along with any projected changes (up or down) to property values or income. The Ellwood J-factor is a curvilinear change in income over the projection period, and typically will increase the cap rate when the income and/or property value is projected to decline. A sample Ellwood equation is summarized for Mr. Slick's apartment complex in Exhibit 6.5.

The inclusion of the change in income (as opposed to just the projected change in property value) is what differentiates the Ellwood model from the Akerson equation. In fact, if the income change over the period for Ellwood depicted in Exhibit 6.5 is removed, the two models produce the same result. Akerson's K factor involves a linear movement of the projected appreciation or depreciation in property value over the projected time period. Akerson's mortgage equity method for Mr. Slick's apartment complex is shown in Exhibit 6.6.

Similar to Ellwood, the Akerson model is not utilized as much these days. Appraisers are opting for a combination of market and academic cap rate derivation models, but are generally staying away from Ellwood and Akerson owing to its computational complexity. Subjectivity enters into the equation for what the projected change in income or property value will be over the holding period. The upside of these models is that when sales come to a halt owing to a significant

Y	= Annual Rate of Yield of Equity on Cash	=	6.0%
n	= Income Projection Period	=	5
M	= Loan to Value Percent Ratio	=	75%
MTG	= Maximum Available Mortgage Length (Years)	=	20
RATE	= Mortgage Interest Rate	=	4.50%
Rm	= Annual Loan Constant	=	0.0759179
1/Sn	= Sinking Fund Factor at Equity Yield Rate	=	0.1773964
P	= Ratio Paid Off-Mortgage	=	0.1730001
C	= Mortgage Coefficient (Y+P1/Sn-RM)	=	0.0147717
Appreciation/Depreciation	= Property Change in Value Over Projection Period	=	-10%
Income Change	= Change in Income Over Projection Period	=	-5%
J Factor	= Adjustment Factor for the Change in Income Over Projection Period	=	0.5528322
Rate	= $\frac{Y-MC +/- DEP/APP * 1/Sn}{1+I*J}$	=	0.0685559
Rate	=	=	6.86%

Exhibit 6.5 Ellwood's Mortgage Equity Method.

Y	=	Annual Rate of Yield of Equity on Cash	=	6.0%
n	=	Income Projection Period	=	5
M	=	Loan to Value Percent Ratio	=	75%
MTG	=	Maximum Available Mortgage Length (Years)	=	20
RATE	=	Mortgage Interest Rate	=	4.50%
Rm	=	Annual Loan Constant	=	0.0759179
1/Sn	=	Sinking Fund Factor at Equity Yield Rate	=	0.1773964
P	=	Ratio Paid Off-Mortgage	=	0.1730001
Appreciation/Depreciation	=	Property Change in Value Over Projection Period	=	-10%
Rate	=	(M * Rm) + [(1-M) Y] - M [P (1/Sn)] -DEP/APP (1/Sn)	=	0.0666609
Rate	=		=	**6.67%**

Exhibit 6.6 Akerson's Mortgage Equity Method.

market change, either of these models allows for the current market data to be changed to yield a new projected cap rate based on projected market movements.

6.2.3 Finalize that cap rate!

As you can see from this section, cap rate derivation is much more than taking your property's NOI and dividing by the purchase price. In order to estimate what a market comparable cap rate would be, the appraiser has at their disposal numerous models that have varying strengths and weaknesses. In the final analysis, the concluded market cap rate is typically some sort of average of what the various models produce.

In our next section, we turn our attention to discount rates.

6.3 Discount rate mysteries revealed

As is typical of discount rate discussions, I will start with the answer. In Chapter 5, the appraiser utilized a 10% discount rate in the discounted cash flow model to value the property at $2,370,000. In most finance problems, the discount rate is provided. This is so pervasive that sometimes we forget how to go about selecting our own desired rate. Sometimes students have trouble telling the difference between the cap rate and the discount rate. As we just discussed, cap rates are a point in time measure of return where the higher the level of risk, the higher the corresponding cap rate. Discount rates are also a measure of risk but are used to discount the cash flow received over the investment holding period. The internal rate of return is the discount rate required to make the net present value of a project equal to zero.

As the discount rate changes, so does the value calculation for the subject property. Exhibit 6.7 illustrates the impact of subtle discount rate changes on the DCF valuation of Mr. Slick's apartment complex. Given the range of values depicted in that exhibit, having a regularized process for discount rate selection seems like a good idea.

Rate	8.00%	9.00%		10.00%	11.00%	12.00%
Value	$2,580,000	$2,470,000	$	2,370,000	$2,270,000	$2,170,000

> **Exhibit 6.7** Impact of Discount Rate Change on DCF Value.

Let's pretend that you are Mr. Slick (or Ms. Slack) and you are completing your discounted cash flow analysis for the apartment complex analyzed in Chapter 5. You have done all of your projections in terms of how you expect the future property to play out, and you have even decided on the appropriate holding period for your investment. In order to determine the property value in a situation where the income is expected to be received in different years in the future, the selection of a discount rate is important. What process might you go through to select the appropriate discount rate? Realizing that the more uncertain the future looks, the higher discount rate you should consider, but the question remains about how to obtain that rate. The following section attempts to add clarity to this selection process.

6.3.1 Market-based discount rate construction

Similar to cap rates, market rates for a given metropolitan area can be obtained from third-party data providers. They typically will list the discount rate as the IRR for a given market, and the same issues that correspond to the cap rate data are also equally in place for the discount rate data, namely, that the properties are located only in metro markets and are typically of institutional quality. The small investor not located in a metro market is again on their own to interpret how to draw a conclusion between the closest metro market information.

As alluded to earlier, many investors come up with their own discount rates based on certain rules of thumb or based on conversations with other investors or commercial lenders. When devising a plan to estimate a discount rate in practical terms, the idea of opportunity cost comes into play. If an investor is contemplating investing equity into a commercial real estate venture, there exist a myriad of alternate investments that they could do instead. Thus, reviewing the latest returns on stocks, bonds, or more appropriately real estate investment trusts (REITs) may shed some light on the current market relative risk parameters. Additionally, reviewing these alternate investment returns can provide guidance on what investor hurdle makes the most sense.

6.3.2 Academic discount rate construction

Similar to cap rates, there are also more academic discount rate construction models. One is the weighted average cost of capital approach, and the other is the built-up method. Both models will be discussed in this section of the chapter.

6.3.2.1 Weighted average cost of capital (WACC)

The weighted average cost of capital (WACC) is utilized in numerous contexts in finance, and it also appears in light of discount rate uncertainty. The basic model consists of estimating the cost of debt, estimating the cost of equity, and then weighting those costs based on the amount of leverage.

For commercial real estate transactions, most lenders consider a 75% loan to value to be desirable, so we will assume here that the debt component of the calculation is weighted at 75%. Required inputs for the cost of debt calculation include the current borrowing rates in the market along with the estimated tax rate for the investor. Investors can utilize their knowledge of commercial real estate lending terms or access free internet sources which provide summaries of current interest rates on offer for commercial investment properties. The investor's tax rate should be known to them, otherwise they can access governmental tax tables to get a good estimate for the marginal tax rate that would correspond to the projected NOI for the subject property.

Based on our estimate of the typical leverage for a commercial real estate property, we will assume that the cost of equity capital is weighted at 25%. Required inputs for the equity or debt calculation include the current estimate for the risk-free rate (US treasuries are often a utilized benchmark), the overall beta for stocks, and the estimated long-term average for stock market returns. This area of the weighted average cost of capital model contains much subjectivity, especially as concerns the chosen stock beta and the estimate for the long-run market average return for the stock market. Since we are contemplating the discount rate for a commercial real estate project, the investor might choose to utilize the beta for just commercial real estate investment companies, or they might utilize a consideration for the entire stock market return. Exhibit 6.8 shows a hypothetical version of this model.

What is interesting about this approach is that based on the current low lending rate environment, the output for this model seems very low. Most appraisals that I have seen do not utilize such low discount rates, as by so doing the future cash flow would not be discounted as greatly as when utilizing more common discount rates from 8 to 10%.

6.3.2.2 Built-up method

The built-up method assumes that the overall unleveraged discount rate is comprised of three things: the risk-free rate, the cap rate spread, and the appreciation spread. The risk-free rate benchmark is often the ten-year US treasury rate, while the cap rate spread is defined as the difference between average cap rates in the market

Risk Free Rate (rf)	2.00% US Treasury (normal times)	
Overall Beta for stocks	1.00 Focus on CRE sector	
Expected market return (rm)	8.00% Long-term market average	
Cost of Equity Capital (Ke)	**8.00%** Ke = Rf + Bi (Rm - Rf)	25% Equity
Cost of Debt in Market (Kd)	6.00% Borrowing rate today	
Tax Rate of investor (1-t)	28.00%	
Cost of Debt (Kd*)	**4.32%** Kd* = Kd (1-t)	75% Debt
WACC	**5.24%** Discount rate assumption	
	5.25% Rounded Discount Rate	

Exhibit 6.8 Weighted Average Cost of Capital for Discount Rate.

Period	Avg. Discount Rate (IRR)	Prior Qtr 10 Yr Treasury	DR Spread Over 10 Yr Treasury	Avg. Cap Rate	CR Spread Over 10 Yr Treasury	Appreciation Spread (DR Less CR)
Most recent Q1	9.50%	2.20%	7.30%	6.50%	4.30%	3.00%
Most recent Q2	9.30%	2.10%	7.20%	6.25%	4.15%	3.05%
Most recent Q3	9.30%	2.05%	7.25%	6.50%	4.45%	2.80%
Most recent Q4	9.00%	2.00%	7.00%	6.76%	4.76%	2.24%
5 Yr Avg	9.38%	2.68%	6.70%	6.50%	3.82%	2.88%
10 Yr Avg	9.27%	2.00%	7.27%	6.00%	4.00%	3.27%

Spot 10 Year Treasury	2.00%
Cap Rate Spread	4.00%
Appreciation Spread	3.27%
Discount Rate	9.27%
Rounded DR	9.25%

Exhibit 6.9 Example of Built-Up Method for Discount Rate.

today and the most recent ten-year treasury rate. The appreciation spread consists of the difference between the average discount rate reported for the market and the most recent cap rate information. The average discount rate reported in the market typically consists of the IRRs that are reported in third-party market reports. The built-up method allows for investors to add an additional return generated from NOI growth or owing to changes in the underlying prices (similar to the concepts of the Ellwood cap rate derivation model).

Thus, the built-up method has at its heart the use of third-party market reports which, as we discussed in Section 6.2.1.2, can be of varying use depending on the location, quality, and size of the investment property being considered for investment. Exhibit 6.9 provides an example of the use of this model.

Since the built-up method starts with the reported average discount rate in a given market, and also includes the average cap rate seen in the market, this model could be considered a market-based approach. But it seems better suited for an academic model given that the rate is calculated rather than simply observed. Subjectivity exists in this model given the reliance on third-party data which are collected from an amalgamation of sources in varying ways.

Interestingly, this blended market and academic approach provides a higher estimate for the current discount situation. The built-up method arrives at a discount rate (rounded) of 9.25% versus the 5.25% which resulted from the weighted average cost of capital model. The final discount rate, which was selected by the appraiser in Mr. Slick's apartment, was 10%, and this choice could have been the result of all of the models that we have discussed in this section.

In our next section we move to highlighting the subjectivity of the debt yield – a lending metric seen in commercial banking in recent years.

6.4 Riddle of the debt yield

What if the loan default problems of the recent past could have been avoided if only one simple change had been made in how commercial real estate lenders underwrite income-producing property secured loans: *moving from the traditional debt coverage ratio to the debt yield metric.* This exciting claim has been made numerous times by many market participants, and it is worthy of a closer examination. Does the debt yield offer a simpler method for banks to improve their underwriting prowess and to lower their default rates? Or might there be hidden flaws in the debt yield which could surface when it is implemented in a traditional banking setting? This section helps to solve the riddle of the debt yield for banks that keep their loans on balance sheet.

6.4.1 Debt coverage ratio versus debt yield

Before we delve deeper into the questions raised above, it is helpful to discuss the difference between the debt coverage ratio (DCR) and the debt yield (also known as the constant carried). The debt coverage ratio is calculated by dividing the NOI of a property by the annual debt service for the loan being underwritten. The basic idea is to have a higher level of NOI relative to annual debt service, so if the property experiences vacancy or increased operating expenses, the debt service on the loan could still be paid. A benchmark for the DCR is 1.25× whereby there is 25% more NOI than annual debt service. The debt yield is calculated by the same starting point as with the DCR: NOI, but instead divided by the loan amount. The idea is to get the percentage of the loan that the NOI represents, and then compare this with a benchmark (say 10%) for approval. The debt yield hurdle increases with the riskiness of the underlying property.

If you were to query "debt yield in commercial real estate" and scan the first few short articles that appear, you might see statements such as these:

- The loan amount is more straightforward relative to annual debt service, as the annual debt service can be manipulated while the loan amount cannot.
- The debt yield represents the lender's expected return if they were to take back the property.
- CRE and CMBS investors want to make sure that low interest rates, low cap rates, and high leverage never again push real estate valuations to sky-high levels.

Let's take each of these claims in turn. For the first bullet point, it would appear to be true that annual debt service is more apt for manipulation than the loan amount. For example, if a given property was projected to produce an NOI of $100,000 and the loan amount was $1 million, the debt yield would be 10%, while the first year's debt coverage ratio would be 1.26× if the loan was priced at a fixed rate of 5% over an amortization of 20 years. If the loan amortization was increased to 25 years, the debt yield would remain constant at 10%, but the debt coverage ratio would increase to 1.42×.

The second bullet point is more problematic. When was the last time that a lender made a loan where the NOI was $100,000 at origination, and the NOI stayed at this same amount when they were forced to take back the property? In most cases, the primary reason that the property is being taken back is owing to poor performance, so the NOI would have dropped relative to when the loan was originated. The debt yield might provide an initial impression of return, but it may not represent the actual return in a liquidation scenario.

The third bullet point sounds great, and it would truly be wonderful if one simple measure such as the debt yield would ensure that these euphoric desires were met. The debt yield, in its simplicity, cannot impact the level of interest rates or leverage experienced in the marketplace. The debt yield was created in the commercial mortgage-backed security (CMBS) industry for classifying the loan-specific return for loans packaged together and sold to investors. Since CMBS investors are buying interest in a pool of real estate mortgages, the debt yield helps in assessing how each loan was performing at origination in a clean and easy format. While CMBS loans are heterogeneous in terms of the type of property and the geographic location, they are typically homogeneous in terms of one key measure: loan amortization.

Most CMBS and other securitized lenders offer loans based on a single amortization period (i.e., 30 years). Traditional lenders will often have a variety of amortization structures depending on the age and condition of the properties securing their loans, and the strength of loan sponsorship. So the third bullet assumes that utilizing the debt yield somehow shields lenders from the vagaries of low interest rates, low cap rates, and high leverage. From a cap rate perspective, the debt yield would not seem to preclude investors from overpaying for properties. And since borrowers are paying banks based on a stated interest rate and amortization, the debt yield would not seem to offer the panacea for low interest rates or high leverage.

6.4.2 Debt yield and heterogeneity

Here is a point that traditional banks may want to consider if they plan on utilizing the debt yield as an underwriting mechanism: you get different levels of comfort when the debt yield is compared with the debt coverage ratio as the loan amortizations change.

Exhibit 6.10 compares the debt yield and the debt coverage ratio for a $1,000,000 loan at an interest rate of 5.00% over 25 years, where the debt yield hurdle rate is 10%.

In this case, the 10% debt yield results in a substantial debt coverage ratio of 1.43× over a 25-year amortization. The 25-year amortization is the shortest length for the loans that are securitized (as most conduit lenders utilize 30 years). Twenty-five years were utilized here as this is typically the longest amortization offered by traditional lenders. Exhibit 6.11 shows the same scenario as depicted in Table 1, only this time the loan amortization is reduced to 20 years.

In this scenario, the debt coverage ratio is still acceptable, but not quite as robust as in the 25-year amortization scenario. Since traditional banks often finance properties not deemed to be of institutional quality, this implies that the properties may sit in non-metro markets and that they could be older than those that are part of the mortgage pools offered in the CMBS market. The result is often 20-year amortizations. Sometimes banks offer amortizations even shorter than 20 years. The point of caution with the debt yield is made plain in Exhibit 6.12 which changes the scenario depicted in Exhibit 6.11 to a 15-year loan amortization.

The debt yield of 10% is clearly not adequate for the same loan size when the loan is structured over a 15-year amortization. The resulting debt coverage ratio is only 1.05×, clearly too thin for even the most aggressive lender.

Loan	1,000,000		
Interest	5.00%		
Amortization	25		
DY	**NOI**	**ADS**	**DCR**
5%	50,000	70,151	0.71
6%	60,000	70,151	0.86
7%	70,000	70,151	1.00
8%	80,000	70,151	1.14
9%	90,000	70,151	1.28
10%	100,000	70,151	1.43
11%	110,000	70,151	1.57
12%	120,000	70,151	1.71
13%	130,000	70,151	1.85
14%	140,000	70,151	2.00
15%	150,000	70,151	2.14

Exhibit 6.10 Debt Yield versus Debt Coverage Ratio over 25 years.

Loan	1,000,000		
Interest	5.00%		
Amortization	20		
DY	**NOI**	**ADS**	**DCR**
5%	50,000	79,195	0.63
6%	60,000	79,195	0.76
7%	70,000	79,195	0.88
8%	80,000	79,195	1.01
9%	90,000	79,195	1.14
10%	100,000	79,195	1.26
11%	110,000	79,195	1.39
12%	120,000	79,195	1.52
13%	130,000	79,195	1.64
14%	140,000	79,195	1.77
15%	150,000	79,195	1.89

Exhibit 6.11 Debt Yield versus Debt Coverage Ratio over 20 years.

6.4.4 Debt yield and sensitivity analysis

Summing up what we have said so far, the debt yield works well when all loans are on the same amortization, but not so well when amortization periods differ within a lender's portfolio. The DCR is much lower relative to a static debt yield as amortizations condense. Additionally, the debt yield would not appear to have much use in terms of sensitivity analysis. For lenders originating loans today, it is clear from Exhibit 6.13 that rates are still at or near historical lows.

Based on Exhibit 6.13, any prudent lender would want to underwrite at an interest rate higher than the prevailing rate today. The debt yield is supposed to remove this risk from the equation, but there is still the risk that the annual debt

Loan	1,000,000		
Interest	5.00%		
Amortization	15		
DY	NOI	ADS	DCR
5%	50,000	94,895	0.53
6%	60,000	94,895	0.63
7%	70,000	94,895	0.74
8%	80,000	94,895	0.84
9%	90,000	94,895	0.95
10%	100,000	94,895	1.05
11%	110,000	94,895	1.16
12%	120,000	94,895	1.26
13%	130,000	94,895	1.37
14%	140,000	94,895	1.48
15%	150,000	94,895	1.58

Exhibit 6.12 Debt Yield versus Debt Coverage Ratio over 15 years.

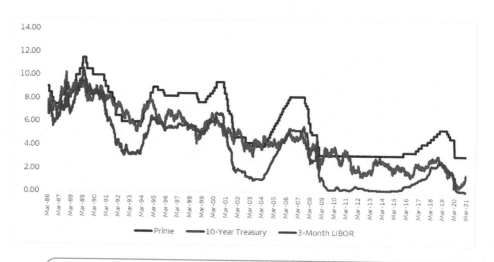

Exhibit 6.13 Thirty-Five year View of Interest Rate Lending Indices.

service at loan maturity (for ballooning loans) will be significantly higher than what we see in today's market.

Traditional lenders utilizing DCR for loan underwriting will often compute a "supportable loan amount" by taking the NOI of the property and dividing by a desired DCR, then dividing by the mortgage constant. The mortgage constant considers the interest rate and amortization of the loan. As interest rates rise, mortgage constants will increase and supportable loan amounts will fall, all other things being equal.

An article by a professor at Cornell University shed some light on the mathematical relationship between the debt yield (DY) and the DCR. If we restate these equations in terms of the loan amount (LA), and then set them both equal to each other, Exhibit 6.14 shows the results.

In Exhibit 6.14, NOI stands for net operating income and MC stands for the mortgage constant. When the equations are simplified and solved for the debt yield, it is shown that the debt yield is equivalent to the DCR multiplied by the mortgage constant. Given the issues with one debt yield hurdle rate in the presence of heterogeneous loan amortizations, the annual mortgage constant for a given interest rate and amortization combination can be multiplied by the desired debt coverage ratio to obtain the implied debt yield that would produce the desired DCR depending on the interest rate and amortization offered.

Some might say that the debt yield considers interest rate sensitivity in the following manner: let's assume that a given loan is being structured based on a 25-year amortization and an interest rate of 5.00%. This equates to an annual mortgage constant of 7.02%. If the lender desires a debt service coverage ratio of at least 1.25×, then the resultant debt yield would be 8.77%. If the bank's debt yield hurdle is 10%, there is a difference of 123 basis points relative to today's implied debt yield based on the example. A debt yield of 10% was often cited as a benchmark for lenders utilizing the debt yield. In a previously published *RMA Journal* article, benchmarks of the debt yield being at least twice the loan underwriting rate, and at least 200 basis points over the prevailing cap rate were discussed (Gordon *RMA Journal* 2015).

Exhibit 6.15 illustrates the point that as the amortization of a given loan declines, the debt yield hurdle rate needs to increase in order to achieve the same debt coverage ratio. Since interest rates are expected to increase, underwriting rates should be higher than prevailing market rates, or lenders may be overexposed when interest rates substantially increase.

Assume LA = NOI/DY
and LA = (NOI/DCR)/MC
Then...
NOI/DY = (NOI/DCR)/MC
NOI (MC) = NOI (DY)/DCR
DCR (MC) = DY

Exhibit 6.14 Debt Yield in Terms of DCR.

Amortization (years)	25	20	15
Mortgage Interest Rate	5.00%	5.00%	5.00%
Annual Mortgage Constant	7.0151%	7.9195%	9.4895%
Desired Debt Coverage	1.25	1.25	1.25
Implied Debt Yield	8.7689%	9.8993%	11.8619%
Desired Debt Yield	10.00%	10.00%	10.00%
Cushion Implied vs. Desired DY	1.231%	0.101%	-1.862%
New DY Hurdle Rate	11.00%	12.00%	14.00%

Exhibit 6.15 Solving for DY Hurdles at Various Loan Amortizations.

In the 25-year amortization example mentioned earlier, there was a 123 basis point difference between the implied debt yield (annual mortgage constant multiplied by desired debt coverage ratio) and the desired debt yield (debt yield hurdle rate selected by the lender). This cushion goes almost entirely away at a 20-year amortization at the same level of interest rates. Interest rate sensitivity analysis is typically concerned with the term of the loan rather than the amortization, but this example illustrates that moving to the debt yield entirely may create issues relative to the amortization utilized in a given loan structure. Obviously the desired debt yield of 10% for the 15-year amortization is clearly insufficient in producing a debt coverage ratio of 1.25× or providing any level of interest rate sensitivity protection over the loan term. The "new DY hurdle rates" shown in Table 6 are rounded and based on a 200 basis point cushion over the implied debt yield. This cushion is only an example as the use of a sensitized interest rate should consider the current and projected interest rate environment, the loan term, and other subjective factors.

For the 20-year amortization example in Exhibit 6.15, if interest rates increase higher than 5.12% (thus moving the mortgage constant to above 8.00%), the 10% debt yield hurdle will no longer produce a DCR of 1.25×. In this way, lenders should utilize some cushion as shown in Table 6, owing to the likely increase in interest rates over the next few years.

6.4.5 Debt yield riddle answered

In Greek legend, the Sphinx devoured all travelers who could not answer the following riddle: "What is the creature that walks on four legs in the morning, two legs at noon, and three in the evening?"[1] In banking, the debt yield is the answer to the following riddle: *what is the bank credit performance metric which leads to happiness in a uniform setting but to tears when things get more complicated?* Given its origins in the secondary market, the debt yield is an adequate measure for the initial performance of a loan, but must be utilized in conjunction with the debt coverage ratio and mortgage constant when the loans in a given portfolio have heterogeneity in loan amortizations. Portfolio lenders that utilize the debt yield should consider having different hurdle rates depending on the amortization being requested. The shorter the amortization, the higher should be the debt yield utilized to qualify for financing. In a rising interest rate environment, some consideration should also be given to the impact of rising mortgage constants on debt yield hurdle rates. Without addressing these issues, lenders might be surprised to find that the simple and easy debt yield has created leverage problems similar to those of recent years, which we hoped were left in our rear view mirrors forever.

6.5 Chapter conclusion

In this chapter, we have discussed the subjective elements of a few very important "little numbers" in the property value and loan suitableness process for investors, appraisers, and lenders. Cap rates, discount rates, and the debt yield all have importance in the valuation process, and all three of these concepts contain much subjectivity in how they are chosen and interpreted. When an investor is contemplating the purchase of a specific property, a market cap rate must be derived to estimate whether the investor is overpaying or not. Both sales in the market and more academic models can be utilized to make this determination. Discount rates also can be observed in the market and built-up relative to data that are available. Finally, debt yields, while typically a lender evaluation tool, have use in that regard but are not immune to the subjectivity of value. In our next three chapters we begin to focus on more specialty properties. Chapter 7 discusses hotel valuation, Chapter 8 highlights for-sale investment projects, and Chapter 9 sheds light on mortgage-backed securities.

Questions for discussion

1. Explain the differences between a capitalization rate and a discount rate. Include how the perception of risk helps determine the final rate selected in each case.
2. Describe the strengths and weaknesses of the debt yield as a lender underwriting metric.
3. Provide examples to show the relationship between a property's cap rate and the perceived risk by the investor.
4. Elaborate on the strengths and weaknesses of the market extraction cap rate derivation model. Provide examples for when the weaknesses are most likely to materialize, and elucidate examples of how to rectify this situation.
5. Outline the components of the band of investments cap rate derivation model. Discuss which of these components are most subjective from the perspective of the lender and the investor.
6. Describe the components of the lender's yield cap rate derivation model. Discuss the strengths and weaknesses of this approach.
7. Describe basic differences between the Ellwood and Akerson cap rate derivation models. In which market situations are these approaches the most and least useful?
8. Explain the differences between the weighted average cost of capital and the built-up method of discount rate estimation. Elaborate on some common other practices for deciding on a discount rate for an investment real estate property.
9. Outline the differences between the debt service coverage ratio and the debt yield. Include strengths and potential for subjectivity in these distinct calculations.
10. Describe how the presence of loan amortization heterogeneity in a lender's loan portfolio can create potential problems when utilizing the debt yield as a loan underwriting metric. Include some possible solutions to this debt yield riddle in your answer.

Chapter 6 Market vignette

Cast of characters: Tom (investor), Jerry (banker), Spike (waiter)
 Act: Local restaurant

Scene one: cooking up a market cap rate

JERRY: Hi Tom, thanks for meeting me for lunch today. I am excited to hear about your latest investment property.

TOM: Good to see you Jerry. I appreciate you being willing to meet with me on such short notice. I am negotiating the purchase of an office building. The property is located in the central business district and consists of multiple professionally oriented tenants. Right now I am considering a purchase price of $1.2 million.

JERRY: That's great. How much are you looking to finance for this purchase?

TOM: Right now I would like to finance $900,000. The rest will come via equity investment on my part.

SPIKE: Speaking of equity investments, here are your lunch orders! Chicken cordon bleu with all the fixings on the one hand, and a ham and cheese sandwich with chips on the other.

TOM: Oh, those lunches look so good! Jerry I am really hoping we can work together on this deal.

JERRY: (Munch, munch.) Yes, I agree. Have you run any numbers yet on your first year projected net operating income?

TOM: I believe that I should clear $75,000 annually on this property in terms of net operating income. I am really looking to finance this deal for as long as possible, Jerry.

JERRY: We might be able to finance up to as long as 25 years on the loan amortization. Just to give you an idea, we typically require that the property produce a debt service coverage ratio of at least 1.25× as a condition of loan approval.

SPIKE: Your waters are looking a bit low, let me pour you some into your glasses.

JERRY: I had the Italian sparkling water if you please. Tom just had the regular water.

TOM: What kind of interest rates would you be looking to charge?

JERRY: That is a great question, Tom. As you know, we always try to get our best customers like you the most desirable lending rates possible. We are living in interesting times. Our central bank aims to please with low lending rates, but this could change at any moment really. I bet we could get you a rate somewhere near 4.50% annually, but of course we would need you to complete a loan application so we can go through the process of review.

TOM: That rate sounds reasonable. I will certainly send over the financial information and sign whatever I need to get the process started. I am wondering about what level of cap rates you have been seeing lately, Jerry?

JERRY: As you know the capitalization rates can vary depending on the type of property, the age and condition of the asset, and the durability of the income stream. I have seen rates in the local office sector vary from as low as 5% to as high as 7% recently.

SPIKE: Speaking of wide ranges, I am happy to present you with today's lunch bill.

TOM: Ha that is so true, what the waiter just said as he walked off. Those are some wide ranges on the market cap rates. As you are paying for our lunch Jerry, I hope that you can tell me how we might narrow our calculations to settle on the appropriate market cap rate for this transaction.

JERRY: Yes, Tom, I am happy to walk you through how we can utilize market information to derive a cap rate for any transaction.

Questions for discussion

1. What is the going in cap rate for this purchase?
2. Given the known data, which cap rate derivation tools can be best utilized for this transaction?
3. What are the limitations of using the cap rate tools in this case?
4. How could these limitations be removed?
5. Elaborate on other methods for deriving a market-based cap rate.

Note

1 Oedipus had the correct answer: Man (baby, adult, elderly).

Bibliography

Adegoke, O. J. (2016) Effects of Valuation Variance and Inaccuracy on Nigerian Commercial Property Market. *Journal of Property Investment & Finance*, 34(3), 276–292. doi: 10.1108/jpif-08–2014–0056

Amidu, A.-R., & Boyd, D. (2018) Expert Problem Solving Practice in Commercial Property Valuation: An Exploratory Study. *Journal of Property Investment & Finance*, 36(4), 366–382. doi: 10.1108/jpif-05-2017-0037

C-Loans. Debt Yield Ratio. http://www.c-loans.com/debt-yield.html, accessed June 5, 2015.

Corgel, J. (2012) Demystifying Debt Yields. *CREF Report Series*, 1(4), June 2012.

CRE Finance LLC. http://cre-finance.newswire.com/cre-finance-llc-explains-how-the/271543, accessed June 5, 2015.

Gabauer, D., & Gupta, R. (2020) Spillovers Across Macroeconomic, Financial and Real Estate Uncertainties: A Time-varying Approach. *Structural Change and Economic Dynamics*, 52, 167–173. doi: 10.1016/j.strueco.2019.09.009

Glennon, D., Kiefer, H., & Mayock, T. (2018). Measurement Error in Residential Property Valuation: An Application of Forecast Combination. *Journal of Housing Economics*, 41, 1–29. doi: 10.1016/j.jhe.2018.02.002

Goddard G. J. (2016). The Riddle of the Debt Yield. *RMA Journal*, December 2015–January 2016, pp. 30–34.

Goddard, G. J. & Marcum, B. (2011). The Crowd is Untruth: The Problem of Cap Rates in a Declining Market. *RMA Journal*, March 2011, pp. 26–32.

Goddard, G. J. & Marcum, B. (2012) *Real Estate Investment: A Value Based Approach*. Springer, Berlin, Heidelberg.

Gordon, A. R. (2015) Debt Yield: An Underutilized Ratio at the Community Bank Level. *RMA Journal*, December 2014–January 2015, pp. 48–51.

Tagore, R. (1919) *Stray Birds*. Macmillan and Co. Limited, London.

Wells Fargo Securities, 30 Year Views of Various Interest Rates as of March 15, 2021. Information accessed via the Bloomberg database.

Zyga, J. (2019) Object and Objective of Property Appraisal and their Effects on Valuation Methods and Databases. Geodetski vestnik, 63, 92–103. doi:10.15292/geodetski-vestnik.2019.01.92-103.

Subjectivity in hotel property valuation

Chapter highlights

- Hotels, the fifth food group
- Hotel service quality
- Hotels and their guests
- Hotel valuation subjectivity
- Upstart challenges to hotels

> Values are always relative, subjective, and human, never absolute, objective, and divine.
>
> Ludwig von Mises

7.1 Hotels: the fifth food group

Traditionally, banks make investment real estate loans secured with apartment buildings, retail shopping centers, office complexes, and industrial properties. These are sometimes referred to as the "four food groups" of investment real estate. The purpose of this chapter is to highlight subtle differences in valuation between these traditional properties and hotels, and how subjectivity significantly influences valuation. When viewed in this context, hotels are the fifth food group of investment real estate lending and investment, with concentrations of hotel exposure ranging from limited to significant, depending on the location of a given lender and their tolerance for risk. Some hotels cater to leisure travelers and are located in coastal areas or other locales with implied tourist demand. Other hotels cater to customers in transit, such as those located near highways in the hopes of attracting weary road travelers on their way to and from business trips and vacations. Other hotels cater

DOI: 10.4324/9781003083672-7

to business travelers or large groups and are traditionally located in the central business district of large to mid-sized cities.

I like to call hotels the "infantry of real estate". Similar to the military operations when the infantry are the first soldiers venturing into combat, hotels are the first commercial real estate property to experience a significant change in economic conditions. Since hotels are rented for short increments, these properties are leading indicators of future commercial real estate economic performance. Given the short tenancy in these properties, valuation can be tricky when viewed in terms of the income approach. While many smaller hotels are family businesses where the owner may live on-site, the larger, nationally and internationally known "flags" are operated as franchises where the owner's residence is separate from the hotel premises.

7.1.1 Hotels via the income approach

When beginning to value a hotel via the income approach, it is helpful to consider the primary methods by which a hotel earns revenue. Certainly, the first income source that comes to mind is room rentals. The duration of stay can vary, from one day to many weeks, depending on the type of client and the location of the hotel. Properties with tenancy of longer duration are known as extended stay properties. In the following example, let's assume that the guest occupancy pattern resembles a more traditional hotel operation, rather than an extended stay format which caters to business professionals seeking longer-term living arrangements.

Additional sources of revenue for a hotel include meals (both in the restaurant and via room service), telephone usage, internet and cable television service (when not gratis), parking or boat slip rentals, vending machines, and the various selections in the mini-bar inside the room. It is this last revenue item that serves as the first basic hotel valuation technique via the income approach. In the "Rule of 100,000", the primary variables required in estimating hotel value are the number of rooms and the price of a can of soda in the mini-bar in the room.

If we assume that our subject property consists of 50 rooms located in a coastal region catering primarily to tourists and that the all-important soda can sells for $1.25, the following value is estimated via this process:

$$50 \text{ rooms} \times \$1.25 \times 100,000 = \$6,250,000$$

While this approach is fun and easy, to paraphrase Confucius, its method is much like using a cannon to kill a mosquito. If the value of the in-room soda can rises to $1.75 (as apparently the hotel owner is planning on selling the property and likes this valuation method), the hotel value increases to $8,750,000. The lucky hotel owner is able to achieve a 40% property value appreciation via this method by raising the price of soda in the room! Obviously, this approach focuses on only one component of the hotel's revenue stream, and so this technique is more for fun than for serious valuation. This fun and subjective model does help put the Mises quote at the start of this chapter into perspective.

Traditional income valuation methods for hotels include room rates, meals, and other sources of income. Let's start with room rate revenue. Obviously, existing hotels with limited seasonality factors will have historical revenue information, which makes for an easy projection for the next year (and ensuing investment holding period). Once seasonality enters into the equation (and it usually does), simple gross revenue estimates must be tempered with market averages and the consideration of the subject property's occupancy history for the entire year.

Now, let's return to our 50-room coastal hotel. Let's further assume that the hotel is located on the East Coast of the United States, situated in an area where the months May through September constitute the high-volume season, with the remaining months historically being very slow in terms of tourist demand. Given its size and location, tourist travel is the primary demand generator for this property.

When deciding where to stay during a trip, the daily room rental rates for hotels are apparent to the customer. If room revenue is considered to be a composite of all of the various room rentals each day over the period of one year, the hotel operator can determine their average daily rental (ADR) rate. This obviously does not take into account unrented rooms during the year. In order to estimate the gross room revenue for a hotel for any given year, the ADR must be converted to revenue per available room (RevPAR), as is shown in Exhibit 7.1.

When the number of rooms is multiplied by 365, the total potential room rentals are obtained (18,250 in Exhibit 7.1). Based on the hotelier's accounting system, the total number of rooms rented for each year is known, so that the total annual occupancy rate for the hotel is obtained (45% in Exhibit 7.1, or 8,213 rented rooms divided by 18,250 potential rooms). When the occupancy rate of 45% is multiplied by the ADR of $120, the RevPAR is estimated at $54. The ADR, occupancy percentage, and RevPAR for the subject property should be compared with market averages and comparable properties in the local market in order to verify the soundness of financial performance. RevPAR is a key metric in assessing the utilization rate of the hotel.

For purposes of our income approach valuation, total room revenue is estimated by taking the ADR of $120 and multiplying by the room nights sold at 8,213, to achieve $985,560 for the first year (rounded to $985,500 in Exhibit 7.2). Total income for the hotel is obtained by estimating annual receipts from other income generators such as meals and in-room sales. Total property revenue is shown in Exhibit 7.2.

Number of Rooms	50
# of Days	365
Potential Room Rentals	18,250
Occupancy Rate	45%
Room Nights Sold	8,213
ADR	$ 120.00
RevPAR	$ 54.00

Exhibit 7.1 Conversion of ADR to RevPAR

Revenue		% of Sales
Room Revenue	$985,500.00	
Other Revenue	$ 12,500.00	1.25%
Total Revenue	$998,000.00	

Exhibit 7.2 Total Revenue for 50 Room Hotel.

7.1.2 Estimation of hotel expenses

Once the total revenue for the hotel is obtained, the next step is to estimate the total variable expenses for the hotel. These variable expenses are typically broken into two primary categories: departmental expenses and undistributed operating expenses. The departmental expenses are those operating costs that directly relate to the sources of revenue at the hotel. Given that our hypothetical hotel contained two primary revenue sources (room and other revenue), the departmental expenses are estimates for room and other expenses which directly relate to the occupancy levels present at the subject property. As is shown in Exhibit 7.3, room expenses are estimated at 30% of total room revenue, while other expenses are estimated at 30% of the other revenues shown in Exhibit 7.2.

The second category of variable expenses for a hotel is traditionally broken out as undistributed operating expenses. These expense items, while typically varying with the operating performance of the hotel, are not directly related to specific categories of hotel revenue. These expenses contain traditional operating expenses found in other forms of investment real estate, such as repairs and maintenance (estimated at 5% of total hotel revenue), energy costs (estimated at 7% of total hotel revenue), advertising expenses, administrative and general expenses, management fees, replacement reserves, and franchise fees.

The last three of these expense categories require further explanation. The management fee is what the owner of the property pays for the daily operation of the hotel. For smaller hotels such as our subject, the owner may manage the property themselves. Appraisers and lenders will assume some level of management expense regardless, as the next owner of the property may not wish to be actively involved in running the hotel operations. Similar to the earlier example of increased soda costs in the room mini-bar, the absence of a management fee should not be a value creator for the current owner.

Replacement reserves are essentially a sinking fund that is maintained annually to account for the general wear and tear of the hotel property or the furniture,

Departmental Expenses		
Room Expenses	$ 295,650	30.00%
Other Expenses	$ 3,750	30.00%
Total Dept. Expenses	$ 299,400	30.00%
Departmental Profit	$ 698,600	70.00%
Undistrib. Op. Expenses		
Advertising	$ 49,900	5.00%
Admin & General	$ 29,940	3.00%
Energy	$ 69,860	7.00%
Repairs & Maintenance	$ 49,900	5.00%
Management Fee	$ 39,920	4.00%
Replacement Reserves	$ 39,920	4.00%
Franchise Fees	$ -	0.00%
Total Undistrib. Expenses	$ 279,440	28.00%
House Profit	$ 419,160	42.00%

Exhibit 7.3 Variable Expenses for 50-Room Hotel.

Number of Rooms		50		Safe Rate		3.00%
Replacement Reserve Estimator						
Item		Cost	Eco Life	Sinking Fund Factor		Reserves
Façade maintenance	$	35,000	10	$0.0872	$	3,053
Shingle roofing replacement	$	257,500	15	$0.0538	$	13,845
Common area carpeting	$	7,500	5	$0.1884	$	1,413
Common furnishings	$	5,000	5	$0.1884	$	942
Room carpeting	$	50,000	5	$0.1884	$	9,418
Room vinyl flooring	$	25,000	5	$0.1884	$	4,709
AC/Heat Replacements	$	75,000	10	$0.0872	$	6,542
Total Replacement Reserves	$	455,000			$	39,921
				Per Unit	$	798.43

Exhibit 7.4 Replacement Reserve Estimator.

fixtures, and equipment in the property. Prudent appraisers and lenders will require that the owner provide a schedule of planned capital expenditures for the next few years in order to both gauge the regular maintenance conducted on-site and assess necessary replacement reserves. Like most hotel expenses, replacement reserves can be either viewed on a per room basis or as a percentage of total revenue. Sometimes appraisers assume a market estimate for replacement reserves, but there is a more refined way of doing this, which is summarized in Exhibit 7.4.

If the hotel owner (or appraiser) obtains estimates for the primary items that would need to be replaced during the holding period of their investment, the replacement reserve calculator can be utilized to estimate how much money per unit should be held aside in order to save for these expected replacement items. The model tends to focus on only those items that need replacement infrequently (i.e., not every year), as more frequent repairs appear in the repairs and maintenance expense category. The replacement reserve sinking fund will provide the level of reserves needed to be set aside annually in order to achieve the total replacement cost of the item over the economic useful life of the product. The safe rate is the assumed rate of interest on the account where the funds are placed. For the first row in the table, the reserves would be calculated assuming ten annual compounding periods, an annual interest rate of 3.00%, and a future value of $35,000.

Turning to franchise fees, for our small hotel, we assume that the owner is an independent and not carrying a major hotel "flag" (or brand) which brings with it certain operating guidelines and an annual franchise fee. Franchise fees are certainly a cost item for a hotel, but those hotels that are listed under a major hotel brand also allow for some consistency in service delivery and guest demand flow given the expectations that the hotel will offer a quality service similar to others in the franchise. For hotels operating under a franchise agreement, there can be a profound impact on the durability of the hotel's income stream, as long as the time remaining on the franchise agreement is lengthy and the franchisee maintains service quality expectations as set by the franchisor.

Fixed Expenses			
Insurance	$	44,910	4.50%
RE & Personal Taxes	$	24,950	2.50%
Total Fixed Expenses	$	**69,860**	85.00%
Net Operating Income	$	**349,300**	35.00%
Cap Rate			8.50%
Estimated Value	$	**4,110,000**	

Exhibit 7.5 Calculation of NOI and Hotel Value.

As is shown in Exhibit 7.3, once the variable expenses have been estimated, house profit (a.k.a. gross operating income) is obtained by subtracting total departmental profit by the total undistributed operating expenses.

Once gross operating income for the hotel has been estimated, the next step is to estimate the fixed expenses to arrive at the NOI of the hotel. This calculation is summarized in Exhibit 7.5.

Fixed expenses typically will include the insurance for the property, as well as the real estate and personal property taxes associated with the hotel and the furniture, fixtures, and equipment (FFE) at the location. Unlike traditional investment real estate property, the FFE in the hotel is considered as part of the property value, as the hotel is essentially a hybrid between an operating entity (i.e., owner occupied) and an investment property (i.e., third-party income and expenses). Real estate taxes include city and county tax assessments on the building and land, while the personal taxes consider tax assessments on the FFE at the hotel.

Once the total fixed expenses of $69,860 are subtracted from the total house profit of $419,160, NOI of $349,300 is achieved. Assuming a cap rate of 8.50%, the estimated value of the hotel via the income approach is $4,110,000 (rounded).

7.1.3 Return of the cannons

Now that we have covered the basics of estimating the value of a hotel via the income approach, we will discuss the importance of sensitivity analysis and benchmarking when it comes to valuing a hotel property. In the words of former Wachovia Bank CEO John F. Watlington, Jr., *"it is ok to eat peas with a knife if you know better"*. Given the large value differences that can ensue when valuing hotels by just changing a few basic assumptions, this thought has never been more appropriate.

Returning to our 50-room small hotel property, Exhibit 7.6 shows the property value differences via the income approach when changing only two basic assumptions: hotel occupancy and the ADR.

In Exhibit 7.6, the subject property is valued via the direct capitalization approach at the same cap rate of 8.50% utilized earlier. For year 1, this represents the valuation that we have previously discussed. For each successive "year", subtle changes have been made to the occupancy rate and the average daily room (ADR) rate in order to achieve property values that span a range of almost 1 million dollars! When the occupancy rate and ADR increases relative to year 1, the year 2 valuation is $4,750,000, while when only changing the ADR relative to year one from $120 to $110, the value of the hotel in year five becomes $3,780,000.

	Ex 1	Ex 2	Ex 3	Ex 4	Ex 5
Occupancy Rate	45%	50%	48%	50%	45%
Room Nights Sold	8,213	9,125	8,760	9,125	8,213
ADR	$ 120.00	$ 125.00	$ 115.00	$ 110.00	$ 110.00
RevPAR	$ 54.00	$ 62.50	$ 55.20	$ 55.00	$ 49.50
Total Revenue	998,000	1,153,500	1,020,661	1,017,409	917,444
Total Property Expenses	$ 648,700	$ 749,775	$ 663,430	$ 661,316	$ 596,339
Net Operating Income	$ 349,300	$ 403,725	$ 357,231	$ 356,093	$ 321,105
Debt Coverage Ratio	1.35	1.57	1.39	1.38	1.25
Property Value (via direct cap)	$4,110,000	$4,750,000	$ 4,200,000	$ 4,190,000	$ 3,780,000

Exhibit 7.6 Sensitivity Analysis in Hotel Valuation.

Exhibit 7.6 does not include changes in property operating expenses, which is another very important part of property valuation. Should occupancy rates and/or ADR decline in a given year while at the same time the level of expenses increase, the resultant property value could become even lower than in year five in Exhibit 7.6. The prevalence of high fixed expenses relative to income can also have a profoundly negative effect on the hotel's NOI.

To mix metaphors, given that eating peas with a knife can produce appraiser and lender cannon fodder when valuing hotels, it is very important that the subject property be compared to its relevant peer group in terms of occupancy rates, ADR, RevPAR, and operating expense ratios.

7.2 Hotel service quality

Given the differences in operating performance that can be experienced at a given hotel, the assessment of hotel management is crucial for success. Third-party hotel industry reports are available to investors, lenders, and appraisers. Some of the more popular reports provide weekly to monthly reviews of hotel industry benchmarks such as ADR, occupancy rates, and RevPAR. Data are segmented by the region of the United States where the property resides, and can be further segmented by state and primary metro market. Additionally, properties are classified according to other commonly referenced classifications as is shown in Exhibit 7.7.

Independent hotels can run the gamut of price and location, with the primary common bond being the lack of a franchise agreement by a reputable national or regional chain. Hotels catering to airports are typically within five miles from the airport and derive the majority of their demand from airport customers. Interstate hotels are those that are not situated in urban or suburban environments whereby the primary demand is generated from road travelers. Small metro markets are defined by population, with a target of 150,000 people or less typically achieving this segmentation.

Utilizing reports such as these can help demystify hotel valuation and provide useful benchmarks for hotel operators as well. Once the lender or appraiser has isolated the location, price, and chain scale of a subject property, current weekly reports and a sampling of monthly reports throughout the year can provide evidence of any possible seasonality in the hotel's demand pattern. For example,

Chain Scale	Price	Location
Luxury	Luxury	Urban
Upscale	Upscale	Suburban
Midscale	Midprice	Airport
Economy	Economy	Interstate
Independents	Budget	Resort
		Small Metro/Town

Exhibit 7.7 Common Hotel Segmentations.

Lodging Quality Index		
Tangibility	Responsiveness	Security
Reliability	Competence	Access
Credibility	Courtesy	Communication
	Understanding	

Exhibit 7.8 Lodging Quality Index Service Quality Dimensions.

resort locations should experience a spike in demand during warmer months and on weekends generally, but third-party reports allow for opinions to become observable facts.

From the hotel management perspective, the best performing hotels are those that truly understand the needs of their target customers and strive for constant improvement in service delivery. Whether the hotel employee is at the front desk, bar, or laundry, the customer's perception of the quality of their experience is shaped by all of their encounters with hotel personnel. Quality in service industries is more challenging to define owing to three things unique to services: intangibility, heterogeneity, and the inseparability of production and consumption. The hotel guests' interpretation of their experiences at the hotel can differ widely based on gaps between the client's perception of what a quality experience *should* be and what they perceive that the quality actually *is*. The "*should vs. is comparison*" can be utilized by hotel management to identify any gaps in the hotel's service delivery to its clients. From a service quality perspective, the lodging quality index (LQI) has been created to help hotel managers assess the customers' perceptions of service delivery. The LQI expands on the original SERVQUAL five-dimension framework to include the characteristics as shown in Exhibit 7.8.

The purpose of the SERVQUAL and LQI is to convert "quality" into tangible dimensions that can be measured via customer surveys relative to how a given hotel has met the perceived quality requirements of a given customer. Tangibility refers to the general appearance and functionality of the property, while reliability refers to the extent to which employees can be depended on to perform services correctly and consistently. Credibility concerns the honesty and believability of the service provider, while responsiveness measures the efficiency of problem-solving during the guest's visit to the hotel. Competence involves the ability to perform a job accurately, while courtesy measures the friendliness of the service provider. Security helps to add the element of safety to the service quality dimensions, while access includes whether employees are approachable and easy to find when problems or needs arise. Communication helps measure the degree to which employees can keep customers informed regarding hotel amenities and other concierge types of concerns. The final service quality dimension of the LQI is that of understanding. This dimension measures the perception of how much effort is being made by hotel management in order to better understand the needs of their clients. Paraphrasing total quality management guru W. Edwards Deming, quality begins in the board room, but it is surely everyone's responsibility.

These service quality dimensions are helpful for hotel managers and investors so they can pinpoint any large discrepancies between perceived and actual service quality, and are helpful for lenders in order to gauge whether the occupancy and ADR levels of the past are reflective of what the future may hold. In a highly competitive industry such as lodging, large gaps in service quality could result in declining occupancy rates. Understanding the needs of customers comes with experience, and those hotel owners with proven cycle-tested performance are generally more successful in reacting to changing market conditions relative to less experienced hoteliers. There is not a wholesale need to order reappraisals on hotel properties as the best strategy is for an interactive communicative relationship between the lender and hotel property owner/investor.

7.3 Hotels and their guests

The marketing strategy and ideal location placement for a hotel depend on the types of guests it hopes to obtain. Some hotels are visited mainly for business purpose, and some hotel stays can vary from a single day to an extended stay. In this section, we will discuss the five primary groups by which a hotel guest can be classified. They are itemized as follows:

- Business
- Transitory
- Leisure
- Resort
- Extended stay

7.3.1 Classification of hotel room demand

Business travelers typically seek out hotels located in central business districts (CBD), with the primary employer of the guest typically paying for the expense. These hotels should be equipped with the most modern telecommunications technologies, conference space, and typically an on-premises restaurant. For business travelers, unless they are utilizing the conference space on-site, the bulk of the time during the visit will be spent elsewhere. The customer's choice of hotel will often depend on how close the business office is to the subject property, and how much the rental rates are compared to proximate competition.

Transitory, or in-transition, guests are those that are stopping at a hotel for a brief respite along a longer journey. The proximity to a highway, railway, or airport is a key order winner in terms of locations. While the amenities offered are important, they are not as crucial as for the business traveler. These hotels are subject to wide swings in occupancy, depending on the time of the year, the economic situation, and how many competitor hotels are located nearby. These are the hotels for the proverbial weary traveler, who decides on a whim to pull into a property when and where convenient.

Leisure guests can stay at really any of the hotels on offer, but they are certainly a distinct type of guest from a categorization standpoint. These can be tourists or people on vacation, individuals visiting friends and family, members of religious festival gatherings, or just guests who are visiting the area for personal reasons outside of work obligations. Similar to the transitory guest needs, the vacation traveler is typically not staying at the hotel very long during their stay, as they have other things to do outside of the property.

Resorts differ from vacation or touristic properties in that the premises is often a primary part of the vacation. Take for example Cancun, Mexico, where there are numerous competing resorts available. These properties offer entertainment, fine dining, beach access, and access to world-class swimming pool and recreational facilities. While other hotel properties have pools and workout rooms, this is a truly important feature for resort properties as the bulk of the guests' time may be spent on-site. The amenities on offer at resort properties are the primary order winner for sales, as is the general location of the resort.

Extended stay guests can require longer stays at hotels for either business or personal reasons. Someone may have transferred their company office to a new location and requires a place of residence while they search for a home. In any event, the amenities on offer for extended-stay hotels have more of a full-time residence feel, as guests are concerned with the quality and size of the kitchen, living spaces, and proximity to their full-time employment or raison d'être.

7.3.2 Hotel matching game

Let's test our knowledge of the link between hotel location and the demand for rooms in the matching exercise shown in Exhibit 7.9. The goal of this exercise is to review the exhibit and assign the specific characteristic to each of the three categories. Some of the characteristics will be included for more than one of the three types of hotel room demand generators. For this example, we consolidated the types of guests into the primary three: leisure, business, and resort. Please note that just below the exhibit is a list of the answers, so review the exhibit first,

---

Match the type of hotel to the location and demand consideration:

Leisure		Business	Resort
Proximity to CBD	Seasonality	Airport	Strength of economy
Shopping	Interstate access	Suburban bus parks	Sporting and cultural events

---

Exhibit 7.9 Hotel matching exercise

Example of Hotel Seasonality and RevPAR Impact												
	January	February	March	April	May	June	July	August	Sept	Oct	Nov	Dec	Totals
Rooms Sold	310	350	465	825	930	1,275	1,395	1,395	1,050	698	600	388	9,680
ADR	$ 90.00	$ 90.00	$ 95.00	$ 100.00	$ 110.00	$ 140.00	$ 150.00	$ 150.00	$ 140.00	$ 100.00	$ 95.00	$ 95.00	$ 112.92
Occupancy %	20.0%	25.0%	30.0%	55.0%	60.0%	85.0%	90.0%	90.0%	70.0%	45.0%	40.0%	25.0%	53.0%
Rooms Available	1,550	1,400	1,550	1,500	1,550	1,500	1,550	1,550	1,500	1,550	1,500	1,550	18,250
RevPAR	$ 18.00	$ 22.50	$ 28.50	$ 55.00	$ 66.00	$ 119.00	$ 135.00	$ 135.00	$ 98.00	$ 45.00	$ 38.00	$ 23.75	$ 59.89

Exhibit 7.10 Hotel Room Demand Seasonality and RevPAR Impact.

formulate your responses, and then once done with that, proceed to reading the rest of the section.

For those scoring at home, leisure guests have an element of seasonality, seek sports and culture, have their demand tied to the strength of the economy, seek shopping, and crave the convenience of easy interstate access. Business travelers seek proximity to the CBD, seek proximity to suburban business parks, their travel demand ebbs and flows with the strength of the economy, and airport and interstate access both are base requirements. The resort guests also experience an element of seasonality; seek sports, culture, and shopping venues; and the demand changes with the general economy. While this game may not be a new reality show in the making (match that hotel!), it does help to reinforce a couple of basic tenets of the hotel investment paradigm: hotels ebb and flow with the general economy and there is often an element of seasonality associated with their demand patterns.

7.4 Hotel valuation subjectivity

Given the high correlation of hotel room demand with the strength of the economy and the recurring seasonality factor in many hotel properties, hotel valuation is often wrought with subjectivity. Once the basic question has been answered concerning what type of hotel guest is most likely to visit a given hotel, the next important question concerns the appropriate assumptions for the subject properties RevPAR calculation. Part of this calculation subjectivity involves how best to account for rental rate and occupancy rate changes over the year, and another with specifically which revenues should be included in the calculation.

7.4.1 Seasonality factor in hotels

As Exhibit 7.10 illustrates, as the occupancy rate percentages and average daily rental rates vary, so does the corresponding revenue per available room and the estimated property value based on the income approach. In fact, in the five examples shown in that exhibit, the span of final estimated property value was almost 1 million dollars, and these were based on seemingly subtle changes in RevPAR. This underscores the importance of an investor, appraiser, and a lender needing to spend time to cull existing market data and property performance in order to provide the best estimates when valuing a hotel property.

Returning to our 50-room coastal hotel example, there would certainly be a seasonal pattern to the room demand as the large majority of the hotel customers are leisure travelers looking for access to the beach during the warm weather. Sometimes hotel guests venture to the coast during off-seasons because of more favorable rental rates and the dearth of other customers on-site. But as is shown in Exhibit 7.10, the hotel receives just over half of its annual hotel room reservations over the months from June to September.

The subjectivity in hotel valuation mainly concerns what final estimate to make concerning annual estimates for ADR and occupancy percentages, and based on Exhibit 7.10 there could be a wide range of possible values concluded. A lender may opt for the final estimates of an occupancy rate of 45% and an average daily rental rate of $120 for a final property value of $4,110,000, as concluded earlier in the chapter. An investor may take a look at the last 12 months' operating performance of the hotel and decide that an average of 53% for occupancy and just under $113 per night in room rent are appropriate conclusion. These inputs would lead to a RevPAR of $59.85 and an estimated property value of $4,560,000.

The market participant who is attempting to estimate the hotel's property value may resolve to expand the analysis to numerous years, and to include a comparison of the hotel's operating performance with market averages as noted in third-party report competitive sets. Others may conclude a need to reduce the impact of the lower months in some sort of weighted average format based on the number of rooms rented relative to the total for the year. What is clear is that valuation subjectivity is inherent when estimating a hotel's annual averages for occupancy percentages and for average daily rental rates. From here, our subjectivity discussion on hotels moves to which revenues to include in the analysis.

7.4.2 Which revenue?

Our discussion in this chapter has heretofore revolved around a hypothetical small operation with 50 rooms, but what about much larger hotels? The larger the hotel, the more likely that it is subject to a franchise agreement from one of the well-known brands throughout the world. These larger hotels are often better equipped with a fully operational restaurant, conference space, and other revenue sources. The presence of these additional significant sources of income has led to the expansion of the RevPAR model to something called the gross operating profit per available room (GOPPAR) model.

Exhibit 7.11 illustrates the expanded revenue source version of a hotel industry benchmark which focuses on comparing various properties relative to their gross operating profit per available room. The GOPPAR model increases the scope of revenue consideration for the hotel to incorporate everything that contributes to the gross operating profit of the hotel property.

For the hypothetical hotel property, food and beverage as well as other income represents a third of the hotel's revenue source over the period shown in Exhibit 7.11. While not negating the importance of the RevPAR metric, the expanded measure of GOPPAR can serve as a helpful comparison tool for the performance of competing hotels. Given the presence of two metrics regarding hotel RevPAR, the revenue category represents our final area of hotel valuation subjectivity as discussed in this chapter.

How might an investor respond to a situation when they are comparing two hotels for purchase and one has a higher RevPAR but a lower GOPPAR? As is the case in most subjective encounters, the answer to this question really depends on what sort of property the investor wants to own, and their experience level in running a hotel enterprise. In terms of Shackle, the experience of the decision maker

	Hotel A	%	Hotel B	%	Hotel C	%	Hotel D	%
Number of Rooms	200		200		100		100	
Number of Days in Period	365		365		365		365	
Number of Rooms Available/Year	73,000		73,000		36,500		36,500	
Occupancy	70%		76%		70%		75%	
Average Daily Rental Rate	100		95		100		100	
RevPar	70		72		70		75	
Revenues		%		%		%		%
Rooms	5,110,000	64%	5,270,600	66%	2,555,000	32%	2,737,500	34%
Food and Beverage	2,000,000	25%	1,200,000	15%	750,000	9%	1,000,000	13%
Other Departments	850,000	11%	900,000	11%	500,000	6%	500,000	6%
Total Revenue	7,960,000	100%	7,370,600	93%	3,805,000	48%	4,237,500	53%
Deparmental Expenses								
Rooms	1,022,000	20%	1,054,120	20%	638,750	25%	684,375	25%
Food and Beverage	1,200,000	60%	720,000	60%	487,500	65%	650,000	65%
Other Departments	400,000	47%	423,000	47%	250,000	50%	250,000	50%
Total Departmental Expenses	2,622,000	33%	2,197,120	30%	1,376,250	36%	1,584,375	37%
Total Undistributed Expenses	1,600,000	20%	1,600,000	22%	900,000	24%	900,000	21%
Gross Operating Profit	3,738,000	47%	3,573,480	48%	1,528,750	40%	1,753,125	41%
GOPPAR	51		49		42		48	

	Normal	%	Decline	% Change
Number of Rooms	1,000		1,000	
Number of Days in Period	365		365	
Number of Rooms Available/Year	365,000		365,000	
Occupancy	70%		67%	-5%
Average Daily Rental Rate	100		95	-5%
RevPar	70		63	-10%
Revenues		%		
Rooms	2,555,000	67%	2,305,888	-10%
Food and Beverage	750,000	20%	727,500	-3%
Other Departments	500,000	13%	485,000	-3%
Total Revenue	3,805,000	100%	3,518,388	-8%
Departmental Expenses				
Rooms	638,750	25%	622,590	-3%
Food and Beverage	487,500	65%	472,875	-3%
Other Departments	250,000	50%	242,500	-3%
Total Departmental Expenses	1,376,250	36%	1,337,965	-3%
Total Undistributed Expenses	900,000	24%	900,000	0%
Gross Operating Profit	1,528,750	40%	1,280,423	-16%
GOPPAR	4.19		3.51	-16%

Exhibit 7.11 GOPPAR Model.

is crucial to what they value and in how these preferences contribute to their valuation assumptions.

7.5 Upstart challenges to hotels

For this final section on our hotel chapter, we will focus on new challenges to hotels that have been seen in recent years. While rental houses have always had the ability to compete with hotels, today there are inchoate models of technology and design that make this process much more successful at eroding the hotel industry dominant market share on short-term residential rentals.

7.5.1 Rental property technology applications

Hotels came into existence as previously there were no aggregated places where travelers could go to temporarily lease space. And if space existed, the problem in the past was that it was hard to connect the sellers of the short-term residential space with the renters of that space. With the progress of technology, homeowners can now sufficiently advertise their homes, rooms, cabins, and other properties to a mass audience quickly and conveniently. Technological platforms (or as they are often called applications) have made it easier for willing renters to determine available properties in desirable locations very quickly. While hotels have also capitalized on these same technologies, one result is that new competitors have been created.

One example is Airbnb. Via this technological platform application, would-be renters can peruse available properties and also review the comments of prior visitors to ascertain the quality of the service offering as depicted in the glossy pictures of the property available on the site. Another benefit of a company like this is that they have taken out one of the primary objections to leasing single-family rental properties, that is, the lack of standardization of the service. Now customers know that properties being listed on this and other sites require that the owners adhere to strict cleaning, service quality, and other factors to standardize the user experience.

Additionally, services such as these also provide the landlords with guidelines of making the guest stay better, and can even serve as a sounding board for what rents to charge given the known competition in the area. Airbnb and competing applications have provided a whole new way for homeowners to monetize their properties during their time of ownership, and with the success of these platforms, have taken away demand from the traditional hotel sector.

From a valuation standpoint, owners who rent out their homes are required to report earnings as taxable income, so when these owners go to sell their properties, there should be a history of success in terms of rental and expense information. When an appraiser is engaged to determine a value for a rental home, the sales approach is still the predominant form of value. This is owing to their being more owner-occupied homes in the market versus rental homes. While there are some communities in resort destinations that specialize in rental properties, most residential neighborhoods cater to owner-occupied housing. The traditional viewpoint is that owner occupants tend to treat their properties better than renters, so the prevalence of more renters than owner occupants in a given market would tend to exert negative pressure on the average home values. With the advent of technological platforms catering to vacation rentals, owners are required to maintain their properties in a more sustainable way, as the inability to do so would cause those properties to be delisted from the site.

An appraiser can still consider the income approach to value for rental properties if this is the predominant way that the property has been utilized for the last few years, and the property sits in a viable vacation market. The appraiser would need to assess the rental rates in conjunction with market rates in order to complete an income approach valuation, but typically the final assessment of value would most likely lean heavier on the sales approach given the single-family residence orientation of the space.

7.5.2 Tiny homes

As a follow-up to our last section on rental property upstart challenges to the traditional hotel industry, one final mention will bring this chapter to a close – tiny homes. Tiny homes are a relatively recent entrant into the vacation rental space, having their origins in owner occupancy. In recent years, there have been numerous reality shows concerning the construction and life-changing potential of tiny homes. These homes are typically smaller than a studio apartment and are typically manufactured similar to a mobile home, albeit with typically more higher-end fixtures keeping in mind the environmental sustainability.

Tiny homes are nothing new, as back in the Middle Ages, the average dwelling size was much smaller than what we see today, primarily owing to families owning much less things to store and tending to be more nomadic than seen in present day. Comedian George Carlin used to say, "*you can't have everything, where would you put it?*" which clearly resonates with owners of tiny homes.

In an effort to provide a short history of tiny homes, the concept got its start millenniums ago when people had less need for storage and were more nomadic. In modern times, homeowners who also own recreational vehicles (RVs) which they use to satisfy their wanderlust began to look for better alternatives that might capitalize on real estate property appreciation. Instead of driving around all over and sleeping in their RVs, they could instead purchase a plot of land in some isolated yet aesthetic community and construct a small mobile home for use on the land. These tiny homes could be made to order from manufactured housing companies, or could be built from scratch by more industrious owners.

Tiny homes are typically mobile and as such are not considered to be real estate proper. These assets are typically titled in a similar manner to the traditional mobile home or RVs from which their idea was born. Once the basic idea of a tiny home was instituted, the next step was to permanently affix these homes on the site similar to a mobile home park. Some owners, shown on the reality shows aired on television, desired tiny homes in order to avoid a large mortgage debt, and others desired them as a cheaper way to own a vacation home. From there it was only a small step (pun intended!) to the beginnings of a tiny home rental market.

This short vignette on tiny homes should bring at least two questions to mind. Are traditional lenders financing tiny homes, and how might an appraiser attempt to value these if they are considered true real estate collateral for said loan? Lenders are typically not financing tiny homes, unless they already have experience in lending in the manufactured home business. This implies that the owners of these tiny homes are financing the construction of these units via personal equity, or some consumer credit such as credit cards, or via equity lines on traditional owner-occupied real estate.

While the future may not look bright in terms of traditional lenders financing tiny homes, let us recall that in the early part of the 20th century in the United States, owner-occupied home lending was atypical for commercial banks, with the typical structure at that time being a five-year bullet loan where 80% of the purchase price was owner equity, and not the debt of today. It was only after the great depression and the creation of the secondary mortgage market in the United States that lending terms for traditional homes tended to liberalize into what we know of today.

Returning to traditional (i.e., not tiny) rental homes for a moment, this asset class has been helped in recent years by third-party research that aggregates market rental information. This aggregated rental and expense data made rental homes more palatable to commercial lenders, and in the last few years there has been a successfully launched and paid out mortgage-backed security entirely comprising rental homes. Single-family residence rental homes are now financed by lenders and packaged into mortgage-backed securities and sold to investors.

It would seem that in order for tiny homes to become a viable alternative to other vacation rental options (including traditional hotels), the first step is in making them viewed as true real estate as opposed to a mobile home alternative. Then lenders would begin to lend against these properties and begin to experience repayment history such that the risk tolerance for these tiny homes can be compared with other real estate asset classes. From there, a secondary market for tiny homes could be created, if the paradigm for single-family residential rental property is any indicator of the pathway to success.

If an appraiser was presented with an opportunity to opine on the value of a permanently affixed tiny home with a history of rental success, the valuation would, you guessed it, be wrought with uncertainty and subjectivity. Some of the rental rates charged for tiny homes would likely be considerably higher than the market rents for traditional properties. Similar to traditional rental homes, the absence of strong rental comparable properties would lead the appraiser to utilize the sales approach valuation as the predominant determination of value. The cost approach might also be utilized as many of the tiny homes are new construction with higher-quality fixtures. The first tiny home appraisals might produce higher-income approach valuations relative to the sales and cost approaches. What we have learned from experience is that when one of the three approaches to value comes in significantly higher than the other forms of value, a market correction might be in order. This comment is applicable when an overall market exhibits an imbalance in values from the three approaches to value (sales, income, cost), rather than just one particular property. One tiny home does not a market correction make, but if the entire asset class appears imbalanced with the income approach so far out of line, the tiny homes could create a splendid splash. For now, tiny homes remain an interesting case study, but similar to the rental home market alternative, the hotel industry would appear to be sleeping soundly about their current status and their continued place in the sun.

By way of a chapter conclusion, hotels can be viewed as a hybrid between traditional operating businesses and traditional investment properties. By using proper benchmarking and understanding the metrics of hotel valuation, the cannon fodder of faulty estimation of future operating performance can be replaced with more accurate estimates that take into account market considerations of risk, and the quantity, quality, and durability of the income stream. The primary areas of subjectivity regarding hotels lie in assessing the RevPAR, determining the type of guest that typically stays at the property, and in how these variables interplay into the final valuation. In our next chapter, we turn our focus to the subjective valuation components of more specialty properties before turning our attention to the subjectivity in valuation for mortgage-backed securities in chapter 9.

Questions for discussion

1. Itemize factors that differentiate hotel valuation from other commercial properties.
2. Describe the different types of hotels relative to the different types of consumers that serve as customers.
3. Explain the difference between RevPAR and GOPPAR and highlight the elements of uncertainty in estimating each for a given year.
4. Describe different situations where the seasonality of hotel demand is a large and small concern for different hotel properties.
5. Elaborate on the replacement reserve, how it is calculated, and how the anticipated expenses differ from traditional repairs and maintenance expenses.
6. Discuss the lodging quality index framework and how each component can contribute to the success of a hotel property.
7. Discuss the primary areas of value subjectivity for hotels that were outlined in the chapter. How might these uncertainties best be addressed during the hotel valuation process?
8. Research hotel brands and franchise agreements and outline the top brands in the current environment.
9. Describe how technology has contributed to the increased success of rental homes in eroding hotel market share.
10. Outline the trajectory of the tiny home movement and offer thoughts on the future success of this inchoate challenge to the dominance of hotels.

Chapter 7 Market vignette

Cast of characters: Joey (appraiser), Dee Dee (hotel employee), Johnny (hotel owner)
   Act: Appraiser visiting a hotel.

Scene one: making contact

DEE DEE: Welcome to Hotel California!
JOEY: Very funny. This is the Camelot Inn, correct?
DEE DEE: Yes, it sure is! Please sir, remember to put on your face mask as a safety precaution. Face masks are required for all who enter the premises. How may I help you?

JOEY: Oh right, I keep forgetting about the mask. I am a commercial property appraiser and am here to meet the owner. But first I have a few general questions that you can help me with, if you don't mind.

DEE DEE: Yes, I will let Johnny know you are here. What questions might you have for me?

JOEY: Basically I am interested in how many rooms you have in the hotel, and what your average daily rental rate has been as well as your occupancy rate over the last few months.

DEE DEE: Let me check our software real quick. I am sure Johnny will provide you with the financials of the hotel in order to conduct your appraisal. We have a total of 85 rooms for rent at Camelot Inn, and our current daily rental rate is $85.00. Looking at our software, it looks like the rental price has stayed constant over the last few months, but back in the summer we increased rents to around $90.00 a night. Our occupancy has stayed around 70%, but in the summer it increased to around 80%.

JOEY: Well that does make sense given your coastal location. Do you have a mini-bar in the room, and if so, how much do you charge for a can of soda?

DEE DEE: Yes we do. Customers really like that feature. It also comes with pretzels, and other nice things guaranteed not to cause a stir. Our sodas are $1.50 a can I believe.

JOEY: What sort of safety protocols are you taking these days?

DEE DEE: Well, as you know we require face masks. We also put our rooms through an extensive cleaning process in between each tenant's stay. In fact, we try to not lease the room for 12 hours after someone has left to ensure any harmful effects are removed from the room.

JOEY: Has there been a history of sickness at the hotel?

DEE DEE: No, and we attribute this to our strong safety protocols. In fact when tenants check out, we require that they put their plastic room cards in an ultraviolet box to remove any harmful germs.

JOEY: Sounds like a hypochondriac's dream. Is the ultraviolet box that strange looking box on the table with the button at the center?

DEE DEE: Yes it is, but what was that other comment, sir?

JOEY: Oh nothing, just mumbling to myself. Thank you.

Scene two: meet the owner

DEE DEE: Oh here comes Johnny now. Johnny, the appraiser is here to visit with you if that is ok.

JOHNNY: Thanks Dee Dee. Yes I was expecting Joey, and I have a package of the last three years' financials on the hotel's operating performance.

JOEY: Thank you for your help Dee Dee, and it is nice to meet you Johnny. Do you mind if I walk through the hotel after our discussion to snap a few photos for the appraisal?

JOHNNY: Yes that is fine. I can have Dee Dee get you access to some of our few vacant units so you can get an idea for how those look.

JOEY: That would be great. Actually I have stayed here before. Do you still leave those great cookies on the pillow upon arrival?

DEE DEE: We had to stop that in conjunction with our cleanliness protocols. We now provide virtual cookies upon request, just kidding there, Joey.

JOEY: That's too bad, I loved those cookies. Virtual cookies upset my stomach.

JOHNNY: Let's go to my office to discuss what questions you have, Joey.

(Joey and Johnny leave Dee Dee at the front desk and proceed to Johnny's office on the first floor.)

JOHNNY: What questions do you have for me as you glance over the last few years' financial statements for the hotel?

JOEY: I see that you have a small dining room onsite. How much revenue does that bring in each year?

JOHNNY: Breakfast is part of the total room charge, so there is not additional income associated with breakfast served on-site. We offer continental breakfast to our tenants.

JOEY: Oh that makes sense. I have a joke that they call it the continental breakfast because when you are done eating, regardless of which continent you are on, hunger soon follows.

JOHNNY: You are a real card, Joey!

JOEY: Ha, thank you! So from what Dee Dee told me, your occupancy rates and rental rates both go up in the summer. What impact is there on your operating expenses?

JOHNNY: During most of the year, our operating expenses run about 60% of our revenues. In the summer, the expenses slightly increase to 65%, given the increase in cleaning and the hiring of additional seasonal employees.

JOEY: Were your operating expenses typically at 60% of revenues before the move to the heighted cleaning regime?

JOHNNY: I like how you put that. Yes, our expenses really did not move that much as we already had full-time employees on-site and our commitment to a sanitized living environment was mandated by the state.

JOEY: I know that once the pandemic hit, many hotels were immediately affected. How did your hotel fare?

JOHNNY: Those were trying times for sure. Our occupancy fell to almost nothing overnight. We requested a 90-day payment deferral from our lender as we couldn't make our regularly scheduled mortgage payments during those dark days.

JOEY: Dark both literally and figuratively it would seem.

JOHNNY: Yes, that is for sure. If you are ready to tour the property, I can show you where to start and which rooms you can visit.

JOEY: I believe in miracles Johnny! Onward and upward!

Questions for discussion

1. Based on the information provided in the case, estimate the value of the hotel under the normal times scenario as well as for the summer months' scenario.
2. What is the value of the hotel using the rule of 100,000?
3. What additional questions would you have for the hotel owner and employee?

4. What should the appraiser do with the information about the occupancy drop and bank loan payment deferrals? How might your valuation change if three months of revenue is taken out of the analysis?

5. Since the pandemic is an outlier event, what other mechanism could the appraiser utilize to account for the drop in occupancy without adversely impacting the value of the property?

Bibliography

Alserhan, B. A. (2011) *The Principles of Islamic Marketing*. Gower Publishing, Surrey.

deRoos, J. & Rushmore, S. (2012) Hotel Valuation Techniques. http://www.hvs.com/Bookstore/HotelValuationTechniques.pdf, accessed December 5, 2012.

Ford, J. & Gomez-Lanier, L. (2017) Are Tiny Homes Here to Stay? A Review of Literature on the Tiny House Movement. *Family and Consumer Sciences Research Journal*, 45, 394–405. 10.1111/fcsr.12205. https://www.fcs.uga.edu/docs/Ford_et_al-2017-Family_and_Consumer_Sciences_Research_Journal.pdf

Gasparini, G. (2011) Understanding Hotel Valuation Techniques, October 2011. http://tourism.blogs.ie.edu/files/2011/10/IE_Hotel_Valuation_Techniques_October_2011.pdf, accessed December 5, 2012.

Getty, J. M. & Getty, R. L. (2003) Lodging Quality Index (LQI): Assessing Customer's Perceptions of Quality Delivery. *International Journal of Contemporary Hospitality Management*, 15(2), 94–104.

Goddard, G. J. (2013) Hotels: The Fifth Food Group. *RMA Journal*, April 2013, pp. 40–45.

Goddard, G. J. & Marcum, B. (2012) *Real Estate Investment: A Value Based Approach*. Springer Publishers, Heidelberg.

Mises, L. (2006) *Bureaucracy*. Liberty Fund, Indianapolis, IN.

Parasuraman, A., Berry, L. L., & Zeithaml, V. A. (1985) A Conceptual Model of service quality and its Implications for Future Research. *Journal of Marketing*, 49 (4), 41–50.

Raab, G., Ajami, R. A., Gargeya, V. B., & Goddard, G. J. (2008) *Customer Relationship Management: A Global Perspective*. Gower Publishers, Aldershot.

STR Monthly Hotel Review, Glossary of Terms, October 2020.

Weir, D. (2010) Have You Checked Your Hotel Loan Lately? *RMA Journal*, February 2010.

Younes, E. & Kett, R. (2003) GOPPAR, a Derivative of RevPAR! HVS International. https://www.hvs.com/content/913.pdf, accessed December 19, 2020.

Chapter 8

Discounted sellout and subjectivity

Chapter highlights

- For-sale projects versus for-lease projects
- The skyscraper's curse – for-sale projects and the macro economy
- The case of the discounted sellout
- Valuation subjectivity in for-sale investments

> The caution and sleepless nights of the investor are the driving forces of capitalism.
>
> Hans Werner Sinn

8.1 For-sale projects versus for-lease projects

The preceding chapters have focused on either owner-occupied real estate or investment property which is held for lease. The goal of the previous discussions on investment real estate was for the owner to lease out the space to third-party tenants in an effort to produce a revenue stream sufficient to maintain the property, service any associated debt, and provide equity cash flow to the investor. The primary discussion in Chapter 8 will be investment properties where the goal is to sell off the units to make profit for the investor.

8.1.1 Condo project pathways

Properties where the investor intends to sell the units for a profit can fall into numerous categories, as this section will describe. Traditional investment projects where space is leased to third-party investors all have the end goal of selling the

DOI: 10.4324/9781003083672-8

property at some point. There are obvious differences between "for-sale" – condominium projects – and the typical "for-lease" investment – real estate project. For-sale project valuations are inexorably linked to the timing of the unit sales. The intent here is to build and sell the units, pay back the lender, and generate a profit as quickly as possible. Conversely, "for-lease" projects tend to be more long-term in nature in that the units are built and then leased to a third party or parties. The key difference is that an investor in a "for-lease" project retains ownership of the property and earns a profit over a relatively extended project life. In "for-sale" scenarios, the entire property may be sold off in parts over the holding period of the investment, and in some cases the only portion of the assets remaining in the control of the developer are common areas that are shared by all members of the condo association.

If a project has an investment holding period of two years or less, it is typically deemed a more speculative investment with the investors who specialize in these short horizon deals, known as flippers. Some flippers focus on purchasing owner-occupied residences at a discount, owing to the age and condition of the property. Once the property is acquired, these short-term investors improve the properties in order to achieve a profitable resale quickly. Other short-term investors might instead focus their efforts on a short-run opportunistic investment in commercial property with a similar paradigm for success. In either case, "for-sale" investments are deemed speculative as the profitability of the investment largely depends on the final resale price of the property. When the investment holding period is short, the investor is not as focused on making money during the investment holding period, such that it earns the speculative moniker.

"For-sale" projects can take a number of forms. One type entails purchasing tracts of unimproved land, dividing it into individual lots, making infrastructure improvements such as roads and sewers, and then selling the lots to builders. In another variant, investors might finance vertical improvements, that is, buildings, on the site and then sell the land and improvements together or separately. A common form of project entails building a multi-tenant complex and subsequently selling the component units as condominiums (condos) to individual owners. Condo projects such as these can involve new construction or the purchase of an existing building with plans for renovation and conversion into separately titled units for resale.

The large majority of the remaining for-sale investment pathways involve the improvement of either acreage or separate units in an existing building with the intention of selling portions of the property over time. One area that has historically been popular in this space is the creation of new homes. If you imagine a tract of land heretofore not utilized (maybe it was raw land previously), investors can focus on any number of ways to sell off portions of the land for profit. If we assume that a given tract of land was deemed suitable for 15 homes of relatively equal size, one investor strategy in the "for-sale" side of the business is to legally differentiate the acreage such that the land now consists of 15 different parcels of land. An investor might purchase raw land from someone who was not interested in home building, and if this is the case, one of the first steps in this process is to change the zoning of the land from the general category of unimproved land, to a categorization which will support the construction of numerous homes (or commercial properties if that is the intended path).

Exhibit 8.1 serves as an illustration of the various pathways to profit in for-sale investments. Once the raw land has been acquired, the investors will decide whether the location and market demand supports a residential development or a commercial

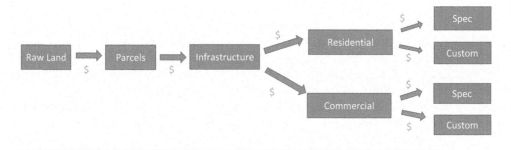

Exhibit 8.1 Pathways to Profit in For-Sale Investments

complex. Investors typically will decide this fairly early in the process, as obtaining zoning clearance from the local municipality can either clear a pathway to success or provide significant obstacles. Given the significant element of speculation in for-sale investments, the pathway to profit could instead become the pathway to bankruptcy if the investor misses their targeted buyer.

The next step in the pathway is to convert the acreage into separate legal parcels where single lots can be sold off at any point in the pathway. You will notice the little dollar signs at each step in Exhibit 8.1. This signifies that an investor could sell the property at any stage along this process. The longer along the pathway an investor journeys, the higher the level of potential profit and loss.

An investor may decide that rather than selling the parcels for an immediate profit, it makes economic sense to continue along the pathway depicted in Exhibit 8.1 and improve the parcels with the various infrastructure needed to support the eventual properties that will be constructed on-site. Infrastructural improvements can consist of creating roads, sewer and utility lines, and other things that make the lots ready for the intended use.

Once the infrastructure is in place, the pathway has its first fork, depending on whether the intended use is residential or commercial. In either case, the units being created on-site for resale can be either custom or speculative properties. Custom-made homes and build-to-suit commercial units are considered less risky as there is a designated buyer for the property prior to construction. Speculative residential and commercial construction offers the plan of building first, and then finding willing buyers. This does not assume that the investors invest little time in market research, as failure to understand the market equilibrium for the supply and demand of space can lead to catastrophic results.

Regardless of whether the construction is speculative or custom, prudent lenders (and investors) will typically require presales at some level to commence a for-sale project, and it is seen as less risky if those buyers signing presale contracts have equity at risk if they were to walk away. All the better in terms of the lender risk assessment is when the required presales have already been approved for financing or have the funds available to purchase their properties upon completion.

8.1.2 The missing reversion

What may not be clear from the section above is the difference between how for-lease and for-sale valuation differs. In prior chapters, we have reviewed income valuation methodologies such as the direct capitalization model and the discounted cash flow which are utilized when valuing for-lease properties. The direct capitalization model provides a one-year projection for NOI, with value being estimated after the NOI is divided by a capitalization rate. The direct capitalization model assumes that the projected NOI will continue in perpetuity with value being derived when capitalizing the NOI. The discounted cash flow provides a multi-period model that estimates how NOI will change during the expected holding period of the investment. Value is based on the present value of the NOI projected during the holding period plus the net present value of the assumed sale (aka reversion) at the end of the holding period. In the parlance of Chapter 8, both of these models assume that the project has value to the investor when the holding period ends.

Since the discounted cash flow model contains a more explicit reversionary cash flow calculation, we will focus on this income valuation model before introducing the primary differences with for-sale projects. Appraisers have two distinct ways of calculating the final sales price within the discounted cash flow model. One approach we will call the "appreciation reversion", while the second we will term the "terminal cap rate reversion".

Assume that you are creating a discounted cash flow for a for-lease investment property with a five-year holding period. If the first year's NOI is projected at $250,000, and annual inflation is expected to be 3% each year, what would the sales price of the property be at the end of year five? There are two ways to determine the future sales price. In the appreciation reversion scenario, the initial purchase price is increased by a compound annual growth factor that equates to the expected inflation over the holding period of the investment. If we assume that the original purchase price was $2,750,000 and that the expected inflation (or appreciation) rate over the five-year holding period is 3% annually, the appreciation reversion is calculated as follows: $2,750,000 \times (1.03)^5$ which totals $3,188,004, which might then be rounded to $3.2 million.

The second method is the terminal cap rate reversion. In this model, the NOI has to be projected for the first year after the assumed property sale after year five. That year six NOI (which would be the first year for the next owner of the property) is then divided by a terminal cap rate to determine the reversion value. Since NOI was projected at $250,000 for the first year, if we assume the same 3% appreciation rate, the year six NOI is calculated as follows: $250,000 \times (1.03)^5$ which totals $289,819. The terminal cap rate is the estimated capitalization rate at the end of the holding period. If the cap rate at purchase was 9%, typically the terminal cap rate is higher given uncertainty of the future economic climate as well as for the increased age of the property. Both of these factors contribute to increased risk which requires a higher estimate of the cap rate at the end of the investment holding period than at the outset. If the terminal cap rate is assumed to be 9.25%, the terminal cap rate reversion is calculated as follows: $289,819/0.0925$ which totals $3,133,179. This might then be rounded to $3,150,000, for final valuation purposes.

Two things require comment at this juncture. First, note that the appreciation reversion is higher than the terminal cap rate reversion. While this is only an example, if you had to pick between the two reversion methods, which seems to be more accurate? The terminal cap rate is calculated based on the existing leases which project the annual NOI from the property. The appreciation reversion assumes the starting point of value to be the original purchase price of the investment. The terminal cap rate estimation is subjective, as how many basis points are added to the going in cap rate is up for discussion. One rule of thumb is that the terminal cap rate should be 25–50 basis points higher than the going-in (current day) cap rate, but selections can vary. The appreciation rate is also subjective. What the appreciation rate should be is open for interpretation from various sources. Since the terminal cap rate utilizes the NOI as projected from the current tenant leases, it is seen as a more accurate approach. Typically when the appreciation method is utilized, it is because the appraiser is having trouble getting the property to appraise at the desired value, so they can utilize this approach to inflate the final value conclusions.

The second thing that requires comment is that for investments that are planned to be sold off during the holding period, there is no reversionary cash flow at the end. This is the primary distinction between the valuation methods for investment properties held for lease versus those held for sale. If the discounted cash flow model is available to value the investment property held for lease until sold, is there another model that can provide clarity to value considerations for an investment property where the goal is to sell out the various units over time?

8.1.3 Discounted sellout model

Let's return to our 15 lot valuation example. Assume that an investor purchases acreage in the mountains and has segmented the land into 15 distinct parcels. The plan is to sell the lots to buyers who will construct their own mountain homes for either themselves or to sell or rent to others. As far as our investor is concerned, she is cashing in her investment in the "parcels" phase of Exhibit 8.1. It makes no difference what the buyer intends to do, for our investor is planning to sell the 15 lots for an average price of $125,000 each. If she is somehow able to sell all 15 lots at once (unlikely!), the valuation is easy: take the 15 lots at $125,000 each, for a total of $1,875,000. From a valuation standpoint, an appraiser would assume some level of selling costs (assume 5%), so the lots would be valued at $1,781,250 at the time of sale.

But what if the lots are not all sold at once? The element of time has now been introduced whereby the investor would need to discount future cash flows in a similar method to the discounted cash flow. Exhibit 8.2 illustrates how the discounted sellout value is estimated, assuming that the lots are sold out over a period of four years.

Given the 10% discount rate and the four-year sellout period, the total value after discounting for time of $1,481,627 is much less than the net sales cost of

Total Lots		15			Discount Rate	10%	Avg. Sales Price $	125,000	
	4 Year Discounted Sellout						Sales Revenue $	1,875,000	
Year		1	2	3	4		Less Sales Cost $	93,750	5%
# Units Sold		4	3	4	4	15	Net Sales $	1,781,250	
Avg. Sales Price	$	125,000	$ 125,000	$ 125,000	$ 125,000				
Total Monthly Sales	$	500,000	$ 375,000	$ 500,000	$ 500,000				
Discounted Value	$	454,545	$ 309,917	$ 375,657	$ 341,507				
Total Value	$ 1,481,627								

Exhibit 8.2 Discounted Sellout over Four Years.

Total Lots		15			Discount Rate		10%	Avg. Sales Price $	125,000
	4 Month Discounted Sellout							Sales Revenue $	1,875,000
Month	1	2	3	4					
# Units Sold	4	3	4	4	15			Less Sales Cost $	93,750 5%
Avg. Sales Price	$ 125,000	$ 125,000	$ 125,000	$ 125,000				Net Sales $	1,781,250
Total Monthly Sales	$ 500,000	$ 375,000	$ 500,000	$ 500,000					
Discounted Value	$ 454,545	$ 351,914	$ 484,365	$ 488,227					
Total Value	$ 1,779,051								

Exhibit 8.3 **Discounted Sellout over Four Months.**

$1,781,250. The lot sales for each year are discounted based on the projected year of sale.

Our investor might wonder what would happen to the value if she was able to sell all of the lots in four months rather than over four years. The resulting value is summarized in Exhibit 8.3. The lot sales for each month are discounted based on the projected month of sale. The amount of the discount is significantly less here as compared to Exhibit 8.2, since the time for sellout is so much shorter in Exhibit 8.3.

Under the shorter sellout period, less of the value of the lots is reduced owing to time. Since there is no reversionary cash flow under investments valued "for sale", the key factors driving value are the lot price, the time to sell the lots, and the discount rate employed. The discounted sellout model is speculative in nature, as how many lots can be sold, when, and at what price are only educated guesses unless the investor has firm prospects when the model is employed. Whether valuing the sale of lots, improved lots, or lots with completed buildings, the basic valuation is the same. Given the lack of a reversionary cash flow, the value swings as the assumptions in the discounted sellout model change are much wider than for the traditional discounted cash flow model utilized in for-lease investment property valuation.

8.2 Skyscraper's curse

Considering the speculative nature of the discounted sellout model, the time has come to discuss an anomaly in commercial real estate history known as the skyscraper's curse. When large buildings are contemplated for construction, whether residential or commercial, the property developers have to assess how much of the space will be leased and how much will be sold. New properties do tend to attract tenants residing in nearby existing space, but when the construction project is very large, the odds are fairly certain that by adding this much space to the market, the supply and demand function in the market will be impacted where there will be new space to absorb. For this reason, new skyscrapers are often a mix of traditional for-lease and for-sale spaces. Since office buildings are much taller and larger than residential buildings, in this section we will focus only on new large office buildings (also known as skyscrapers).

The premium spaces (often near the top) may be so desirable that the intended user would prefer to purchase rights of ownership rather than obtaining leasehold rights via the leasing option. It is for this reason that the skyscraper's curse is discussed in this chapter. The more that the new space being constructed is pre-leased or presold, the less is the risk of default for the investor and lender. The larger the office building being contemplated, the less likely that all of the space will be spoken for before construction commences. From a marketing perspective, gaining market acceptance of a new property involves providing a factor of differentiation, and in the case of skyscrapers, building the tallest building in the area is a plus. For the few buildings that have sought the world's tallest building designation, the skyscraper's curse has been observed.

The skyscrapers curse is the observed trend through history where once the height of a new building eclipses the previous world record high, that economic calamity ensues. This does not purport that the construction of a new world's tallest office building causes economic duress. Skyscraper construction is seen as more of a symptom of the cheap money and loose credit terms that help create the boom and bust economic cycles (or in the parlance of Chapter 3, the Minksy moment). Exhibit 8.4 provides illustration of how the world's tallest building has grown considerably throughout history.

The first noted example of the skyscraper's curse commenced when the seven-story Equitable Life Assurance building was planned, built, and opened in 1869–1870. When the new building was planned for construction, the economy was humming along seemingly well. But by the time the new building opened for business, the economy was in shambles following the wake of the first Black Friday

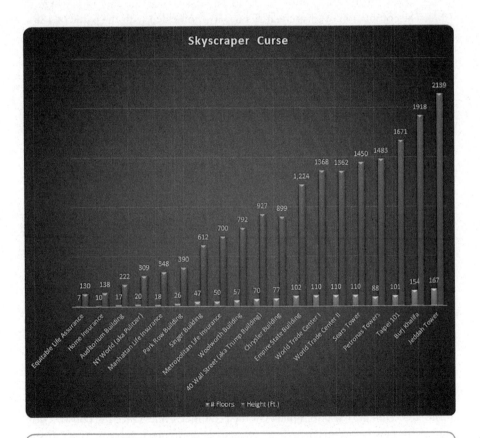

Exhibit 8.4 Tallest Skyscrapers Through History.

Building	Location	# Floors	Height (ft.)	Record Completion	Crisis
Equitable Life Assurance	NYC	7	130	1870	Black Friday Sept 24, 1869
Home Insurance	Chicago	10	138	1884	Panic of 1884/Depression 1882-85
Auditorium Building	Chicago	17	222	1889	Panic of 1890 (Baring Crisis)
NY World (aka Pulitzer)	NYC	20	309	1890	Panic of 1890 (Baring Crisis)
Manhattan Life Insurance	NYC	18	348	1894	Panic of 1893
Park Row Building	NYC	26	390	1899	4th largest quarterly GNP decline just before opening
Singer Building	NYC	47	612	1908	Construction just before Panic of 1907
Metropolitan Life Insurance	NYC	50	700	1909	Construction just before Panic of 1907
Woolworth Building	NYC	57	792	1913	23 month contraction prior to start of WWI
40 Wall Street (aka Trump Building)	NYC	70	927	1930	Great Depression
Chrysler Building	NYC	77	899	1930	Great Depression
Empire State Building	NYC	102	1,224	1931	Great Depression
World Trade Center I	NYC	110	1368	1973	1970s Stagflation
World Trade Center II	NYC	110	1362	1973	1970s Stagflation
Sears Tower	Chicago	110	1450	1974	1970s Stagflation
Petronas Towers	Malaysia	88	1483	1999	Asian Financial Crisis
Taipei 101	Taiwan	101	1671	2003	Dot-com/Tech Bubble
Burj Khalifa	Dubai	154	1918	2010	Housing Bubble/Great Recession
Jeddah Tower	Saudi Arabia	167	2139	2021	COVID-19 Lockdowns

Exhibit 8.5 Skyscraper Curse Through History.

stock market collapse of September 24, 1869. The second example of the skyscraper's curse came with the completion of the Home Assurance building in Chicago in 1884. The completion of this ten-story property coincided with the panic of 1884. From these inauspicious beginnings, Exhibit 8.5 provides a chronological view of the ensuing eclipsing of office building height records and the associated economic troubles.

As Exhibit 8.5 illustrates, the skyscraper curse has proven resilient to the passage of time. As the buildings became taller and taller, the financing methods used changed. In the 1920s and 1930s, the construction financing of skyscrapers were done by a mortgage company underwriting the debt financing, and then issuing bonds (i.e., skyscraper bonds) to small investors through a retail sales force. For investors too cautious to invest in the bubbling equity markets of the 1920s, skyscraper bonds seemed like the perfect alternative. More buildings over 200 feet in height were built in New York between 1922 and 1931 than in any time period before or since. While the substance of construction financing changed, the skyscraper curse remained unaffected. Once skyscraper records began to be eclipsed after the Great Depression, the various entries in the 1970s into Exhibit 8.5 were also prone to opening during economic low notes.

The most recent example is the Jeddah Tower in Saudi Arabia, which was conceived and planned in more pristine economic conditions than the world found itself in 2020–2021. I have steered clear from lengthy discussions of COVID-19 in this book, with the hope that by the time of publication, the misery of this debacle would be only a memory. It was also wished that in the heady days of early 2020, that the skyscraper's curse would prove to be illusory, but this has not been the case by any stretch of the imagination. The curse of the giant skyscraper is still in effect even in present day.

The basic construction of the skyscraper's curse is as follows. The ground-breaking for a new record building construction project typically commences during the twilight of a boom phase of the economic cycle. Once the construction eclipses the new record heights, there are signs of economic trouble on the horizon. When the building opens, the economic situation is significantly depressed as compared to when the construction project commenced. The construction of the new tallest skyscraper in the world does not cause economic calamity. It is more a symptom of cheap money, loose credit, and investor risk-taking that are the hallmark of the end of the economic boom cycle.

What this section illustrates is that the speculative fervor which mounts at the end of a boom period tends to create more for-sale speculative projects that need to be worked through once the project is completed and is offered to the public for sale after the exuberant music of economic good tidings has stopped.

8.3 The case of the discounted sellout

In order to be profitable, condominium projects require thorough knowledge of the local market, qualified presales of units, and more often than not, more than a little luck. In the immediate aftermath of the Great Recession, many investors, as well as lenders, found themselves ensnared in projects that were finalizing construction at the worst possible time – just as the economic expansion ended. In most cases this led to a slower than expected "sellout" of the units, and often the expected sellout did not occur at all. In this section, we will discuss valuation considerations for properties experiencing what Sherlock Holmes might call *the case of the discounted sellout*. For banks finding themselves in a workout condo project, one course of action is the "lease it until you sell it" scenario. The discounted sellout valuation technique is utilized when a project contains four or more units/lots as it reflects that an estimate for the time and cost of carrying the lots must be estimated.

8.3.1 Absorption periods and qualified presales

The amount of time required to sell or lease a new unit in a given market is known as the *absorption period*. The absorption period can vary widely depending on the economic strength of a given market as well as the location of a project within that market. Obviously, some market absorption periods may be much quicker than others. Using the Bounty Paper Towels™ "quicker picker upper" slogan as a guide, a 20-unit condo complex facing an assumed absorption period of three months per unit, that is, on average four units per year, will require a five-year sellout period, while an absorption period of just two months per unit will drop the sellout period to just over three years. Alternatively, if the absorption period increases to six months per unit, then the sellout period for the 20-unit project balloons to ten years! In the latter scenario, the absorption period might more closely resemble the "leading brand" from the famous television commercial, that is, it is not performing too well in terms of effective and efficient absorption.

A key component of any "for-sale" project is the number of *qualified* presales versus the number of speculative (spec) units. Qualified presales represent buyers who have been credit qualified by a lender and who have also provided an equity deposit that is lost should they renege on the purchase. Typically, lenders prefer to see some minimum percentage of qualified presales prior to a loan commitment on a condo project as evidence that the loan can be repaid via the sellout of units over the stated period of time. Because "for-sale" projects preclude the long-term ownership component of the developer (or investor) present in "for-lease" projects, long horizon amortizations are rare. Consequently, lenders tend to structure the repayment of the loan to coincide with the intended sellout of the units and often require a minimum monthly or quarterly principal curtailment, regardless of the unit sellout projection.

The existence of qualified buyers with "skin in the game" provides some assurance that the units will sell, so rather than a relatively long amortization loan structure, a for-sale condo project may require that the entire loan be repaid within three to five years, with payments that depend on the timeline of the project's construction and projected sales.

8.3.2 Payback ratios

Lenders may devise a payback ratio which requires that an additional amount of principal be repaid when a unit is sold. In this case, the total loan amount typically is viewed on a per unit basis so that the additional percentage of the loan principal to be repaid allows payback of the balance to occur before all of the units are actually sold. For example, for a 20-unit condo project with a loan amount of $1 million, a payback ratio of 1.25 achieves a pay down per unit of $62,500, where the loan per unit is only $50,000. Under this financing scenario, the loan would be repaid after the sale of the sixteenth condo unit. Depending on the risk of the deal and the general economy, the payback ratio can be raised or lowered to fit the situation.

To effectively structure a "for-sale" project loan, the lender must make a rather precise assumption regarding the selling price of the units. Nevertheless, if market conditions deteriorate between the outset of a project and its completion, the realized unit sales prices may be far less than projected. Under depressed economic conditions, the intended sales may not occur at all, which is especially true for more speculative projects. For example, assume that a developer plans to purchase an older building and renovate it into 20 condominium units, each comprising 1,500 square feet with similar amenities. Further assume that comparable properties in the local market are selling for $150,000, or $100 per square foot. If the developer pays the lender 100% of the net sale proceeds until the loan is repaid, then a loan of $1 million will require that seven (7 units × $150,000/unit = $1,050,000) of the 20 units be sold for the principal to be repaid.

Obviously, if qualified presales exist, the investor and the lender have more certainty regarding the term and risk of the loan when assessing the loan repayment structure, especially if the number of qualified presales is greater than or equal to the number required to extinguish the loan balance. In this circumstance, the lender might initially provide interest only financing to allow time for the renovation. Also, once the project is complete, the lender can provide a principal reduction schedule that essentially matches the borrower's timeline for completion and sale of the units.

Typically, a lender will require quarterly principal reductions equal to the projected net proceeds from the sale of the units. Also, the lender might establish payback ratios that are based on the riskiness of the project and the credit or financial strength of the principals. Regardless, if the number of presales is relatively small, the lender may require the developer to provide additional equity to reduce the initial credit exposure. If the project does not produce the number of qualified presales to allow what the lender considers to be a reasonable repayment projection, there are other underwriting alternatives.

For example, given the $1 million loan on the condo renovation project, seven units must be sold to repay the loan. If the developer, however, can generate only four qualified presales, the lender might be willing to assume that the final three units required to pay back the loan will be sold in the quarter following the last qualified presale already in place. Alternatively, the lender may change the payback ratio to 2.00 so that the loan balance is paid when the 10th unit is sold *(i.e., payback of $100,000 per unit when the loan per unit is $50,000)*. The argument in favor of this approach is that the developer has provided some actual sales evidence that demand exists for the project, thus reducing the lender's risk. Of course, if the developer cannot produce any qualified presales, or if the number of presales is significantly lower than the minimum necessary to repay the loan, the project becomes almost entirely speculative, thereby increasing the lender's risk. Most commercial real estate lenders view speculative projects as exceptions to their institutional credit policies.

So, in the event of insufficient qualified presales, what are the key assumptions necessary for a lender to ascertain the appropriate repayment schedule on a loan financing a "for-sale" project? Furthermore, what assumptions are implicit in the investor's decision to undertake such a project?

8.3.3 Field of dreams

Clearly, knowledge of the sales price per square foot of the units as well as the timing of the sales is crucial for effectively valuing a project. Quick presales indicate a level of market anticipation for the project and strong future sales. Alternatively, if presales begin to slow or stop, both current and potential buyers may become hesitant because a slowdown could signal that early buyers overpaid. For example, if a few units sell at a given price per square foot, but then further sales fail to materialize, it may be inevitable that the subsequent price will have to fall to rekindle interest. One approach sometimes used to determine the "gross sellout value" of a project, that is, the value of a project given the completion of construction and sellout of all of the units, is to use the last observed per square foot, market sale price, assume that price holds for the remaining units, and discount back from the projected sellout date. Of course, the sellout date largely depends on the fluidity of the unit sales comprising the project and general activity in the local market.

Another component of project valuation is the assessment of operating expenses. The expenses incurred depend on whether the project is entirely for sale, or if some of the units are intended for lease, in which case the developer/borrower will most likely also manage the condo association. Condo association fees typically are assessed monthly and are paid by all condo owners. These fees cover landscaping and other common area maintenance and provide a savings mechanism for any future expenditure necessary for general repairs of the building(s) that may be shared among the owners. Expenses incurred by the developer alone include the costs of marketing and sales commissions paid to brokers. Additionally, if the project includes a for-lease component, the developer also will incur real estate taxes as well as expenses associated with leasing those units.

More often than not, for-sale condo projects that include a for-lease component often are the result of insufficient unit sales. If a developer has completed the construction or renovation and has sold only a small portion of the project, usually the only way to maintain project momentum and viability is to attempt to lease the remaining units. The field of dreams scenario ensues when a developer has constructed new units, but the buyers have not materialized (i.e., the "if you build it and they don't come" scenario). Valuing in this type of situation is covered in the following section.

8.3.4 Discounted sellout complexities

Consider a hypothetical, 20-unit condo project on which a developer is seeking a $1,000,000 loan with an equity investment of $850,000; the developer has presold five units. The units are identical in terms of size and amenities. Unfortunately, during the last phase of construction, unit sales have ceased and general market conditions have deteriorated. Nonetheless, the five presales are expected to occur within the first year. The five presales are expected to yield $100 per square foot for a selling price of $150,000 per unit. The developer intends to sell out the units, but until then the remaining units will be leased on an annual basis. Of course, lessees have the option of purchasing the property at the end of the lease term, but the developer maintains the right to terminate a lease with 60 days' notice if the sale of a leased unit occurs. Exhibit 8.6 provides the anticipated timeline as well as sales expectations for the units over a five-year holding period.

Given the slowdown in the condo market, it is projected that only 3 units will sell in the second year of the holding period and that the expected selling price will be 25% lower than that of year one. In years three through five, however, the market should begin rebounding so that the number of units sold as well as their price should increase. These projected unit sales prices are obviously subjective.

With regard to the leasing potential of the property, local market rents for comparable space currently are about $0.75 per square foot per month, but this should increase at a rate of 3% per year over the remaining four years of the projected sellout. Other details concerning the rental units are shown in Exhibit 8.7.

The annual rental revenue per unit in the first year is found by multiplying $0.75 per square foot by the 1,500 square feet per unit and then multiplying across the 12 months in a year. In this example, the condo leasing expenses are assumed to be variable, requiring 35% of each unit's annual rental income, while real estate taxes per unit are assumed at $2,500 in the first year, increasing by 3% annually. HOA dues

	Year 1	Year 2	Year 3	Year 4	Year 5
Units Sold	5	3	4	4	4
Avg Unit Sale Price	$ 150,000	$112,500	$115,875	$119,351	$122,932
Units Leased	15	12	8	4	0

Exhibit 8.6 **Expected Sales and Leasing.**

	Year 1	Year 2	Year 3	Year 4	Year 5
Annual Rental/Unit	$ 13,500	$ 13,905	$ 14,322	$ 14,752	$ -
HOA Dues/Unit	$ 1,350	$ 1,391	$ 1,432	$ 1,475	$ 1,519
RE Taxes per unit	$ 2,500	$ 2,575	$ 2,652	$ 2,732	$ 2,814
Condo Leasing Exp	$ 4,725	$ 4,867	$ 5,013	$ 5,163	$ -
Total Units	20	15	12	8	4

Exhibit 8.7 **Expected Operating Performance of Leased Units (in dollars).**

Discounted Sellout Analysis						
	Year 0	Year 1	Year 2	Year 3	Year 4	Year 5
Condo Sales Revenue		750,000	337,500	463,500	477,405	491,727
HOA Revenue		27,000	27,810	28,644	29,504	30,389
Condo Leasing Revenue		202,500	166,860	114,577	59,007	-
Total Gross Revenue		**979,500**	**532,170**	**606,722**	**565,916**	**522,116**
Commissions	5%	38,850	18,266	24,607	25,345	26,106
Marketing Costs	2%	15,540	7,306	9,843	10,138	10,442
Overhead & Contingencies	2%	15,540	7,306	9,843	10,138	10,442
RE Taxes		50,000	51,500	53,045	54,636	56,275
Homeowners Dues		27,000	20,858	17,187	11,801	6,078
Leasing and Op Exp		94,500	97,335	100,255	103,263	-
Total Expenses		**241,430**	**202,570**	**214,780**	**215,322**	**109,344**
Net Operating Income		**738,070**	**329,600**	**391,942**	**350,594**	**412,772**
Aggregrate Principal Reduction		500,000	800,000	1,000,000	1,000,000	
Annual Principal Reduction		**500,000**	**300,000**	**200,000**	**-**	**-**
Interest Expense	5%	$ 50,000	$ 25,000	$ 10,000	$ -	$ -
Debt Coverage Ratio		1.34	1.01	1.87		
Net Cash Flows	(850,000)	188,070	4,600	181,942	350,594	412,772
BTIRR On Equity	8.40%					
Discounted Cash Flows		163,539	3,478	119,630	200,453	205,221
Property Value		$ 1,550,000.00				
% of Loan Outstanding	100%	50.00%	20.00%	0.00%	0.00%	0.00%

Exhibit 8.8 Discounted Sellout Model for Workout Condo Project.

represent fees collected by the project developer/owner from the respective owners of the individual units and are a source of cash for maintenance and insurance on the shared community property. It should be noted that if the units are being leased, these charges may show as operating expenses for the owner until units are sold.

Exhibit 8.8 illustrates the importance of the repayment structure. In this case, although viewed as a five-year project, the payback ratio is set at 2.00, so that the loan will be repaid during the third year. The annual principal reduction on the loan is defined in terms of the number of units sold and the principal curtailment requirement for each unit. Based on a loan of $1 million, a project comprising 20 condo units and a payback ratio of 2.00, the principal balance on the loan will be reduced by $100,000 ($1,000,000/20 units × 2.00 =$100,000) upon the sale of each unit. So, the five presales that are completed in year one generate a principal reduction of $500,000 ($1,000,000/20 units × –2.00 × 5 units = $500,000). In this case, the lender could require an additional principal payment of $175,000 at the end of the first year in order to affect an early loan repayment. As depicted in Exhibit 8.8, the payback period is assumed to be 2.00 without any additional principal reduction. Interest expense is calculated based on an annual rate of 5%, with the beginning of year balance carried until the end of the year. For example, interest expense during the first year is estimated to be 5% of the total loan amount of $1 million, while year two is based on the amount of the remaining loan at the beginning of year two.

The before tax internal rate of return (BTIRR) delineates the developer's pre-tax return on the equity investment. The BTIRR is the discount rate that equates the value of the initial equity investment with the pre-tax residual cash flows, that is, cash flows after all expenses, but before federal taxes, generated by the project over time – in this case, over the five years. Given the $850,000 equity investment, the project's internal rate of return over the five-year holding period is 8.40%.

The value or present value of the project is determined by applying a discount rate to the net cash flows produced (positive or negative) over its life. When considering the discount rate for sellout projects, appraisers typically will include a provision for entrepreneurial profit. The provision for entrepreneurial profit recognizes the need to compensate the developer/investor for their expertise and for bringing together the capital and materials necessary to complete the project as well as financial risk and time. Because relatively few units were presold (i.e., 25%), the project carries with it considerable risk that future sales will not occur, so a discount rate of 15% is applied. Conversely, if the project had been entirely presold, the risk to the entrepreneur would be near-zero. Discount rates should reflect the overall risk of the project over the investment time horizon, and should be compared to rates earned by comparable investments in the market at the time.

8.3.5 When sellouts become workouts

The purpose of this section was to evaluate alternatives for lenders holding problem condo projects. Ceteris paribus, the higher the level of presales, the better the market acceptance for a particular project; the stronger the sales history for a given type of project in a given market, the higher the probability of success. However, many condo lenders have found themselves with relatively few units sold, and many units unsold but under lease. This hypothetical example of a "lease it until you sell it" approach may be the most practical mechanism for converting a non-performing asset into something more closely resembling a profitable venture for all involved.

8.4 Valuation subjectivity in for-sale investments

In this chapter we have discussed how for-sale investment properties are different from for-lease investment properties from a valuation perspective. During the course of this chapter, we have highlighted that often construction projects have a mix of for-lease and for-sale scenarios, and that the more speculative investments are planned and financed during the twilight of economic boom phases (i.e., at exactly the wrong moment). What remains is a brief summary of the various components of for-sale investments and how these elements impact the subjectivity of real estate value.

For-sale investment is easy to develop, finance, and earn economic profit as long as the investor and lender have three things under their strict control. If it can be accurately predicted when the units will sell, how many will sell by a certain date, and how much those units will sell for, for-sale investment project success would be similar to hunting fish in a barrel. As countless investors and lenders will attest, the "fish in a barrel" concept does not work in reality. In fact, the barrels that the strictly controlled fish are swimming in can become more of an ocean of uncertainty, with the fish getting lost in the tumult that is economic reality.

One attempt at regulating the consistency and profitability of for-sale investments is to focus efforts on custom build-outs rather than purely speculative plays.

Even with customized sales, there is the possibility that prospective buyers may change their minds, especially if they do not have any money at risk when they decide to pull out of the project. While sometimes the change of opinion for the prospective buyer concerning purchasing a unit is based on their own personal financial situations, the typical reason for the change of tune is souring economic prospects as the construction projects linger on the vine. Depending on the level of presales, an investor/developer team may get more favorable financing than offered for more speculative ventures.

The perceived riskiness of a given project will also impact the discount rate utilized within the discounted sellout model, and should influence the payback period and general loan structure on offer from the commercial lender. As alluded to in the skyscraper curse section, as the scope of for-sale projects has increased over the years, so has the lender response to financing these ventures. What began as a commercial banking endeavor, eventually became an investment banking securitization scheme. What has remained constant is that the better conceived projects at the right times will obtain better financing owing to their more secure future probability of success.

Each of the various components that impact value contributes to the subjectivity of valuation of these for-sale real estate ventures. If the negotiation between the lender and the investor at the inchoate stages of these projects is any indication, there is a constant interplay between the lender wanting to get their loan principal back as soon as possible and at a reasonable return, and the borrower wanting the certainty of financing should the projected sales prove illusory from either a demand, price, or timing perspective.

The quote that started our chapter deserves a mention as this chapter concludes. Investors who endeavor to take on speculative ventures is a key component to the capitalistic economic model. Those that find the right product in the right moment deserve the profits that they achieve. While this chapter spent time in assessing the risk of speculative ventures, without these projects our economic system would result in a boring certainty of servitude to past successes where nothing new is attempted owing to the pervasive fear of failure. Change is often good, and well-researched projects can be handsomely rewarded.

In our next chapter, we will turn our focus to the subjectivity of valuation for mortgage-backed securities. The prior chapters have all focused on the subjective elements of valuation for specific properties, but as will be discussed in Chapter 9, subjectivity in valuation is also very much at play when a series of properties are financed, packaged together, and sold to investors.

Questions for discussion

1. Discuss the various for-sale investment property paradigms while noting the strengths and weaknesses of the various pathways.
2. Explain the difference between the appreciation reversion and the terminal cap rate reversion.
3. Outline how the lack of a reversionary cash flow in the for-sale investment property valuation model can bring increased uncertainty and increased valuations ranges.

4. Compare and contrast the discounted sellout valuation model with the discounted cash flow valuation model.

5. Identify the root cause of the skyscraper's curse and what it says about the economic cycle.

6. Provide examples of how the skyscraper's curse impacts other areas of the economy.

7. Describe how a lender can utilize the payback ratio to structure for-sale project financing.

8. Describe the types of presales and how their presence can shape the risk profile for a particular for-sale property venture.

9. What is market absorption and why is it a key ingredient for success in for-sale ventures?

10. What are the primary areas of subjectivity in for-sale investment property projects?

Chapter 8 Market vignette

Cast of characters: Ebenezer (Eb) and Bob (real estate developers)
Act: Contemplation of the creation of the new big thing...

Scene one: site selection

EB: Bob, I think I may have found a strong possible site for our next development project.

BOB: That's great Eb! What have you found for us this time?

EB: I have found some reasonable looking property for sale in southern Virginia right over the North Carolina border. It's in a town called Saltville.

BOB: I have never heard of that place. What's the hook?

EB: Well the town is situated in the Appalachian Mountains and is near some good hiking and biking trails. Also the land and properties look very reasonably priced by today's standards.

BOB: I know that there has been much success in the nearby North Carolina mountains in developing small towns as tourist attractions. Remember the white squirrels of Brevard?

EB: Ha! Yes you keep talking about those squirrels. Have you seen any of those yet?

BOB: Only in other people's photos or in the gift shop. Tell me more about this new target location.

EB: Saltville had historical importance during the U.S. Civil War, and it seems ripe for a for-sale real estate investment. While it is a small town, much of the construction is older and in need of refurbishment, and there are plenty of good site locations still undeveloped.

BOB: I assume that you are considering this spot for residential development or might you also be contemplating retail?

EB: I think that both are needed. We might decide to build the retail site as a for-lease project, but I think the best play for the residential property is for sale.

BOB: Why is that, Eb?

EB: Since the town is so small, the current demographics of the town don't really matter to us. What I mean is, if the current residents are older or younger is of no concern for us. But I do think that we should develop a plan to construct and sell off the residential units. Nothing too large. I am thinking of maybe building from 30 to 50 homes and concurrently developing a retail center in the area to help spur sales of the residential properties.

BOB: What do we know about the town's zoning restrictions? What I mean to say is, can we build multifamily or would the single-home option be preferred?

EB: I am thinking that the multifamily option might be met with objections from town officials. Plus given the small size of the market and the trail blazing nature of this development, going small seems like the best avenue for success.

BOB: That does make sense. I guess what we need to do after exploring the details of this project is to form a Saltville investment company, and seek equity investors to help contribute to the purchase of the acreage from which this idea will spring to life.

EB: Yes! Now let's consider what our target audience should be after doing a bit more research on the location.

Scene two: target demographic

BOB: As it turns out, there are only a few multifamily properties in Saltville, so I do like your idea of focusing our efforts on single-family homes. Also, I found it interesting how Saltville got its name. Basically there was so much salt millions of years ago, and the area where Saltville is today was a shallow inland salt water sea. This led to a boom in development two centuries ago, surrounding all things salt.

EB: I think we could use this as part of our marketing for the property. Maybe name each street in the subdivision after some famous event that occurred in the town over the years. I envision something cool like the "salt palace" where the community members can gather for some recreational fellowship.

BOB: Sounds like you have already envisioned this in your mind Eb.

EB: Yes, once we get equity investors lined up, we can purchase the ten acre tract and start planning on the 40 residential homes that we can build on that land.

BOB: That would bring us to four homes per acre which should be sufficient for the zoning ordinances in Saltville. But should we build custom or speculative homes?

EB: I think we can build a combination. Once we purchase the land, we can begin to advertise the final plans to see what type of initial interest we get.

BOB: Do you have an opinion on whether we should target the over 55-year-old community, or wealthy individuals looking for vacation homes?

EB: To me the 55 years and over community seems the most appropriate. We would take care to specify that the intended buyer of the homes should desire outdoor activities such as biking and hiking, as opposed to an assisted-living situation.

BOB: This would also make the supporting retail easier as well. I know Saltville has a grocery and dollar store, but we would want to include a pharmacy which caters to the community along with coffee shops and luxury retail outlets.

EB: What should be our price point for the homes, Bob?

BOB: Well, the area runs the gamut from lower priced to expensive homes, so if we come in around $250,000 for the speculative homes, we can gear the custom homes to the plans that we get for the construction.

EB: How long do you think it would take for the homes to sell, Bob?

BOB: I would think we would want to be out in five years. If our average price point per home is $250,000, we could plan on selling eight homes a year in a worst-case scenario. Hopefully, we will get strong initial interest from the presale market to make this timeline much more condensed.

ED: For the retail properties, I am thinking we could buy a two acre tract nearby and plan on a 25,000 square foot building with ample parking. We would want to make sure that we get a well-known pharmacy to sign a pre-lease, and then we could fill in the other tenants. We should plan on a total of five tenants all with equal square footage rented, at least for starting our planning.

BOB: I think we can shoot for a retail annual rent of $22.00 per square foot.

ED: That sounds about right to me. I am excited to get this project off the ground!

Questions for discussion

1. Discuss the plans for development in Saltville. Are Eb and Bob forgetting anything significantly important at this stage of planning?
2. Discuss the planning stages in light of the pathways for profitable for-sale relationships model highlighted in the chapter.
3. Does the plan for making the residential properties for-sale, but planning for the retail properties as for-lease make financial sense? Present both sides and defend your argument.
4. Discuss how you might construct a discounted sellout model for the homes and any pitfalls in the valuation. What basic assumptions are still unknown from this case?
5. Discuss how you might construct a direct capitalization income approach model for the retail space. What basic assumptions are still unknown from this case?

Bibliography

Ambrose, B. W., Diop, M., & Yoshida, J. (2016) Product Market Competition and Corporate Real Estate Investment under Demand Uncertainty. *Real Estate Economics*, 45(3), 521–590. doi: 10.1111/1540-6229.12150

Anglyn, W. T., Moreyra, R., & Putnam, J. C. (1988) Subdivision Analysis-A Profit Residual Model. *Appraisal Journal*, January, pp. 45–59.

Camis, C. (2020) *Veblen: The Making of an Economist Who Unmade Economics*. Harvard University Press, Cambridge, MA, and London.

Ditchkus, L. & Biadasz, S. (1996) Rethinking Speculative Subdivision Valuation for Loan Purposes. *Appraisal Journal*, July, pp. 263–272.

Eichholtz, P., Holtermans, R., & Yönder, E. (2015) The Economic Effects of Owner Distance and Local Property Management in US Office Markets. *Journal of Economic Geography*, 16(4), 781–803. doi: 10.1093/jeg/lbv018

Fan, Q., Hansz, J. A., & Yang, X. (2015) The Pricing Effects of Open Space Amenities. *The Journal of Real Estate Finance and Economics*, 52(3), 244–271. doi: 10.1007/s11146-015-9508-1

Goddard, G. J. & Marcum, B. (2014) The Case of the Discounted Sellout. *RMA Journal*, February, pp. 43–47.

Goetzmann, W. N. (2016) *Money Changes Everything: How Finance Made Civilization Possible*. Princeton University Press, Princeton, NJ & Oxford.

Goetzmann, W. N. & Newman, F. (2010) Securitization in the 1920s, NBER Working Paper Series, Working Paper 15650. National Bureau of Economic Research, Cambridge, MA. https://www.nber.org/system/files/working_papers/w15650/w15650.pdf

Gould, T. R. & Smith, H. C. (1995) Entrepreneurial Profit Incentive and Marketwide Obsolescence: Are They Mutually Exclusive? *Appraisal Journal*, January, pp. 53–59.

Kapplin, S. D. (1992) Entrepreneurial Profit, Redux. *Appraisal Journal*, January, pp. 14–24.

Lovell, D. D. (1983) Condominium and Subdivision Discounting. *Appraisal Journal*, October, pp. 524–539.

Melser, D. & Hill, R. J. (2018) Residential Real Estate, Risk, Return and Diversification: Some Empirical Evidence. *The Journal of Real Estate Finance and Economics*, 59(1), 111–146. doi: 10.1007/s11146-018-9668-x

Robin, E. (2018) Performing Real Estate Value(s): Real Estate Developers, Systems of Expertise and the Production of Space. *Geoforum*. doi: 10.1016/j.geoforum.2018.05.006

Sinn, H. W. (2014) *The Euro Trap*. Oxford University Press, Oxford.

Thornton, M. (Spring 2005) Skyscrapers and Business Cycles. *The Quarterly Journal of Austrian Economics*, 8(1), 51–74.

Thornton, M. (2018) The Skyscraper Curse: And How Austrian Economists Predicted Every Major Economic Crisis of the Last Century. Mises Institute, Auburn, AL https://mises.org/library/skyscrapers-and-business-cycles, accessed December 24, 2020.

Wolski, R. (2018) Listing of Developer Companies as a Predictor of the Situation on the Residential Real Estate Market. *Real Estate Management and Valuation*, 26(4), 12–21. doi: 10.2478/remav-2018-0032

Xu, R.-h. & Lai, R. N. (2018) Optimism-driven Decisions of Real Estate Developers under Demand Uncertainty. *The Journal of Real Estate Research; Sacramento*, 40(2), 267–308.

Chapter 9

Mortgage-backed securities and subjectivity

Chapter highlights

- Types of mortgage-backed securities (MBS)
- Residential MBS and subjectivity
- Commercial MBS and subjectivity
- MBS and investor preference

> It is not when the truth is dirty, but when it is shallow, that the lover of knowledge is reluctant to step into its waters.
>
> Friedrich Nietzsche

9.1 Types of mortgage-backed securities

In this chapter, we turn our attention to the valuation subjectivities associated with groupings of mortgages secured with real estate. While the preceding chapters have focused on the valuation inflection points for single properties, this chapter will concern mortgage-backed securities. When a property owner seeks a loan secured with their property, there are typically two avenues for lender support: traditional lenders who keep the loans on their balance sheets, and lenders who package up and sell loans to investors.

Mortgage-backed security (MBS) investors seek cash flow from a pool of properties which make up the specific bond of which they are investing. MBS investors can receive financial benefit from the mortgage industry without having to own real estate property directly. In this chapter, when we speak of investors, we are concerned with those who are buying shares in securitized products that will be itemized in this section.

DOI: 10.4324/9781003083672-9

9.1.1 Collateralized mortgage obligations (CMOs)

Collateralized mortgage obligations (CMOs) are the category header within the overall securitization market nomenclature for mortgage loan pools. The wider net of securitized products would include loan pools secured with business loans (collateralized loan obligations or CLOs), various forms of debt (collateralized debt obligations or CDOs), and specific loans secured with vehicles or other collateral (asset-backed securities or ABS). Exhibit 9.1 provides a summary of the securitization universe, and where CMOs are positioned within this universe.

CMOs can consist of either residential or commercial loans. CMOs can also entirely consist of commercial real estate loans, or can include business purpose loans secured with real estate. The difference between CMOs and some of the other categories of securitized products (CLOs, CDOs, ABS) is their exclusivity of being secured by mortgage loans. The basic structure of the mortgage bonds does not change when the loans move from the residential category to commercial loans, with the exception of the prevalence of government guarantees in the residential space. After the meltdown of the securitization market after the Great Recession, loan pools that contained unsecure or esoteric collateral became virtually obsolete. While CMOs vary greatly in their complexity, in the aftermath of the Great Recession the number of tranches (or slices) and the heterogeneity of the loans included in a given pool have greatly been reduced.

Regardless of the classification of the mortgages held in the pool, the basic process of asset formation is as follows. A property owner seeks financing for a property deemed worthy of inclusion into a mortgage bond pool. The lender provides loan funds and takes a security interest in the subject property. The loan balance is held temporarily in a warehouse line of credit at the financial institution until such time when critical mass is achieved in terms of the aggregate loan balance available for all of the various loans held in the temporary account. The warehouse line of credit balance is reduced, and the associated mortgages are packaged up and sold to investors. During this process, the loans are removed from the lender's

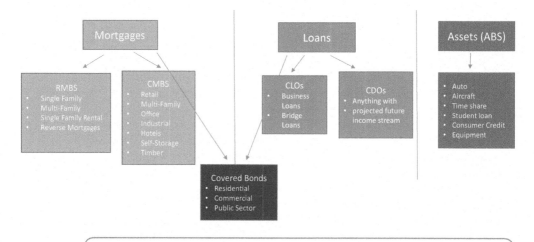

Exhibit 9.1 Securitization Nomenclature.

balance sheet and placed into a special purpose vehicle known as a real estate mortgage investment conduit (REMIC). The REMIC is underwritten by an investment bank for resale to investors. Part of this process is the inclusion of internal and external credit enhancements which provide sufficient incentive and certainty of future repayment performance in order to achieve the desired debt rating by the rating agencies (Moody's, Standard and Poor's, and Fitch). Internal credit enhancements include situations where the originator provides protection in the form of financial support to cover potential losses. These include things like additional interest, cash, or over-collateralization. External credit enhancements consist of agency guarantees for certain RMBS mortgage pools or generally any guarantee or pledge of collateral by an outside entity, whether it be an insurance company, financial institution, or hedge fund.

The REMIC itself is not subject to federal taxation in the U.S.A. as long as there is no tinkering with the specific loans in the pool once the REMIC has been created. The permanency of the loans included in the mortgage bond pool makes the structure and credit enhancements that make up the mortgage bond asset all the more important.

9.1.2 Residential mortgage-backed securities (RMBS)

RMBS comprised consumer loans secured with owner-occupied homes, but in recent years, the category has expanded to include single-family residence rental pools. RMBS can be considered either agency guaranteed or private label, with this classification aiding investors in their assessment of risk when considering a new mortgage pool for investment.

Some of these residential mortgage bonds are guaranteed by the U.S. governmental entities such as the Federal National Mortgage Association (FNMA) which is known colloquially as "Fannie Mae", the Governmental National Mortgage Association (GNMA) or simply "Freddie Mac", and the Government National Mortgage Association (GNMA) or "Ginnie Mae". These government-backed mortgage bonds have what is known as agency guarantees, and are seen as of lesser risk given the penchant for bailouts when things go awry. The government-sponsored entities (GSEs) may only purchase loans that conform to certain standards in terms of loan to value, consumer debt to income ratios, and personal credit bureau score limitations, which helps investors ascertain the riskiness of the mortgage pool in question.

Other residential mortgage bond pools do not have government guarantees (whether implicit or explicit), and are known as private label RMBS. These are seen to have higher risk than their government-guaranteed counterparts. Private label RMBS are not subject to mandated limitations on loan to value or other factors such that the return to the investor can be higher relative to agency issues given the linkage between risk and return. While the lion share of RMBS volume is focused on owner-occupied homes, other nascent classes such as rental homes and reverse mortgages are also available.

The mortgage pools for residential MBS are typically stratified by the quality of the borrower from a credit perspective, the geography of the location of the homes, and the size of the loans contained in the pool. RMBS can include a variety of asset classes within the same mortgage pool. Some examples of the varying asset classes that might make up a typical RMBS include jumbo loans (or larger than typical home loans), prime loans (excellent credit scores and initial underwriting metrics such as loan-to-value ratio and the debt-to-income ratio for the borrower), subprime (less than stellar credit history and/or lending metric results), and government-guaranteed exposures. Typically, loan classes such as reverse mortgages and single-family rentals are contained in their own mortgage pools, although they can be included within the other categories.

As is typical for all CMOs, RMBS can contain various tranches whereby investors can opt to receive a prioritization for payment. In these "waterfall" scenarios, the first investors to receive payment receive a lower interest rate, while those that receive their payments later are compensated for their higher risk with a higher interest rate.

9.1.3 Commercial mortgage-backed securities (CMBS)

CMBS stand in contrast to RMBS, as they are assets backed by commercial mortgages. Primary distinctions between CMBS and RMBS revolve around the lack of government agency guarantees (i.e., Fannie Mae, Freddie Mac, and Ginnie Mae) for CMBS, the potential for costless prepayment of the mortgages backing RMBS, and a higher degree of mortgage heterogeneity in CMBS pools. In this context, heterogeneity refers to the various property types (i.e., retail, office, multifamily, industrial, and hotel), geographic diversity, and the varying contract structures in place within the underlying pools.

CMBS pools can take a number of forms. A *conduit* pool consists typically of over 80 loans, with no loan representing more than 10% of the pool balance, whereas a *fusion* pool contains a similar number, but one loan represents over 10% of the total loan value. *Large loan* pool structures usually are composed of less than 30 loans and at least some of the loans represent over 10% of the total principal value. *Floating rate conduits* are pools that consist of any number of mortgages and generate cash flows based on a floating rate benchmark. Other pool varieties include *single asset* structures, where the pool is collateralized by one asset or a small pool of assets, and *single issuer* pools that consist of loans originated by the same entity.

Non-agency RMBS investors have experienced significant losses as a result of the obvious troubles facing the residential housing and, consequently, the corresponding mortgage market; namely, defaults and short-sales. While CMBS pools did not include subprime mortgages, per se, the commercial real estate market generally suffered a decline in loan underwriting quality leading up to the financial crisis in 2008. Accordingly, the "vintage" (or year) that a given loan was originally underwritten is very important. A "2007 vintage" loan is likely to be more highly levered than a loan underwritten at earlier (or subsequent) times.

Following the collapse of the CMBS market in 2008, the single issuer CMBS was the most common form of commercial securitization vehicle. For example, one of the few, early 2010 vintage CMBS securitizations was secured by properties that included the UK grocer Tesco (Thomas, 2010); the value of the offering almost entirely rested on the underlying strength of Tesco. At the time of Tesco issuance, CMBS had become tarnished investment vehicle as a result of the perceived complexity and opaqueness associated with analyzing the mortgages in the underlying pools. Consequently, the first "CMBS 2.0" issuances, which included Tesco, were more transparent because the mortgagor was a publicly traded company, allowing investors to dip their toes into the commercial mortgage market pool once again. The few CMBS issuances that fueled the meager recovery in the

U.S.A. in 2010 were often backed by pools comprising a majority of loans on multifamily properties, because this property sector remained relatively resilient throughout the economic downturn compared to others such as retail and office property. Once the investors began to trust the CMBS product again, the volume picked up again, until recently. The slowness of the recovery of CMBS helps illuminate the quote that appears at the beginning of this chapter.

9.1.4 Covered bonds

A final class of mortgage bond worth mentioning are covered bonds. Covered bonds, while not available in the United States, are very popular in Europe and Asia. Covered bonds can consist of residential mortgages, commercial, or public sector loans, so all of the loans included in the pool are not necessarily mortgage secured. Historically, covered bonds have consisted primarily of residential mortgages, but bond collateral pools exist with commercial mortgage exposure. While similar to MBS, covered bonds have subtle differences, leading to a lack of covered bond defaults for over 200 years. During the EU sovereign debt crisis, when primarily poor-performing countries such as Greece, Ireland, Italy, Portugal, and Spain experienced RMBS and CMBS defaults, the covered bond market performance remained consistently acceptable.

Covered bonds owe their origins to two distinct events in the 18th century. In 1769, Frederick the Great of Prussia decided to pool the specific claims on Prussian estates to increase the flow of credit following the Seven Years' War. To this day, the German Pfandbriefe has an enviable track record of successful repayment. In 1795, after the Great Copenhagen Fire had destroyed much of the primarily wooden buildings downtown, government and banking interests again pooled resources in order to finance the city's reconstruction effort. The Danish covered bonds are also without a default since the concept came into existence.

One interesting feature concerning this shared lineage is that covered bonds began the asset pooling concept in a method that has more in common with the origins of insurance in ancient China than you might expect. In China, local merchants often grouped together to ship shared products overseas in a pro rata basis, such that if a particular boat sunk, the merchants would be equally impacted. The start of covered bonds has this same "we are all in this together" refrain which seems to be contrary to the modern-day RMBS and CMBS where loans are packaged and sold to investors. In those situations, if the mortgage loans within the pool experience unexpected payment troubles, only the investors who invested in that specific group of mortgages are impacted. The extent of their malady in the down cycle depends on what portion of the cash flows a given investor is entitled to receive and by when.

So how is it possible that a European cousin of RMBS and CMBS has not experienced bond payment defaults in over 200 years, while the more modern variety has seen the ebbs and flows to make even the most tranquil investor anxious? You might recall the earlier discussion regarding the formation of REMICs during the process of compiling, packaging, and selling a specific mortgage bond to new investors. For RMBS and CMBS mortgage pools, investors are only purchasing rights to cash flow for specific loans that are only secured by the properties that make up the pool in the REMIC. Covered bonds, since they remain on the balance sheet of the lender, have the feature where poorly performing loans can be removed from the existing pool in the covered bond and can be replaced by better performing loans. So, similar to the restart of the CMBS market after the collapse in 2008, single borrower pools are the answer to success. Unless the issue itself goes bankrupt over the bond term, the covered bond should not experience prolonged payment default. In the case of covered bonds, investors have dual recourse against both the issuer (lender) and the collateral pool.

Given the lack of defaults in the covered bond market, the interest rates provided to investors are lower than those in the RMBS and CMBS markets. Investors in the United States do not have the covered bond investment option, with the last attempt at legislating the creation of the concept failing in 2011. At that time, the sticking point was the impact of making changes to the original pool of assets and the impact on the taxation of the REMIC (or other type entity) where the loan pool would be held.

9.2 Residential MBS and subjectivity

When compared with CMBS, RMBS would seem to have less uncertainty and subjectivity in valuation. RMBS sticks to primarily the same asset class (residential property) unlike CMBS which has numerous different sectors represented (office, retail, hotels, etc.). Additionally, residential loans are typically more homogeneous than commercial loans, as they do not include prepayment penalties, and the performance covenants for the residential market are fairly streamlined. Residential loans typically contain a loan to value stipulation, as well as the general agreement for the borrower to adequately maintain their property. Since the large majority of the loans within RMBS collateral pools are owner-occupied, the risk of significant deferred maintenance for loans included in RMBS would seem low.

The key ingredient for valuation is the ability to project the probability that loans in the collateral pool will be repaid as currently structured. Economic swings certainly impact repayment for RMBS, but these are generally predictable and investors can review the geographic dispersion of the loans in the collateral pool as well as certain loan metrics at origination to evaluate the quality of the assets included. The loan metrics typically specified include the loan to value for the property, and the debt to income and credit score for the borrower. How the economy will impact the mortgage repayment ability of the borrowers in the collateral pool is unknown, but part of the initial underwriting process for the RMBS is to review the recent history of loan repayment associated with economic impact and interest rate changes.

Given the lack of prepayment penalties on residential mortgages, when interest rates drop, borrowers have an incentive to refinance their mortgages. When a loan is refinanced, the existing balance is paid out of the RMBS pool, and the new loan is eligible for inclusion in a new RMBS offering. From the MBS investor viewpoint, loan repayments mean that they are getting an early return of principal. If the interest rate paid to the MBS investor was 4%, but when interest rates drop they are getting paid out when market rates are 3%, this is a negative situation for the MBS investor. Conversely, as interest rates rise, loan prepayments slow down, which is also a negative situation for the investor. In both cases, the movement in market interest rates has the opposite effect on how the MBS investor would prefer to be repaid early: repayment is more likely as rates drop and less likely as rates increase.

Since the investor has to utilize the existing market rates at the time of repayment, receiving more principal early at lower rates than the contract rate of the MBS is a problem, as is the expected decrease in early repayment when interest rates rise relative to the contract MBS interest rate.

9.2.1 Uncertainty of cash flows: RMBS negative convexity

The nonlinear relationship between the change in interest rates and bond price is known as convexity. In most cases, when the interest rate on a bond increases, its price drops. For RMBS, as rates drop there are more repayments of principal early, relative to when interest rates increase. Since convexity can be hard to explain, Exhibit 9.2 offers a simple example of this concept.

If we utilize the simple example shown in Exhibit 9.2, when a $1,000 bond has a starting interest rate of 10%, the price of the bond decreases by 1.76% as interest rates move from 10 to 11%. Conversely, the price of the bond increases by 1.74% as interest rates fall from 10 to 9%. If the initial price of the bond is compared to the prices when rates move up and down, the convexity is calculated at 0.0236% (or mildly positive). In the case of RMBS, the asset price movement as interest rates decline would be expected to be higher than when interest rates increase, which results in negative convexity.

The issue of convexity is present for any bond, but for RMBS it is especially important given the higher expected loan prepayments as rates drop relative to

Making Sense of Convexity			
Bond Yield Data		**Bond Yield Data**	
Face Value	$ 1,000.00	Face Value	$ 1,000.00
Annual Interest Rate	10.00%	Annual Interest Rate	10.00%
Years to Maturity	2	Years to Maturity	2
Coupon	$ 80.00	Coupon	$ 80.00
Value of Bond	$965.29	Value of Bond	$965.29
Bond Yield Data		**Bond Yield Data**	
Face Value	$ 1,000.00	Face Value	$ 1,000.00
Annual Interest Rate	11.00%	Annual Interest Rate	9.00%
Years to Maturity	2	Years to Maturity	2
Coupon	$ 80.00	Coupon	$ 80.00
Value of Bond	$948.62	Value of Bond	$982.41
% Change from Rate Increase		**% Change from Rate Decrease**	
Price at 10%	$965.29	Price at 10%	$965.29
Price at 11%	$948.62	Price at 9%	$982.41
% Change	-1.76%	% Change	1.74%

Convexity	0.0236%
Price if Rate Rises	$948.62
Price if Rate Falls	$982.41
Initial Price of Bond	$965.29

Convexity Formula:
$$\frac{(Price\ if\ Rate\ Rises + Price\ if\ Rate\ Falls) - (Initial\ Price\ of\ Bond * 2)}{((Initial\ Price\ of\ Bond * 2) * (1\%)^2)}$$
Then Multiply result by $(1\%)^2$

Exhibit 9.2 Making Sense of Convexity.

when rates rise. Beyond the need to forecast how the economy might impact the borrowers who have loans in the mortgage pool, an investor also needs to pay attention to how the change in interest rates over the bond period will impact loan repayments and the price of the bond. As you can imagine, there are a multitude of assumptions that can go into forecasting how these expected changes might impact the performance of the RMBS, and this is where the subjectivity of valuing these investments comes to the forefront.

9.3 Commercial MBS and subjectivity

George Orwell said that "*every ideology is a reflection of economic circumstances*". Certainly, the banking industry's loan underwriting appetite shifts with the economy's tide. As the economy's tide rises and prices are high, banks tend to focus on sales volume, but as it recedes, the emphasis becomes credit quality. During a period of prolonged economic expansion, incentive structures in many financial institutions reward sales volume, often at the expense of loan underwriting quality. Conversely, during more uncertain economic times, a bank's lending appetite tends to move away from sales volume and toward more conservative underwriting standards. Neither focal point provides satisfactory results: a financial institution that emphasizes sales volume is inevitably accepting speculative or risky loans, while a financial institution concentrating on credit quality may be turning away good business. Generally, the blend of a strong sales culture guided by sound credit principles is the surest recipe for success. Since the shifting economic tide influences what loans banks approve, it also influences the universe of CMBS investor choices.

When focusing on the highest volumes in Exhibit 9.3, it is clear that between 2005 and 2007, the banking industry was focusing on sales volume. The lack of a pervasive emphasis on quality essentially was driven by the way financial institutions assessed loans. During the early 1990s, banks typically held a real estate secured loan on the balance sheet until the underlying collateral was sold, liquidated, or otherwise paid out. Conversely, this "loan and hold" model began to be dominated by the "loan to distribute" model from about 1995 to 2008 – rather than holding the loans as revenue-generating assets, many were used to collateralize CMBS, and so they were packaged and sold to third-party investors. Consequently, a bank's revenue model generally was as follows: originate a loan, package it (often through an investment banking arm), sell it, and charge a fee for servicing it. In the wake of the Great Recession, CMBS volume has begun to approach levels seen in the early part of the 20th century, but not quite to the levels experienced in the halcyon days of 2005–2007.

Property owners often find CMBS loan terms favorable given the typical non-recourse financing and loan structures that most often are based on ten-year loan terms and 30-year loan amortizations. Of course, inclusion in a CMBS pool entails some restrictions on the borrowers. The fact that the loans are non-recourse means that the equity partners are protected from personal liability should the borrower default. Naturally, the liability protection is in place during the loan term, but some borrowers may discover that they need local knowledge and assistance that typically is not associated with a CMBS loan package.

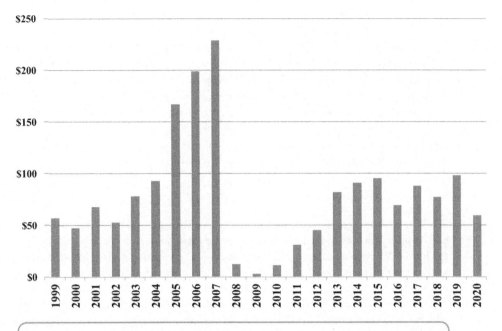

Exhibit 9.3 Highs and Lows in the U.S. CMBS Market (annually in billions).

Exhibit 9.4 Commercial Loan Payment Timeline.

Commercial loans that are included in CMBS structures normally require lockout provisions for a few years that contractually prohibit the borrower from prepaying. As Exhibit 9.4 illustrates, after the lockout period ends, there usually is a stated period when prepayment may occur. Prepayments often take the form of a declining fee proportional to the remaining balance, or a form of yield maintenance that compensates the lender on a net present value basis. Additionally, *defeasance* has gained favor in recent years. Under a defeasance arrangement, the loan can be prepaid if a borrower substitutes other income-producing property (usually U.S. Treasury obligations) for real estate collateral to facilitate the removal (i.e., defeat) of an existing lien without paying out the existing note. Finally, under most commercial loan agreements, borrowers may prepay the loan without penalty during the "open period", which is in place during the final three to six months of the loan's term to facilitate refinancing.

Relative to RMBS, the potential for early repayment of principal in CMBS mortgage pools is significantly reduced given the lockout provisions. Also as compared to RMBS, the impact of economic changes (and the lenders' response to those changes) can also impact the performance of CMBS loans. The loans within CMBS mortgage collateral pools are typically much higher than the average loan size in RMBS. Also there is more heterogeneity in the collateral pools in CMBS as properties securing loans included in the MBS can vary from among retail, office, industrial, multifamily, hotel, and other specialty property types.

As you will see in the next two sections, the differences in CMBS loans relative to RMBS loans impact the ability for investors to adequately forecast the timing and accuracy of payments received by investors, and also the ability to understand how the diversity of the mortgage pool itself will impact future success.

9.3.1 Uncertainty of cash flows: CMO waterfall example

While investors can spend time analyzing the various underwriting metrics of CMBS loans such as the debt service coverage ratio, loan to value, and debt yield, the hardest thing to measure is the probability of receiving payments as scheduled within the mortgage bond. Regardless of whether we are speaking of an RMBS or a CMBS structure, the projection of future cash flows is wrought with subjectivity. Since CMBS loans are larger and have more performance covenants which are known to the investor at the outset, now is a good time to provide an example of a simple mortgage bond with the impact on future cash flow repayments.

Exhibit 9.5 illustrates the layout of a simple waterfall CMO. The term waterfall refers to the hierarchy of payments as each separate class of investor gets paid in order throughout the term of the bond.

If we assume that the CMO depicted in Exhibit 9.5 consists of CMBS loans (so a very small and simple CMBS example), and that the total bond consists of 36% class A, 20% class B, 40% class Z, and 4% in cash, the total weighted coupon of the bond is 10.14%. Different investors will have different reasons for investing in the bond which should translate into investor preferences relative to the various tranches of investment alternatives. For all of the bond tranche classes, individual investors have the ability to purchase bond shares, especially as mutual fund companies begin to open up CMBS funds.

Assets		Liabilities				
CMO Waterfall	Tranche	Maturity	Coupon	Amount		Weighted Coupon
$75,000,000	Class A	2-5 years	9.25%	$27,000,000		3.47%
11% interest 10 year maturity	Class B	4-7 years	10.00%	$15,000,000		2.08%
	Class Z	6-10 years	11.00%	$30,000,000		4.58%
				$72,000,000	Total Bonds	10.14%
				$3,000,000	Total Equity	
				$75,000,000	Total Debt and Equity	

Exhibit 9.5 CMO Waterfall Example.

Class A investors get their principal repaid the quickest and are conversely receiving the lowest interest rate among the investor classes. Some typical investors for class A would be commercial banks, savings and loans, money market funds, and large corporates. The class A properties would be the strongest in terms of performance metrics within the mortgage bond collateral pool.

Class B investors are willing to wait until the class A investors are repaid before they recoup any principal. Typically this investor class will receive interest until such time as the class A exposure is completely repaid. The properties within this class may be of a lesser quality than from what the investors first in line are being repaid. Examples of class B investors could be insurance companies, pension funds, trusts, and international investors.

Class Z investors are also known as the "interest-only" class, and their name stems from the concept of zero amortization (ZAM) mortgages where principal is repaid at the end of the loan amortization period. In our CMBS CMO waterfall example, class Z investors could consist of pension funds, international investors, hedge funds, or any investor class that has a longer range investment horizon. Depending on how the scheduled loan repayments match what actually transpires, the class Z investor may have to wait until the end of the term of the bond in order to have principal repaid. The Z class investors receive no interest until the lockout period ends. The lockout period typically ends once the other tranches have been completely paid off.

The $3 million in cash, which was included in the $75 million bond offering in Exhibit 9.5, is there for two primary purposes. The first is to get a good rating from the agency that is assessing the quality of the MBS at inception. The second is to serve as a backdrop for loans that pay out early or default owing to performance-related issues. As loans pay out early in the pool for whatever reason, the available cash is utilized to supplement the investors for the payments that they were expecting. The ability to project the required over-collateralization at the time of bond issuance is a skill that proved elusive in the wake of the financial crisis. Whatever modeling was used to decide on the appropriate cushion did not include the worst-case scenario of all of the properties declining at once. Returning to our waterfall metaphor, the worst-case scenario is that the barrels that the investors used to protect them in their journey down the waterfall crashed and broke once they hit the river below.

9.3.2 Herfindahl index: a measure of concentration

Evaluating the investment quality of a pool of commercial mortgages, such as those backing a CMBS, entails a host of issues beyond estimating the credit risk of each loan, even if evaluating each loan was economically feasible. A closely related problem is faced by potential investors considering pools of commercial real estate loans that are offered by financial institutions that find themselves overweighted in the asset class.

To some extent, knowledge of the "vintage" of the loans can be part of the credit risk assessment. For example, ceteris paribus, loans originated in 2007 are likely to be more highly leveraged than loans with a subsequent vintage. Also, the presence of secondary financing implies a higher degree of risk, because there usually is less free cash flow available for investors. In tandem with the assessment of underwriting quality, the property types on which the loans are written should be evaluated to assess the level of exposure to particularly risky sectors, as well as the degree of diversification across geographic regions and business sectors. For example, a pool containing a high percentage of mortgages written on retail or hotel properties in areas most severely impacted by the recent financial crisis can profoundly depress the expected cash flows generated by the pool.

The extent to which the total value of a CMBS is *concentrated* among a small subset of loans backing the security is another factor in determining the overall credit risk. In fact, the level of concentration, as measured by the Herfindahl index, or the Herfindahl–Hirschman index (HHI),[1] is a factor employed by some ratings agencies to grade new CMBS offerings. The HHI is an economic measure that is commonly used by the Federal Reserve and the Department of Justice to investigate the level of market competition (i.e., concentration) within an industry. In a market context, it is defined as the sum of squares of the market shares of firms within an industry, where the market shares are expressed as proportions. The measure takes into account the relative size distribution of the firms in a market. An HHI score can range between 0 and 10,000, increasing as the number of firms in a market declines and as disparity in the size between firms rises. A higher score indicates less competition in the market, with a 10,000 result representing a pure monopoly.

The HHI can be used by lenders as a way to determine the level of concentration in a given market and the extent to which the lender is financing it. For example, Exhibit 9.6 represents the total supply of self-storage units catering to military personnel in a hypothetical town. It is immediately obvious that two storage facilities, All American Storage and Semper Fi, encompass over 30% of the supply of units in this market. Summing the squares of the market percentages (Market %) of each facility produces an HHI of 1,006. A market is considered to be less concentrated (i.e., highly competitive) when the HHI is less than 1,500, moderately concentrated when it is between 1,500 and 2,500, and highly concentrated (i.e.,

Herfindahl-Hirschman Index (HHI)

Property	CC Units	Std Units	Totals	Market %
Self-Storage Market Primary Players				
Auction Storage	248	147	395	7.88
All American Storage	204	600	804	16.04
Iron Guard	78	392	470	9.38
Affordable Fred's	150	280	430	8.58
Ayatollah's	150	350	500	9.98
Orange Diamon	120	43	163	3.25
U-Haul	240	49	289	5.77
Semper Fi	325	375	700	13.97
Store More	375	75	450	8.98
Storage Chest	94	247	341	6.81
Storage Camp	66	28	94	1.88
U-Store-It	200	175	375	7.48
Totals	**2250**	**2761**	**5011**	**100.00**
HHI Score				**1,006.20**

Exhibit 9.6 Market Concentration in a Given Self-Storage Market.

less competitive) at scores above 2,500. The U.S. Department of Justice and Federal Trade Commission provide general guidelines related to HHI score increases related to merger activity.[2] In terms of a lender's analysis, a further step might be to compute the HHI of the market in terms of climate-controlled and standard units.

If some of the market participants are unknown, it is often reasonable to assume that the remaining, unidentified portion of the market is divided among numerous firms. Typically, the highest market share assigned to the unknown players is assumed to be less than any of those with an identified share. For example, if the identified market represents 80% of the total and the smallest share held by any one business is 5%, an analyst could assume that the remaining 20% of the market is divided among 20 firms (i.e., 1% each), or 5 firms (i.e., 4% each), or some similar multiple. Regardless, the assumption usually will have little impact on the final HHI score.

The Herfindahl index or "Herf score" is a close cousin of the HHI and is often used as a measure of loan value concentration in a CMBS pool of mortgage loans. The Herf score relates the outstanding balance of each loan to the total outstanding balance of the pool. It is defined as the inverse of the sum of squared proportions of each loan's remaining principal balance to the total principal remaining in the pool, or

$$\text{Herf score} = 1 / \sum_{i=1}^{n} \left(\frac{p_i}{P} \right)^2$$

where n is the number of loans in the pool, p_i is the remaining principal on the ith loan, and P is the total principal remaining in the pool. The Herf score essentially converts pools of loans with unequal remaining principal balances into a number of identically sized loans. Higher Herf scores indicate less value concentration among the loans in a pool. An example comparing five small loan pools will help describe this concept.

Exhibit 9.7 provides the proportional principal weights for loans within five relatively small pools, as well as the resulting Herf score. Pool 1 generates the

Herfindahl Scores of Sample Loan Pools					
Share of the Pool (%)					
Loan	Pool 1	Pool 2	Pool 3	Pool 4	Pool 5
1	10%	25%	40%	60%	30%
2	10%	20%	30%	20%	12%
3	10%	15%	10%	5%	15%
4	10%	10%	5%	5%	7%
5	10%	10%	5%	5%	5%
6	10%	4%	2%	1%	4%
7	10%	4%	2%	1%	4%
8	10%	4%	2%	1%	6%
9	10%	4%	2%	1%	8%
10	10%	4%	2%	1%	9%
Total	100%	100%	100%	100%	100%
Herf	10	7	4	2	6

Exhibit 9.7 Herf Scores for Five Small Loan Pools.

highest score, because all of the loans comprising it carry the same size relative to the total remaining pool balance. To calculate the Herf score, the proportional weight of each loan is squared and then the sum of the squared values is inverted. In the case of Pool 1, there are ten loans with squared weights equal to $(10/100)^2$ or 0.01. Summing these squared values and inverting yields 1/0.10 or 10. The remaining four pools shown in Exhibit 9.7 generate lower Herf scores because of the relatively high concentration of the loan values. Pool 4 generates the lowest Herf score because two of the loans account for 80% of the outstanding total balance.

Obviously, the number of loans in the five exemplar pools is substantially smaller than is typically the case in the market. It is interesting to note that if a pool consists of 30 loans of equal size, the highest possible Herf score is 30. A pool comprising 80 or more loans with a Herf score of 30 implies that some level of concentration exists, but nothing approaching the concentration exhibited in pools three and four in our example. The higher the Herf score (also known as the effective loan count), the lower the risk to the investor as the risk of default is spread out over more of the loans in the pool.

Of course, it is virtually impossible for an issuer to assemble pools of uniform size. Loan opportunities arise in a fairly random fashion, with loan sizes determined by the underlying fundamentals of the borrower and the property. Once a CMBS lender acquires a sufficient supply of outstanding loans, then the pool is issued as a security. So, it would be difficult for a lender to ever construct a CMBS with the maximum Herf score, although smaller loans do tend to improve the score. It would be folly to view a Herf score as the only risk metric, but it is an important starting point for loss probabilities. Thus, the Herf score provides an objective measure for the dispersion of the loans within a CMBS pool. Additional evaluation is warranted concerning the largest loans in the pool, as if the largest loans in pools three and four were to default, investors would truly be in a world of hurt!

9.3.3 Credit barbells

From the preceding sections we have discussed how tricky it can be to project the future repayment of mortgages within the bond pool, and that the presence of large loans within the collateral pool creates an element of risk specific to CMBS structures. As investors began to focus on the Herf scores as a means of assessing risk, issuers began to explore ways to make their new offerings look as palatable as possible.

One method was the inclusion of smaller loans within the CMBS pools. If historically CMBS had been the place for loans above $10 million in exposure, by moving down market the mortgage pool would have small loans which could create more diversity in terms of credit repayment. The idea of surrounding larger loans

Exhibit 9.8 **Credit Barbell.**

with smaller loans to reduce the impact of the large loans in the collateral pool is called a credit barbell. Exhibit 9.8 provides a pictorial example of this concept.

Similar to a weightlifting barbell, the idea here is to create diversity via smaller loans such that they segment out the risk of the two larger loans in the pool.

As the smaller loans found their way into MBS in recent years, the question that arose was as follows: What would happen to the very large exposures? Assume that an MBS originator is contemplating placing a $500 million loan secured with a class A trophy office property in a major metro market. This office property has strong quantity, quality, and durability of cash flow and has proven to sustain high occupancy even over recent years. While at origination this loan looks secure, by placing it in a CMBS loan pool, the rating may get lowered owing to a low Herf score. Should that office property experience a repayment issue (either owing to a fall in occupancy or issues related solely to the borrower), the mortgage pool would be adversely impacted by a default of this size.

What is a possible solution? One recent entry has been to create *"pari passu"* loans, which in Latin means "on equal footing". In order to (potentially) mitigate risk, the $500 million loan can be carved up into pieces and placed in numerous bonds. The idea here is to reduce the amount of indebtedness for the loan that is part of the collateral pool, but does this really reduce the risk of the impact of a large loan going bad? From an industry perspective, the answer would appear to be no. If the $500 million loan defaulted, it would not matter if the loan was split into several collateral pools or contained in just one. If it was contained in just one, the impact of default would only be experienced by the group of investors set to receive payments. If the loan was split up and placed into numerous bonds, each set of investors would have equal claims to the loan in the event of default. The same issue that caused the default would be present in all of the bonds where this loan appeared. It seems to be the equivalent of placing a series of interconnected bombs within a mortgage pool.

Interestingly, the Fitch rating agency reported that these types of loans did not appear in any of the bonds that they rated in 2010, but that by 2017 *pari passu* loans accounted for 45% of the mortgage exposure in bonds they reviewed that year. Since the verdict is still out on how these loans perform in cases of default, it looks like there might be plenty of opportunity for observation of this in the years to come.

9.4 MBS and investor preference

In this chapter, we have discussed the various elements of subjectivity regarding mortgage backed securities. We have also discussed how loan originators and ratings agencies play a part in the determination of the risk profile and credit rating of the bonds created. What remains is a practical example of how an investor might decide between two mortgage pools for investment.

One thing that is probably not going to happen is the investor doing a deep dive into all of the different marketing material available at the time of origination. By way of a humorous example, Exhibit 9.9 highlights just how many pages of material that the discerning investor might have to review in order to get a good handle on the expectations of a collateralized debt obligation that contains RMBS, ABS, and a myriad of other investment choices.

CDO Reading List	No. of Pages
Pages in CDO^2 Prospectus	300
Pages in ABS CDO Prospectus	300
Pages in RMBS Prospectus	200
Number of ABS CDO tranches in CDO^2	125
Number of RMBS in a typical CDO	150
Number of mortgages in a typical RMBS	5,000

Total Pages to Read for CDO^2 Investor:	1,125,000,300
Pages to read for ABS CDO Investor:	30,300
Maximum Number of Mortgages in a CDO^2:	93,750,000
Maximum Mortgages in ABS CDO:	750,000

Exhibit 9.9 CDO Reading List.

A few comments are in order regarding the eternal reading assignment depicted in Exhibit 9.9. This assumes that the CDO^2 is a CDO of an ABS CDO. It also assumes that there is no overlap in the composition of RMBS pools that back the CDO, or in the CDO that backs the CDO^2. This reminds me of when I first started doing research on MBS and came across a shiny, new book at the Wake Forest Library, titled *Synthetic CDOs*. It had apparently never been checked out, and it presented an opportunity to learn all about these collateralized debt obligations that invest in other collateralized debt obligations. After reading about 20 pages, it became clear as to why it had not been checked out. Fancy formulas dominated the landscape, and the reader was left wondering what it all meant in the real world.

9.4.1 Choosing between CMBS alternatives

Investors in MBS can attempt to read all of the various brochures with the "past is not necessarily indicative of future results" caveats, or they can utilize a simple plan to compare the contents of existing CMBS offerings.

Let's assume that an investor has narrowed down their CMBS investment search to two finalists. Both bonds are structured for ten years at an annual interest rate of 4.25%. The loans contained in both bonds are amortized based on monthly interest compounding over 30 years. Exhibits 9.10 and 9.11 summarize the contents of both new bond offerings.

Bond 1 contains a total of 11 loans, while bond 2 contains a total of 17 loans. In a simple case such as this, the investor might be able to quickly review the types and concentration of properties and locations, but if the bonds were much larger this would not be as easy an exercise. Regardless of the size of the collateral pool in the bond offering, the investor should analyze both bonds from an underwriting metric perspective. With the information concerning the tenor, amortization, and interest rate for the debt, the next step is to calculate the debt coverage ratio (DCR), debt yield (DY), and loan to value (LTV). Exhibits 9.12 and 9.13 summarize the results for both bonds.

Type	Location	Loan		NOI		Value
Office	Boston MA	$	8,750,000	$	650,000	$ 11,500,000
Retail	LA CA	$	14,500,250	$	1,100,500	$ 17,850,000
Office	Dallas Tx	$	21,250,500	$	1,450,000	$ 25,600,000
Hotel	Miami FL	$	8,750,000	$	975,000	$ 18,500,000
Apt	Fort Lee NJ	$	21,750,675	$	1,650,000	$ 30,000,000
Retail	Chas SC	$	16,350,735	$	1,350,000	$ 28,750,000
Storage	Seattle WA	$	18,500,725	$	1,550,500	$ 29,500,750
Retail	Montreal Qe	$	26,050,650	$	1,890,000	$ 34,500,000
Apt	Chicago IL	$	32,750,415	$	2,675,000	$ 42,500,000
Warehouse	Baltimore MD	$	16,580,390	$	1,450,000	$ 30,000,000
Office	New York NY	$	35,750,900	$	2,850,000	$ 46,700,000
Totals		$	220,985,240	$	17,591,000	$315,400,750
Herf			9.39			
Loan Count 11		$	20,089,567	Avg. Loan Size		

Exhibit 9.10 Bond 1 Contents.

Type	Location	Loan		NOI		Value
Apt	Hackensack NJ	$	1,000,000	$	85,000	$ 1,250,000
Hotel	Myrtle Beach SC	$	3,500,000	$	265,000	$ 4,650,000
Office	Milwaukee WI	$	65,600,000	$	4,835,000	$ 82,500,000
Retail	Portland OR	$	2,750,000	$	205,600	$ 3,850,000
Warehouse	Kingston ON	$	1,999,000	$	156,500	$ 2,750,000
Apt	Miami FL	$	12,500,000	$	936,000	$ 16,750,000
Hotel	New York NY	$	86,500,000	$	8,450,000	$ 125,000,000
Retail	WS NC	$	4,500,000	$	350,000	$ 6,100,000
Storage	St Louis MO	$	2,710,000	$	207,650	$ 3,650,000
Retail	Austin TX	$	18,500,000	$	1,350,000	$ 28,250,000
Apt	San Diego CA	$	13,750,000	$	1,115,000	$ 21,600,500
Hotel	Vancouver BC	$	65,600,450	$	5,150,000	$ 88,500,000
Office	Quincy MA	$	5,550,000	$	315,000	$ 6,450,000
Warehouse	Shelton CT	$	7,260,050	$	500,000	$ 9,500,000
Storage	Forest Hills NY	$	1,150,060	$	107,500	$ 1,560,000
Hotel	Des Moines IA	$	3,850,000	$	386,985	$ 6,100,000
Totals		$	296,719,560	$	24,415,235	$408,460,500
Loan Herf			5.20			
Loan Count 17		$	17,454,092	Avg. Loan Size		

Exhibit 9.11 Bond 2 Contents.

After reviewing the results of the analysis depicted in Exhibits 9.12 and 9.13, the investor might notice that there is not much difference in the debt coverage ratio, debt yield, or loan-to-value ratio for the two bond choices. The similarity in this regard could be why both of these bonds were selected as the final two choices for this particular investor.

While there are more loans in bond #1 relative to bond #2, the Herf score is higher for the first bond, but the average loan size is lower for the second bond. A higher Herf score for the first bond choice implies that there is less concentration risk as compared to the second bond offering. The second bond offering also has a high concentration in hotel exposure. Given the similarities between the two bonds in terms of debt coverage, debt yields, and loan-to-value, the high percentage of hotel exposure could be cause for concern. Further analysis might be needed by the

Type	Location	Loan	NOI	Value	ADS	DCR	DY	LTV	Property Type %		Herf %
									Office	30%	
Office	Boston MA	$ 8,750,000	$ 650,000	$ 11,500,000	$ 516,537	1.26	7.43%	76.09%	Retail	26%	4%
Retail	LA CA	$ 14,500,250	$ 1,100,500	$ 17,850,000	$ 855,990	1.29	7.59%	81.23%	Apt	25%	7%
Office	Dallas Tx	$ 21,250,500	$ 1,450,000	$ 25,600,000	$ 1,254,476	1.16	6.82%	83.01%	Hotel	4%	10%
Hotel	Miami FL	$ 8,750,000	$ 975,000	$ 18,500,000	$ 516,537	1.89	11.14%	47.30%	W-House	8%	4%
Apt	Fort Lee NJ	$ 21,750,675	$ 1,650,000	$ 30,000,000	$ 1,284,003	1.29	7.59%	72.50%	Storage	8%	10%
Retail	Chas SC	$ 16,350,735	$ 1,350,000	$ 28,750,000	$ 965,229	1.40	8.26%	56.87%	Total	100%	7%
Storage	Seattle WA	$ 18,500,725	$ 1,550,500	$ 29,500,750	$ 1,092,149	1.42	8.38%	62.71%	Region %		8%
Retail	Montreal Qe	$ 26,050,650	$ 1,890,000	$ 34,500,000	$ 1,537,842	1.23	7.26%	75.51%	NE US	30%	12%
Apt	Chicago IL	$ 32,750,415	$ 2,675,000	$ 42,500,000	$ 1,933,348	1.38	8.17%	77.06%	Western	7%	15%
Warehouse	Baltimore MD	$ 16,580,390	$ 1,450,000	$ 30,000,000	$ 978,787	1.48	8.75%	55.27%	SE US	19%	8%
Office	New York NY	$ 35,750,900	$ 2,850,000	$ 46,700,000	$ 2,110,475	1.35	7.97%	76.55%	NW US	8%	16%
Totals		$ 220,985,240	$ 17,591,000	$315,400,750	$13,045,375	1.35	7.96%	70.06%	Central US	24%	100%
Herf		9.39							Int'l	12%	9.39
Loan Count 11		$ 20,089,567	Avg. Loan Size						Total	100%	

Exhibit 9.12 Practical Analysis of CMBS Bond #1.

Type	Location	Loan	NOI	Value	ADS	DCR	DY	LTV	Property Type %		Herf %
									Office	24%	
Apt	Hackensack NJ	$ 1,000,000	$ 85,000	$ 1,250,000	$ 59,033	1.44	8.50%	80.00%	Retail	9%	0%
Hotel	Myrtle Beach SC	$ 3,500,000	$ 265,000	$ 4,650,000	$ 206,615	1.28	7.57%	75.27%	Apt	9%	1%
Office	Milwaukee WI	$ 65,600,000	$ 4,835,000	$ 82,500,000	$ 3,872,551	1.25	7.37%	79.52%	Hotel	54%	22%
Retail	Portland OR	$ 2,750,000	$ 205,600	$ 3,850,000	$ 162,340	1.27	7.48%	71.43%	W-House	3%	1%
Warehouse	Kingston ON	$ 1,999,000	$ 156,500	$ 2,750,000	$ 118,007	1.33	7.83%	72.69%	Storage	1%	1%
Apt	Miami FL	$ 12,500,000	$ 936,000	$ 16,750,000	$ 737,910	1.27	7.49%	74.63%	Total	100%	4%
Hotel	New York NY	$ 86,500,000	$ 8,450,000	$ 125,000,000	$ 5,106,336	1.65	9.77%	69.20%	Region %		29%
Retail	WS NC	$ 4,500,000	$ 350,000	$ 6,100,000	$ 265,648	1.32	7.78%	73.77%	NE US	34%	2%
Storage	St Louis MO	$ 2,710,000	$ 207,650	$ 3,650,000	$ 159,979	1.30	7.66%	74.25%	Western	5%	1%
Retail	Austin TX	$ 18,500,000	$ 1,350,000	$ 28,250,000	$ 1,092,107	1.24	7.30%	65.49%	SE US	7%	6%
Apt	San Diego CA	$ 13,750,000	$ 1,115,000	$ 21,600,500	$ 811,701	1.37	8.11%	63.66%	NW US	1%	5%
Hotel	Vancouver BC	$ 65,600,450	$ 5,150,000	$ 88,500,000	$ 3,872,577	1.33	7.85%	74.12%	Central US	31%	22%
Office	Quincy MA	$ 5,550,000	$ 315,000	$ 6,450,000	$ 327,632	0.96	5.68%	86.05%	Int'l	23%	2%
Warehouse	Shelton CT	$ 7,260,050	$ 500,000	$ 9,500,000	$ 428,521	1.17	6.89%	76.42%	Total	100%	2%
Storage	Forest Hills NY	$ 1,150,060	$ 107,500	$ 1,560,000	$ 67,891	1.58	9.35%	73.72%			0%
Hotel	Des Moines IA	$ 3,850,000	$ 386,985	$ 6,100,000	$ 227,276	1.70	10.05%	63.11%			1%
Totals		$ 296,719,560	$ 24,415,235	$408,460,500	$17,516,183	1.39	8.23%	72.64%			100%
Loan Herf		5.20									5.20
Loan Count 17		$ 17,454,092	Avg. Loan Size								

Exhibit 9.13 Practical Analysis of CMBS Bond #2.

investor to determine if the hotel loans in question are of acceptable enough risk to warrant investment, but the odds are that the investor would prefer the first bond given the higher Herf and more diverse property and regional profile.

The point of this section was that an interested MBS investor can utilize the available information when making an investment decision, but most investors should adopt some formal process of their own in order to shed light on which investment is best for their risk tolerance, future repayment goals, and portfolio concentrations.

9.4.2 Alphabet soup of securitization

This has certainly been a chapter of acronyms, a veritable alphabet soup. By means of a quick end of chapter quiz, let's review the following terms and determine which acronyms are forms of securitization and which are not. An answer key will appear at the end of this chapter.

ABS CLO UO Synthetic CDOs DEVO RMBS CDO^2 HERF
CMO ELO CBGB MBS   CMBS CDO OREO ABBA

While not all of the acronyms listed in this section represent investment alternatives, there are numerous choices from which an investor can choose. Mutual funds now have investment options that focus on the real estate sector (RMBS, CMBS, and REITs primarily). These options may be attractive for investors who are looking to diversify their investment portfolio with real estate, but do not necessarily like the associated debt and ongoing property management needs that owning investment property outright require.

In this chapter we have toured the existing landscape of various MBS and have highlighted that the valuation subjectivity that is present for the single property does not vanish when the investment option changes to a pool of collateral options. For each property in the collateral pool, the subjectivity of valuation that exists at the single property level is still present, but this chapter has highlighted additional uncertainties associated with forecasting future repayment and in assessing the impact of economic, concentration, and interest rate changes on the mortgages present in whichever security option the investor prefers.

ALPHABET SOUP ANSWER KEY

ABS: Asset-backed securities (car loans, credit cards, receivables, etc.)

CLO: Collateralized loan obligations…corporate loan bonds

UO: Urge Overkill. Chicago rock band from the 1990s

Synthetic CDOs: R&B Band from the 1970s… ok not really. These are CDOs that invest in credit default swaps or other non-cash assets to gain exposure to a portfolio of fixed income assets

Devo: 1980s New Wave Band…whip it into shape!

RMBS: Residential mortgage-backed securities including home loans, home equity loans, and some multifamily loans

CDO²: CDOs which invest in other CDOs

HERF: Herfindahl index. A measure of concentration used in CMBS evaluation.

CMO: Collateralized mortgage obligations…mortgage bonds with various tranches.

ELO: Electric Light Orchestra. Hall of Fame Rock band featuring Jeff Lynne

CBGB: Country Blue Grass Blues punk rock club in NYC. Ramones, Talking Heads, and Blondie started here; securitization did not

MBS: Mortgage-backed securities…general category for mortgage bonds

CMBS: Commercial mortgage-backed securities…office, retail, hotel, industrial, multifamily, and so forth.

CDO: Collateralized debt obligations…bonds with all sorts of things in them.

OREO: Other real estate owned, or some good cookies. Either way it's not securitization.

ABBA: 1970s Swedish pop group. Acronym stands for member names.

Questions for discussion

1. Discuss the primary differences between RMBS and CMBS loans.
2. Describe how the Herfindahl index can be helpful in determining the risk of a mortgage bond pool.
3. Elaborate on the benefits and pitfalls of *pari passu* loans within CMBS loan structures.
4. Explain how did the CMBS structures change after the crash of the market after 2008?
5. Describe negative convexity and how it might impact RMBS risk assessment.
6. What is a "CMBS vintage" and how can it be used for comparison purposes?
7. Explain the basic difference between covered bonds and RMBS/CMBS structures.
8. Outline other areas of finance and economics where the Herf score could be helpful.
9. Describe the CMO waterfall concept and how it pertains to investor cash flows.
10. What is an agency guarantee and why are they only present in RMBS versus CMBS?

Chapter 9 Market vignette

Cast of characters: Donald, Daisy, and Daffy (investment bank employees), Charlie, Lucy, and Schroeder (MBS investors)
Act: Efforts to balance risk and return in CMBS pool creation and purchase

---

Scene one: making the initial CMBS pool

DONALD: Good morning Daisy! I think our primary objective today is to determine which commercial real estate loans that were recently approved by our loan underwriting division will best be combined into the creation of a new $1 billion CMBS pool for sale in the market.

DAISY: Hello Donald. Yes I believe that we have our work cut out for us. As you know we are required to try to obtain as high a credit rating as possible for the loans that we package together for sale to investors. What is the composition of the loans currently held for resale?

DONALD: It looks like we have a mix of various property types and loan sizes. As you know the loans come into our underwriting unit in fairly random fashion, but our bank has tried to stay away from riskier property types like hotels. So I would say that the loans available for inclusion in the proposed mortgage bond would consist of office, retail, and some industrial properties primarily.

DAISY: What is the average loan size that we have for this bond composition?

DONALD: That's a good question. I think we will need to ask Daffy to provide more transparency for the loans. Let me see if we can call him jointly now.

(Donald calls Daffy with Daisy on the line.)

DONALD: Hi Daffy! Daisy and I have a few questions for you about the current crop of mortgages that we are looking to securitize.

DAFFY: Hi Donald. I have asked you not to call me Daffy, if that's alright.

DONALD: No problem, Daffy. Daisy and I were interested in hearing more about the average loan sizes for our new CMBS offering.

DAFFY: Oh sure. Most of the loans are between $10 and $25 million, with an average loan of around $17 million. Is this what you are looking for?

DONALD: Yes, thanks Daffy. Are there any really small or really large loans in our current warehouse?

DAFFY: It looks like about 10% of the loans are under $10 million, with the lowest being around $3 million. In terms of the larger ones, there are three loans over $100 million, with one loan being $600 million just by itself.

DAISY: Wow, that is a large loan. I think we are trying to keep our mortgage bonds to about one billion dollars in size, so a $600 million loan would have a hard time getting placed.

DAFFY: Well that particular loan is very strong. It is multi-tenant office and retail in Hong Kong. Most of the tenancy is investment grade and historical occupancy and financial performance has been really stellar.

DONALD: If we took that one loan, our Herf score would probably not allow us to get the bond rating that we are looking for in the current market. Maybe if we took that one loan and a bunch of smaller ones, would that have an impact on getting a more attractive Herf score?

DAISY: Well, I still think the issue would be the large loan relative to the others in the mortgage bond pool. Right, Daffy?

DAFFY: There you go calling me Daffy too! You are correct that including such a large loan would be tough to hide in terms of concentration risk for the investors. We could offer a portion of that loan within the current mortgage bond that you are looking to construct. Would that make sense?

DONALD: It does seem like we would get the benefit of a high-quality deal without the risk of having too much of the investor cash flow being reliant on that one loan.

DAFFY: I agree. We could probably put $100 million for that large loan into your pool. That way your bond would not be too heavily concentrated in that one loan.

DAISY: We also should make sure that the geographic placement of the various properties doesn't expose the investors to undue risk.

DONALD: Right, we will focus on the geographic Herf, as well as the loan Herf, as we look to aggregate the existing loans into a bond to sell to the market.

DAFFY: Since we are offering such a strong cash flow on the large Hong Kong deal, maybe we could put some of the thinner debt service coverage and debt yield deals that we have on the bank's balance sheet as well?

DAISY: I was thinking the same thing. If the bulk of the loans are large and strong, we might have some room to include the lower debt yield deals in the mix.

DONALD: We can also attract investors by offering some interest-only loans in the pool as well. I know our underwriting team has recently approved some interest-only loans in anticipation of this need.

DAFFY: Yes, we could do that as it might differentiate our bond from some of the others and allow us to earn a higher yield on the transaction.

DONALD: That sounds great. We will spend some time reviewing the information that Daffy sent, and then put together a proposed mortgage bond structure.

DAFFY: Ok, but stop calling me Daffy.

Scene two: caveat emptor

(After some time passes and the CMBS is issued, an investor contemplates purchase.)

CHARLIE: Soccer games are so silly sometimes. All this flopping. Every time someone barely touches another player, down they go faking an injury, hoping to get a penalty assessed on the other team.

LUCY: I know it. Flopping is rampant in our culture. Look at politics. The political parties are always trying to blame the others for causing problems for their political gain.

SCHROEDER: That brings us to our investment decision today. Ever since we formed our new MBS mutual fund, it's always interesting to read through the prospectus and new investment offering materials. Sometimes the banks that create the bonds attempt to gain favor by manipulating the overall picture of the bonds included in the mortgage pools.

LUCY: Manipulate seems a bit strong of a term, Schroeder.

SCHROEDER: Yes it probably is. I was just making a joke relative to the earlier flopping discussion. Transparency is nice, but nobody has time to sift through all of the information provided. So I do like these summaries that the bank has provided on our behalf.

CHARLIE: I like the summaries too. For the most part, the bulk of the loans in this new CMBS looks pretty good from a metrics standpoint.

LUCY: Right, the loan to value, debt service coverage ratios, and debt yields all appear reasonable.

SCHROEDER: What does *pari passu* mean?

CHARLIE: Where do you see that, Schroeder?

SCHROEDER: It was noted in the summary and is then referenced again at the bottom of page 237.

LUCY: So after a quick internet search, I found out that it means "on equal footing". What that means in this context, I am not sure.

CHARLIE: Well, we might want to check on that, but otherwise the larger loans look really strong. I also like how they were able to diversify the exposure from a geographic and property sector standpoint.

LUCY: I would have liked to have seen some residential loans included, to be honest. Apartments have been doing really well lately.

SCHROEDER: True, but it was good not to see hotel exposure, as those have, well, been flopping lately. I also like the inclusion of a good mix of industrial properties in this pool.

CHARLIE: Yes, that is very true indeed! I think we should recommend that our mutual fund invest in this new CMBS offering!

Questions for discussion

1. Would a higher or lower Herf score be desirable from a bond ratings perspective and why?
2. Discuss the strategy for creating this new CMBS offering. Are there any improvements that you would suggest?
3. What are some weaknesses of the approach discussed in this market vignette?
4. What might Daffy and Lucy be missing in their assessment of the large loan exposure being included in the mortgage bond?
5. What additional questions might you have when contemplating purchasing a mortgage bond?

Notes

1   HHI was independently developed by economists Albert O. Hirschman (1945) and Orris C. Herfindahl (1950).
2   See U.S. Department of Justice & FTC, Horizontal Merger Guidelines (2010).

Bibliography

Buchanan, B. G. (2017) *Securitization and the Global Economy: History and Prospects for the Future*. Palgrave Macmillan, New York.

Commercial Mortgage Alert (2020) CMBS Annual Volume. http://www.cmalert.com/ranking, accessed December 30, 2020.

Danske Capital (2015) Danish Mortgage Bonds Provide Attractive Yields, January 2015. https://www.danskeinvest.com/web/show_download.hent_fra_arkiv?p_vId=whitepaper-dkmortagebonds.pdf

Fabozzi, F. J. (2008) *Handbook of Finance, Financial Markets and Instruments*. John Wiley & Sons, Inc., New York.

Fitch Ratings (2017) 2017 US CMBS in Review, December 21, 2017.

Goddard, G. J. (2018) *Securitization and the Global Economy: History and Prospects for the Future*, New York: Palgrave Macmillan, 2017, *Journal of Asia-Pacific Business*. doi: 10.1080/10599231.2018.1419046.

Goddard, G. J. & Marcum, B. (2012) *Real Estate Investment: A Value Based Approach*. Springer Publishers, Heidelberg, London, New York.

Goddard, G. J. & Marcum, B. (2013) A World of Herf. *RMA Journal*, pp. 36–42.

Hayre, L. (2001) *Salomon Smith Barney Guide to Mortgage Backed and Asset Backed Securities*. John Wiley & Sons, Inc., New York.

Herfindahl, O. C. (1950) Concentration in the US Steel Industry. Unpublished doctoral dissertation, Columbia University.

Hirschman, A. O. (1945) *National Power and the Structure of Foreign Trade*. University of California Press, Berkley, CA.

Kaplan, A., & Liberman, M. (2018) The Use of Real Estate Trust for Holding of and Management of Property in Israel. *Trusts & Trustees*, 25(1), 135–137. doi: 10.1093/tandt/tty182

Kolb, R. (2011) *The Financial Crisis of Our Time*. Oxford University Press, New York.

Nietzsche, F. W. (2009) *Thus Spoke Zarathustra*. The Floating Press, Auckland.

Schwarcz, S. L. (2011) The Conundrum of Covered Bonds. *The Business Lawyer*, 66(3), 561–586. https://www.iiiglobal.org/sites/default/files/conundrumofcoveredbonds.pdf

Standard & Poor's (2020) US CMBS Q3 2020 Update: New Issue Credit Metrics Mixed, October 13, 2020.

Swiss Re Corporate History (2017) A History of Insurance in China, Company Publication. https://www.swissre.com/dam/jcr:eb1aba5f-05ca-4bd4-bfe6-d42a6ed6b8c5/150Y_Markt_Broschuere_China_Inhalt.pdf

Szumilo, N., Gantenbein, P., Gleißner, W., & Wiegelmann, T. (2016) Predicting Uncertainty: the Impact of Risk Measurement on Value of Real Estate Portfolios. *Journal of Property Research*, 33(1), 1–17. doi: 10.1080/09599916.2016.1146790

Thanh, B. N., Strobel, J., & Lee, G. (2018) A New Measure of Real Estate Uncertainty Shocks. *Real Estate Economics*. doi: 10.1111/1540-6229.12270

Thomas, D. (2010) Tesco Issue Signals Returning Appetite for Mortgage Bonds. *Financial Times*, web edition, June 30. www.ft.com, accessed May 23, 2012.

Udoekanem, N. B. (2018) Valuation of Urban Commercial Properties in Nigeria for Secured Lending: Issues and Developments. *International Journal of Built Environment and Sustainability*, 5(1). doi: 10.11113/ijbes.v5.n1.247

Chapter 10

The provocation of time

Chapter highlights

- Why subjectivity persists
- The provocation of time
- Challenges to subjectivity
- Why subjectivity must remain
- Concluding thoughts and areas of future research

> Without principles, we drift
>
> F. A. Hayek

10.1 Why subjectivity persists

In this final chapter, we will review some of the salient points covered in this book and provide a pathway forward for possible future research. The theme of our oeuvre has focused on how different market participants can view the same investment property very differently. These varied opinions lead to divergent viewpoints as to the final value of the subject property. These differences create a range of possible values among which market participants can reasonably conclude that the optimal property value resides.

In Chapter 1, the historical underpinning of the Shackle Possibility Curve was introduced, owing its lineage to Austrian economics in the 19th century. Carl Menger was the first to discuss that goods, whatever they may be, have exchange value and that the value differences among market participants depend on the importance that each individual assigns to a given good or service. In a barter

DOI: 10.4324/9781003083672-10

economy, the exchange of goods and services takes place when two market participants agree on a reasonable exchange rate. In the fiat money system of today, the final "price" is denominated in the prevailing currency where the trade is to take place. Shackle's Possibility Curve is a graphic illustration of how there can be a myriad of divergent pathways to the final value depending on the person doing the valuing.

10.1.1 Market participant diversity

As Exhibit 10.1 illustrates, each market participant comes to a purchasing decision with a certain set of experiences, risk tolerances, and preferences. Sometimes good experiences lead an investor to increase their risk tolerance from where it was historically. They likely perceive that an additional profit can be made when venturing into investment options that are riskier relative to what they have previously attempted, but these new ventures may differ in significant ways from the experience of the decision maker. Sometimes poor experiences can make an investor less willing to take on risks that they previously have undertaken. As the Shackle Possibility Curve illustrated in Chapter 1, the further that the decision at hand varies from the experience of the market participant, the more likely errors will ensue.

Preferences, whether they consist of the family that desired the cul-de-sac home in Chapter 3, or where Ms. Slack sought to purchase the apartment building in Chapter 4, can vary with experience and the tolerance for risk of the market participant. Sometimes investors build up their preferences based on prior results. For example, an investor might have started out with a few rental homes and then moved into larger and larger multifamily units over time. If an investor has a higher tolerance for risk, the importance of prior success within a given investment option is not as crucial. But typically the link between experience and the preferences desired is positive. This concept links up well with the quote at the beginning of this chapter, as without some mechanism for making decisions, we would all be rendered inoperable. What is clear in Exhibit 10.1 is that the starting point for any personal valuation decision lies with the experience, risk tolerance, and preferences of the market participant in question.

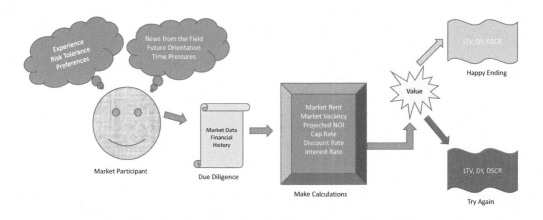

Exhibit 10.1 **Why Subjectivity Persists.**

Another primary component that influences how the individual market participant views the market data and financial records for the subject property is their future orientation and the news from the field that they might hear during the valuation process that slightly sways their decision-making process. A person's future orientation can be linked to their tolerance for risk. Someone with a higher risk tolerance is not as concerned with past failures, so they could have a more positive view of the future relative to someone whose prior mistakes loom large in their mind's eye as they review the next investment option. Additionally, those with a future orientation are likely also planners whereby their daily tasks are more planned than someone without such strong self-efficacy.

Future orientation also involves consideration of the time required to make a decision. If an investor is pressured to make a quick assessment of property value, there is a higher probability that errors will enter into the equation. Sometimes investors are required to complete a transaction within a certain mandated period of time in order to defer the taxation from the sale (i.e., 1031 "like kind" Exchange in the U.S.A.). In other situations, the time table is not as regimented, but the result could be the same. If an investor is actively looking at numerous investments alongside all of the other activities that they are engaged with in a given day, the desire to come to an expeditious value conclusion can be daunting.

News from the field is another Shackle concept, whereby an investor that hears positive news concerning market vacancy, rental, and absorption rates is more likely to estimate lower expenses than in the alternate case where *Chicken Little* has seized the day and negativity abounds. As the commercial real estate perception of value survey results in Chapter 4 helped illustrate, different market participants can look at the same market information (labeled as due diligence in Exhibit 10.1) and form different value conclusions. Ever so slight differences in cap rates, vacancy rates, or other inflection points can sway the final value estimate for market participants, which helps to create the range of values that makes real estate an illiquid asset class. Illiquidity is owing to the time it takes for two market participants (as well as an appraiser and possibly a lender) to agree on a final purchase price. Time pressures and their impact on the subjectivity of valuation will be further addressed in the next section.

The final value determined by the market participant could lead to a good investment result (IRR and NPV above investor's hurdle rates, and LTV, debt yield, and debt service coverage ratio within the requirements of the lender) or a poor result. Typically, if an investor is projecting a poor investment result based on their estimates of the future economic performance for the property (or in the parlance of home purchases if the sales price per square foot is too high relative to the comparable set of properties in the market), then the decision would be to either forego the investment entirely or to sharpen their pencil and revise their calculations for the validity of investing in the subject property.

10.1.2 Philosophical underpinnings

Regardless of how wide the range of values for a property can be, each investor should come to the valuation process with their own methodology for arriving at a value conclusion. Similar to stock investing, where investors can be segmented relative to fundamental analysis (i.e., study prior company results for insight into the future) and technical analysis (i.e., study stock market movements in order to predict future outcomes), real estate investors can also fall into different groups. Early in Chapter 1, we provided a spectrum of valuation, with subjectivity and objectivity on the opposing ends. Some real estate investors prefer quantitative analysis of commercial properties, while others look to market appreciation rates and other subjectivities to gauge future success. For most equity investors, a combination of fundamental and technical analysis is most appropriate. The same is the case for real estate investment, as a combination of subjective and objective factors is the most common approach. The blending of the two schools is common and useful. Or as Kierkegaard would say, "*reasoning is the result of doing away with the vital distinction which separates subjectivity and objectivity*".

G.L.S. Shackle often said that choice involves valuation. In real estate, each component of the valuation process can lead to divergent pathways. Further, Shackle has said

> there is no objective, publicly visible or publicly valid basis for assigning degrees of relative importance to various characters or features of an imagined history to come. Their effect on the chooser depends on his own nature, as on that of history itself

As Exhibit 10.1 depicts, each market participant comes to the valuation decision with their own set of experiences, risk tolerances, and preferences. While market data and property financial history can be commonly viewed by numerous market participants, the survey results in Chapter 4 illustrated that different actors can reach different conclusions when viewing the same information. Additionally, just because information is publicly available, this does not mean that each market participant will assign the same importance to each of the components of that information.

As we conclude this section, one of my favorite Shackle quotes is, "*we are prisoners of the present who must choose in the present on the basis of our current knowledge, judgments, and assessments*". An increasingly important question in the 21st century is how long the present is defined, at least in terms of how long it should take to make a reasonable decision. This idea was termed by Shackle as "duration". From an objective perspective, duration can be seen as any number of distinct moments that have a simultaneous reality for the various market participants. From a subjective perspective, duration is experienced as the individual's solitary moment in-being. The individual alone has the knowledge of these moments and in how they reach and shape their own valuation conclusions. The "stretch of time" when a decision is contemplated and made, while it can be shared among different actors, cannot be summed since we cannot be in two distinct moments at once. Therefore, no meaning can be assigned to the idea of cumulating the actual experiences of successive moments. Regardless of how much time it takes to make a decision, a formal valuation framework is key to success.

10.1.3 Shackle's investment blueprint

G.L.S. Shackle theorized that an investment opportunity, or blueprint, is something that first exists in the investor's mind. The initial characteristics of these blueprints consist at the outset of thoughts which cannot be separated from the individual investor. This would be similar to our discussion of land development in Chapter

1. The land exists, but the eventual repurposing is currently left in the mind of the investor. The thoughts that create the blueprints are influenced by the individual's heredity, tolerance for risk, and life experiences. Each investor shapes their investment blueprint, whereby they focus on the maximum profit and loss potential of a given investment opportunity and project out their maximum offering price for acquiring the asset. The investor would also decide on a timeline for making the initial blueprint a reality.

The further in the future a possible investment opportunity resides, the more the investor can change their blueprints to evaluate how the project would perform as the economic climate, supply and demand patterns, and available land for construction change. An investor would gain satisfaction from the anticipation of their investment blueprint being successful. The investor should consider any future events which could impair the profitability of the investment. Should future changes begin to erode the projected profitability of an investment (i.e., the cost of materials increases substantially from when a blueprint was originally created), the investor will have to determine a specific investment profitability hurdle rate whereby once the projected profits or value of the property falls below this level, the investment blueprint must be abandoned.

As the scheduled blueprint comes close to the construction commencement date, the more likely an investor is to proceed with the project given the various time, money, and effort expended on bringing the idea from its initial stage to just before it becomes a physical reality. This does not mean that plans cannot be aborted late in the process, but typically there would need to be significant changes present whereby the decision to cease construction of a new property, or to stop the redesign of an existing property, is made abundantly clear. If all that was holding back a new construction project from being built was the acquisition of an acceptable site with appropriate zoning ordinances, once the land becomes available the final stumbling blocks keeping the construction project from commencing often quickly fall away. Should costs escalate in terms of buying the land and construction materials, an investor may decide to significantly alter their investment blueprint or move on to another competing project.

In the next section, the importance of time relative to the subjectivity of value is explored.

10.2 The provocation of time

In our increasingly digital society, time is of essence. As financial transactions are increasingly done online, there are a myriad of competing financial institutions, with market and property financial information readily available. This has the impact of speeding up the processing time for loans and contracting the listing period for investments offered at a reasonable price. Market participants, whether they are investors, lenders, brokers, or appraisers, all share the same challenges relative to the time required to find, evaluate, and close new business. The move to a digital society has created what philosopher Byung-Chul Han refers to as the *"digital swarm"*, whereby there is a constant stream of communication that removes the down periods between work and play. The constant *"news from the field"* and the concomitant desire to remain up to date with all of the seemingly relevant data have created what Han terms *"the end of leisure"*. In *The Disappearance of Rituals*, this idea was described thusly: *"If our life is deprived of all of its contemplative elements, we become suffocated by our own activity"*. In Han's *The Transparency Society*, it was noted that *"today, the growing, indeed rampant, mass of information is crippling all higher judgment"*.

Since the onset of the digital swarm is relatively new and the subjectivity of value is not, the point of focus here is how the increasing processing speed and the reduction of contemplative time might impact the accuracy of valuation efforts. If we consider the traditional process flow for an investor finding a suitable investment property and bringing the purchase to closure with the probable concurrent loan to finality, there are a series of market participants involved with making these events come to fruition. The investor would more than likely require a sales agent (or broker), lender, appraiser, and attorney during this process. While it is convenient to assume this process takes a linear format (as depicted in Exhibit 10.2), the real world rarely plays out in this fashion.

What linearity presumes is that each market participant involved in the process works in an orderly flow like a machine might in producing a tapestry; following a strict pattern from start to finish. What is also assumed is that each of the various players in the flow chart has an agreeable amount of time to devote to their particular task in the process with the absence of interruptions. In the 21st century, time is of the essence and multitasking reigns supreme. A recent popular book coined the term "essentialism" for when people focus on getting the right things done as opposed to doing everything all at once (McKeown, 2014).

As shown in Exhibit 10.3, multitasking, or the focus on too many activities, tends to spread energy too thin with limited productive gain. While Exhibit 10.3

Exhibit 10.2 **Linear Investment Process Flow.**

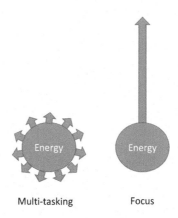

Exhibit 10.3 **Essentialism as Energy Focus.**

makes it clear that those who can obtain the appropriate focus of their attention will accomplish more than those who engage in multiple tasks at the same time, the question that arises is as follows: What are the various tasks that each player in Exhibit 10.2 might be confronted with in a given day? The era of the two-income family with a prevalence for working from home has blurred the time spent each day on personal and work-related activities. Most working adults try to be as productive as they can but still wish to achieve the ideal work–life balance. For simplicity we will only focus on business-related activities for each of our market participants, realizing that this only tells part of the multitasking story.

The start of our flow chart depicted in Exhibit 10.2 is the property buyer (home owner or investor). For a buyer looking to purchase a dwelling for residence, other than the search for an appropriate property, they might be confronted with competing tasks from their full-time job as well as a plethora of tasks that pop up every day in the business world. For the investment property buyer, these same activities exist, along with the analysis of each property that they are considering for investment. For the sales agent (or broker) in our flow chart, they also have multiple activities that pressure their time spent on any particular activity. The investor depicted in Exhibit 10.2 could be just one of a series of investors that the sales agent (or broker) works with on a given day. The same thing could be said for the lender, appraiser, and real estate attorney: our investor is just one of a sea of possibilities for each stop on our flowchart of market participants.

In an attempt to categorize the universe of task duplicity that exists, let's turn our focus to the lender section of Exhibit 10.2. They sit in the middle of our process flow chart, and all of the competing activities experienced by the lender exist for the other market participants in our process flow chain.

10.2.1 Universe of competing priorities

Throughout history, astronomers have used classification systems in order to better understand the universe. As it turns out, some astronomical classifications (such as stars, planets, and comets) can be helpful in explaining the competing priorities experienced by the lender each and every day. As we go through the model, remember that each of these competing priorities exists in turn for the property buyer, broker, appraiser, and closing attorney as well.

The *stars* of the lender universe are certainly new loans. These are what all sales personnel desire, and what all credit analysts aspire to analyze. Who would not get excited about reviewing a new customer loan or a new credit request from an existing customer? The problem for the lender is that these stars are unpredictable in terms of quantity and timing. The lender does not know when the stars will appear or how voluminous they might be. When stars materialize for the lender, there might be a situation where one credit analyst has "capacity" (i.e., the ability to take on an analysis) on Friday, but by the following Tuesday his/her capacity has proven to be a chimera as three new complex stars arrived at the same time. All of this volume has to be handled as soon as possible as each is viewed with equal esteem by the borrower (i.e., "do mine first").

Another set of large tasks in the lender universe are renewal loans. These can be seen as *comets*, or those pesky things in the universe that appear ever so often in a regularly scheduled manner. You might recall Halley's comet's appearance in earth's orbit roughly every 76 years. Renewal loans originally come in as stars (new loans), but when the loans mature, they reappear on the lender's landscape like comets. For planning purposes, renewals are known in advance. So early in the year, the lender can assess how many comets (renewals) will appear and when during the year. In traditional banking, renewals are inevitable with each new loan, unless inefficiencies in handling the renewals cause them to be lost to the competition.

Another group of large components of the lender universe are *planets*. These are large, often complex tasks that are conducted for each customer annually (a.k.a. annual portfolio reviews). Typically the planets are known in advance in terms of quantity and location, but what is variable each year is how complex they might have become. A relationship with three borrowers the previous year may have expanded into a relationship with six borrowers in the current year given new loan originations to entities owned in whole or in part by the same principals.

Heretofore, our lender universe has focused on productive things. Up until now, all tasks were also directly measurable. In astronomy, *dark matter* is something that is known to exist but is difficult to measure. Researchers must rely heavily on models to make informed predictions about the nature of this elusive material. Dark matter in the credit analysis universe consists of any activity that takes time away from the analysis and documentation of new loans, renewals, and annual portfolio reviews. Dark matter can be things like memoranda to file to document various changes, weekly sales team calls, preparation of covenant default letters, "help me" questions from sales personnel better suited for technology support, and third-party report engagement (i.e., ordering appraisals, environmental studies, or legal documents from the other market participants in our process flow chart). While dark matter can never go away entirely, it should be shared across the team. Dark matter is further problematic as each time it arises, the scope of the request is innocuous. Dark matter may not take very long, but as multiple similar requests materialize, the lender finds themselves further and further away from the primary focus of making timely loans. In astronomy, hundreds of dark matter particles zip through our bodies every second. Lender dark matter can have the same feeling to the credit analyst with a mound of productive work to do, but limited time to do it given the competing priorities.

Another element of distraction for the lender is the mass of rules, regulations, and paperwork that exist parallel to the actual underwriting and approval of loans. In our hypothetical lender universe, this is imagined as the "*financial Oort cloud*", an area in the far outreaches of the universe where the alphabet soup of regulations is created for the supposed betterment of all.

Our final component in the lender universe is *asteroids*. Like in astronomy, these are things floating in the universe that can cause lots of damage to stars, comets, and planets upon impact. From a lender perspective, asteroids can be items like *too much detail* in credit write-ups, *too many redundancies* in the credit approval process, *too many meetings*, and *too many interruptions*. Each of these asteroids can severely hinder the performance of a lender, and often the source of these troubles comes from outside of the lending team. The more time we spend talking about something, the less time there is to do it. If credit analysts are overanalyzing or spending too much time on small details (known as "nitter natter") of the customer's financial condition, the big picture may remain unclear or hidden from view. Asteroids matter as they slow down the production time of a lender in completing measurable tasks such as new loans, renewals, and annual portfolio reviews. Asteroids are things to be avoided in the lender's universe.

10.2.2 Projecting future priorities

So far we have presented the different categories of a complicated universe for the lender. The revised process flow is shown in Exhibit 10.4.

Exhibit 10.4 presents a revised and more accurate state of the process flow depicted in Exhibit 10.2. In this illustration, while the basic model is still intact in terms of who does what and when, the lender's universe is depicted as a constant choice between which tasks to prioritize in order to meet the needs of all customers. The customers of the lender include both the traditional external customer and internal customers, and in the cases of many countries of the developed world, the regulators. Regulatory groups have entered into our discussion during Chapter 3 for the various consumer regulations concerning real estate lending, as well as in Chapter 9 regarding agency guarantees for various mortgage-backed securities.

Nonlinearity is often difficult to depict in graphic form, but the primary intention of Exhibit 10.4 is to show that task duplicity and required multitasking of the lender are replicated for each of the other market participants. The investor, broker, appraiser, and attorney all have similar daily (or hourly!) decisions to make concerning which tasks to prioritize when, and often numerous tasks are completed simultaneously. The asteroids shown at the top of Exhibit 10.4 could land anywhere in the process, delaying or derailing the best-laid plans of efficiency and the timely completion of tasks. Not pictured is the ever-present dark matter that lies in the background of the entire process flow diagram. All of these competing priorities lead to time pressures which can result in market participants not spending as much time as they would like when evaluating subject properties being considered for loan or purchase. The provocation of time can lead to valuations errors as well as acceptance of market data or other assumptions without fully investigating the quality of the information.

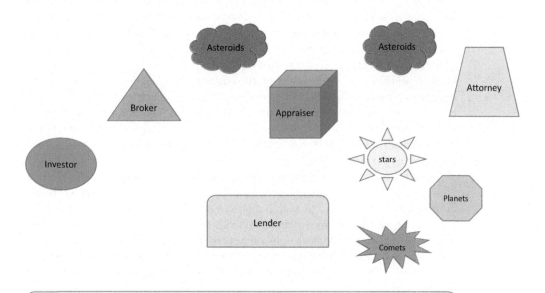

Exhibit 10.4 Revised Investment Process Flow.

Regarding the ability to project the future task volume, some items are known in advance in terms of quantity and timing (renewals, portfolio reviews), others are of unknown quantity and timing (new loans), and still others are not directly measurable (dark matter). What is a lender to do?

One approach is to take things as they come. In this model, lenders will be required to handle any and all requests regardless of what they might entail. In this approach, individual lending team members should raise their hands when they feel like they have too much to handle, realizing that by the time they raise their hands, others may not be in a position to help. While this approach is easy in terms of planning, it leaves to the randomness of time the impact on their daily tasks when the unpredictable volume of stars enters the landscape.

Another method focuses on the knowns and attempts to track for unknowns. Since renewals (comets) and annual portfolio reviews (planets) are known in quantity and timing at the outset of each year, the lender can attempt to distribute their known future task productivity to allow time for the unknown timing of new business. Each lender should review the customers in his/her portfolio in order to classify them based on complexity. This approach uses a one-to-four scale, with four being the most complex/arduous credit analysis. If the quantity and complexity of each lender's monthly volume is estimated in this manner, they can begin to pinpoint early in the year the peaks and valleys in volume in a given portfolio. The goal of all of this planning is to smooth out the known primary tasks such as to reduce the need for multitasking, and to reduce the mistakes that arise from hurried work when volume is higher than is anticipated. This additional complexity nuance allows for the lending team to attempt to load level based on both volume and complexity of the portfolio review (planet) or renewal (comet).

Predicting new loan volume (i.e., the stars in our universe) is not as easy. While most investment prospectus contain the caveat "the past is not necessarily indicative of future results", one first step in projecting new loan volume is to review the past few years' new loan production. This will only capture the universe of closed loans and will not measure new loans analyzed but not closed. Whether the lender wins the business of the property buyer or not, the contemplation of a new loan opportunity takes time. Another star prediction method is to work closely with the sales personnel as they often will monitor leads on new loan production enough to be able to project what they are currently entertaining, when it might come in as a loan request, and the probability of winning the deal. Additionally, each credit analyst should have a list of the new loan requests previously reviewed such that the lender can capture the historical production of the team to include both closed loans and opportunities lost.

Much research has been done in projecting demand in both certain and uncertain production. Some economists like Sinn attempted to use statistical methods to aid in the prediction of future productive activity. Others like Shackle considered the future to be inherently unpredictable and viewed statistical inquiries of the future to be as useful as astrological signs or as precise as the tossing of a pair of dice. Wherever one might fall on this spectrum, new loan requests will be a significant use of the lender's time, so some mechanism for prediction based on historical volumes is desirable.

As should be clear from the preceding discussion, managing workflow for lenders presents many competing goals. On the one hand, lenders wish to help as many internal and external customers as possible by offering assistance in as many areas as possible. Conversely, time is limited such that the lender should attempt to spend their time where it is most useful. If lenders can focus on their primary tasks (stars, planets, and comets), more will be accomplished. That said, the reduction of non-essential activities (i.e., dark matter) and the elimination of redundancies and time wasters (i.e., asteroids) should be the goal for any market participant. What this vignette illustrates is that when an investor is on a short timeline to complete a transaction, as they engage their lender to help facilitate the deal, there is panoply of other things with which the lending staff could be concerned. Each market participant faces a similar smorgasbord of competing activities, all of which contribute to the provocation of time.

10.3 Challenges to subjectivity

If the subjectivity of value persists owing to the diversity of experience, risk tolerance, and preferences of the various market participants, it would appear that this situation is leading to the range of possible value conclusions for a property offered in the marketplace. The range of values is seemingly inefficient and if there was an easier method for arriving at an optimal value for all property, those offered for sale would more quickly be sold and the real estate asset class would no longer be known as illiquid.

While this sounds great, it is wrought with problems. If the great valuation wizard was to produce a model that everyone could believe in, it couldn't be too long before that model was manipulated in order to achieve a higher asking price for the rapacious seller, or a lower price for the sagacious buyer. This section summarizes a few of the market attempts that have cropped up in recent years to relegate the subjectivity of value to the dustbin of history, or at least to raise to prominence the idea of a singularity for the property value.

10.3.1 Government mandates

The most obvious attempt at valuation singularity includes government mandates for "official opinions" of value for real estate. In the United States, the real estate appraisal is seen as the official opinion of value of an appraiser, and this value conclusion is what sets the loan to value at origination. The appraisal process starts with asking what the contract price for sale is between the seller and buyer, thereby setting the tone for the appraisal process to essentially confirm or reject that offering price. Starting a valuation exercise equipped with the final answer once again reminds of the Kierkegaard quote: "*in case he who should act was to judge himself according to the result, he would never get to the point of beginning*".

If you recall the discussion in Chapter 5, there are a myriad ways that a buyer and seller can utilize in order to come to a final purchase price for real estate. Since the bank and the appraiser are often come into the picture after a purchase price has been decided, both parties begin their valuation process while knowing the final desired valuation result. The appraiser must utilize market data to confirm whether the agreed purchase price is considered a market value, or if the property might have been valued incorrectly by the buyer and seller in the transaction. The lender will often assume that the purchase price negotiated between the buyer and seller is reasonable (to be confirmed by the appraiser), and instead will look to verify if other sources of repayment are adequate if the property itself is overvalued.

By mandating that an appraisal is obtained, this represents an attempt to remove the range of possible values and to focus on one particular value opinion. Another area of possible government mandates concerns the use of cryptocurrency and blockchain, which has the potential to both threaten the dominion of fiat currency and the inclusion of a range of market participants, and will be discussed in a subsequent section of this chapter.

10.3.2 Statistical modeling

Another attempt to remove the inconvenience of diverse opinions of value comes from statistical models. The process could entail the use of standard deviations or other paradigms of settling on a final price, or it could utilize discounted cash flow and direct capitalization models that require one final appraised value. Either way these are attempts at achieving the unity of opinion for what a real estate property is worth.

Listing statistical modeling in this section of the challenges of subjectivity could seem misplaced, and I am certainly not attempting to pick a fight with the entirety of the statistics profession. The point here is that statistics helps contribute to the movement away from the range of values to the singularity of the final value by way of statistical procedures. Variation, standard deviation, and other concepts help the user to differentiate the significance of the divergence in values to help them toward a value conclusion. Statistical modeling does aid the investor in reaching a value conclusion, but by its nature is a challenge to the subjectivity of value.

G.L.S. Shackle was not a fan of one particular methodology discussed in chapter two: expected value theory. Shackle wrote that probability is relevant when there are repeated trials as in a clinical trial situation. In that case, hundreds of similar trials bring to importance the probability of an actual result occurring. Shackle did not feel that probability entered into the decision process for individual transactions. If every individual purchasing decision required a series of possible monetary outcomes all tied to a subjectively derived probability, the world would be filled with the people jotting down equations before any decision was made. You can imagine if the patron in front of you waiting to order at the restaurant was slow to the draw on this process, how it might take a while for him to choose between the bologna and cheese and the chicken salad.

A real estate example that Shackle utilized in *Expectation in Economics* involved the market for land adjacent to towns. In this example, Shackle compared how traditional expected value theory fares relative to his own concept of potential surprise. Shackle theorized that potential surprise was a methodology that market participants utilized to narrow the range of possible pathways in an uncertain future state following a purchasing decision. A decision maker would theorize the most likely positive and most likely negative outcome that could ensue whereby they would not be surprised if that result did come to pass. If we imagine a large town that is fully developed with a periphery of land adjacent to the town ready to be built upon in order to satisfy the future demand for housing, office, or other land uses, the two models can be adequately compared. If there was enough space adjacent to the town to account for 50 equal land parcels, but only ten of these would be utilized in the near future for construction, a potential seller of the land might come at the valuation problem from different perspectives. On the one hand, they could utilize expected value theory. Under that approach, the current land could be worth $50,000 in its current state, or could be sold for the future development at a price of $100,000. Since there are 50 parcels that could be utilized for the new development where only ten of them will actually be used, the seller for one parcel might assume that there was a 20% chance that their specific lot would be selected for the new construction site. Expected value theory would value the lot as follows:

Under this theory, the seller would price their lot at $60,000. Using Shackle's theory of potential surprise, the seller would have no reason to believe that their lot would not be selected for the construction project. Therefore, if they listed the land for less than $100,000, they would be selling cheap in the situation where the specific lot being sold was selected for the future construction project. As Shackle wrote:

> in order to enjoy with a high intensity, or even to the full, the anticipation of some gratifying outcome, a person requires only that there should be no solid, identifiable reason to disbelieve in the possibility of this outcome; they do not require solid grounds for feeling sure that it will be the true outcome.

The difficulty in determining the future selling price of lots was the subject of Chapter 8 on the discounted sellout approach. As was elucidated in that chapter, if a developer projects one set of possible selling prices for lots when the economy appears to be growing, there exists much probability of potential surprise when the prices drop when the economy takes a downward turn.

10.3.3 Technological advancement

In Chapter 2, we discussed the progress related to machine learning and artificial intelligence regarding both real estate valuation and commercial lending. If you consider the items highlighted in Exhibit 10.1, the current state of artificial intelligence seems well advanced on the calculations portion of the model, but still struggles with how to best include the combined experience, risk tolerance, and preferences into the technological platforms.

Since humans design the algorithms and financial models being purported as the replacement for the human being, any weaknesses, knowledge gap, or bias present in the creators of the machines should be present in the final automated product.

From a general digitalization perspective, the increasing availability of market and property related data in digital form should make the process of valuation for real estate more transparent. This increase in transparency regarding the information at the disposal of the market participant to effect rendering a value conclusion is also a challenge to the subjectivity of value. In this case, the transparency of the information available, which could aid a market participant in their value assessment, can lead to more uniform property values, in effect decreasing the range of values present prior to the mass of digital information now available. At present, some of the market- and property-related information is available for free and in digital form, while other information is held privately or sold for a fee. The impact of digitalization on increasing the transparency of market information is helped by the internet, but somewhat hindered by the presence of data and information silos often only accessible at a cost to the user.

One specific area of real estate technology which could prove challenging to the subjectivity of value is the use of smart contracts in blockchain ledgers which record land and property ownership and subsequent transactions. The blockchain itself, which is typically associated with cryptocurrency platforms such as Bitcoin, can be expanded to include transparent and unalterable real estate transactions which would reduce the need for intermediaries such as real estate brokers, governmental entities, and possibly closing attorneys and lenders. Since this technology is still in the inchoate stage for real estate transactions, one thing is clear at this juncture. Even if only one intermediary is removed from the real estate property conveyance process, the utilization of blockchain would speed up the transfer of property assets between buyers and sellers. Additionally, cost savings could be seen if the real estate industry decides to utilize blockchain in the future.

When utilizing smart contracts within the blockchain framework, literally anything of value could be exchanged (including real estate) once specified conditions for the sale are met. Given the anonymity of the blockchain platform in terms of its users, government regulation could soon follow which attempts to increase the transparency of the market participants since the transparency of the transaction is a well-known feature of blockchain technology. Future regulatory potential aside, the blockchain could be utilized instead of land registries as supervised by various government municipalities and states.

Any time a procedural change is implemented which speeds up the process of selling real estate, the subjectivity of value can be impacted. Since the range of values for real estate properties is a hallmark of the industry, the speeding up of the buying and selling of property should only result in a narrowing of the possible ranges of acceptable values, owing to the provocation of time.

10.4 Why subjectivity must remain

In this final chapter, we have explored why subjectivity exists, the philosophical underpinnings of why subjectivity exists, and some challenges to the subjectivity of value. What remains is to make the case for why subjectivity must remain and offer thoughts for areas of future research. In the preceding section on the challenges to subjectivity, statistical modeling was provided as an example, to not refute the entirety of statistical analysis but to highlight that methods to explain away value variability from a statistical standpoint stand in contrast to our efforts to understand why the differences in value exist in the first place. A more serious challenge is that of the progresses in artificial intelligence and machine learning regarding real estate valuation.

As highlighted in Chapter 2, the desire to automate the credit process began decades ago, started with the concept of the five Cs of credit, and explored how to best estimate those characteristics of the borrower's persona in historical data form. Today, machine learning attempts to mine the multitude of data collected on consumers every day for inclinations as to their repayment ability. What in the past was a focus on the personal credit report and personal references for a credit application, today social media and other means of assessment attempt to capture a more complete picture of the consumer requesting credit or anything else for that matter. Additionally, modern computing (machine learning combined with artificial intelligence) has tackled the valuation question and seemingly "there's an app for that" to utilize a common phrasing, but the question is how will the computer applications handle the divergent opinions relative to valuation of real estate.

Exhibit 10.5 provides a fun example of one futuristic possibility. The faces that surround the laptop represent various market participants that we have discussed. These faces in the crowd could be the eventual buyer, prospective buyers who did not bid on the property, prospective buyers who bid on but did not win the contract for sale (owing to value concerns no doubt), the seller, the lender (or lenders in a competitive loan bidding process), the appraiser, sales agent (broker), and the real estate attorney. All of these market actors have an interest in the final property value whether it be devised by a human, a machine, or a combination thereof.

If you notice the countenances on the surrounding faces, they represent the multitude of personalities, predilections, and perquisites that could be present in any "moment of decision". Some people will be shocked at the value, others delighted, and others vaguely amused. Given all of the divergent values that could be possible, the final value conclusion will hardly please all actors in our valuation play.

The face on the screen represents how the final opinion of value might compare to each of the differing opinions of value for the market participants involved in the property transaction. The final value would not appear to be a perfect match

Exhibit 10.5 Why Subjectivity Must Remain.

for any one of the market participants in question. This is the fear with an automated valuation decision: the dreaded guy with a funny hat syndrome. The last thing we need is a guy with a funny hat, or a value whereby none of the market participants can agree with the final value conclusion.

The subjectivity of value must remain because different people will inevitably reach divergent valuation conclusions. This may not happen every time in every situation, but the range of values is the most likely result any time opinions differ as to the interpretation of the data at hand. Attempts to "make the computer do it" will continue to progress, but a sale will not transpire until at least two people (a buyer and a seller) agree on a price. Until then, real estate will continue to sit on the market, the exemplar of an illiquid asset.

10.5 Concluding thoughts and areas of future research

This book came together once I realized that much of my research and writing since the publication of *Real Estate Investment: A Value Based Approach* had been focused on the subjectivity of value in commercial real estate. Portions of many of those published papers fit neatly into the broader construct of the narrative of this book. While the subjectivity of value has a long lineage in economic theory and the work of Shackle sits squarely in between Austrian economic thought and Keynesianism, the thought of bringing a book to market that utilized the Shackle Possibility Curve in a real estate context proved too much to resist, and I hope you have enjoyed the process of exploring this idea with me over these pages.

When I began the commercial real estate perception of value survey discussed in Chapter 4, I did not realize at that time that it would lead to a book as the end result. I also did not realize that I would subject so many semesters of students in multiple countries to completing the survey. Certainly other studies of this kind could be undertaken to see if the range of values that I found appear reasonable. Other exercises would require a partnership between academic and private practice, as I envision having different appraiser firms valuing the same property at the same time to see the variability of their value conclusions. Some studies could begin with the appraisers knowing what the contracted purchase price is, and some would not. It would be interesting to see if the value disparity (if there was any) changed with the appraiser's foreknowledge of the contract for sale price.

Finally, the creative process for this book came during the various work-from-home mandates and lockdowns. I have made a conscious decision to limit any references to COVID-19 in this book in the hopes that when this book reaches your hands, those dreary days are distant memories for us all.

Questions for discussion

1. Describe in your own words why the subjectivity of value persists in real estate valuation.
2. Discuss how the provocation of time impacts market participants and how multitasking may lead to errors in valuation.

3. How can market participants best attempt to plan their tasks to avoid duplicity and harried decisions?
4. Provide examples of how machine learning and artificial intelligence can be utilized to reduce the range of property values.
5. Itemize some examples for why reducing the range of property values may not necessarily be a good thing for the real estate industry.
6. Elaborate on some reasons for why reducing the range of property values could be helpful for the real estate industry.
7. Discuss how the Shackle construction blueprint impacts the probability of a project being completed as the length of the project increases.
8. Research current progress on utilizing smart contracts and blockchain technology to facilitate property ownership registration and conveyance. What does its continued use say about the subjectivity of value?
9. In your own words, describe why the subjectivity of value is likely to remain regardless of attempts to eliminate it.
10. What other studies could be undertaken to study the subjectivity of real estate property value?

Chapter 10 Market vignette

Cast of characters: Hobbes (appraiser), Shaggy (customer), Calvin and Scooby (children), Velma (Banker)
   Act: To be constructed property appraisal

Scene one: a new assignment

HOBBES: Calvin! Tell the man at the counter what you want for lunch.
CALVIN: I want a hot dog, no, I want a hamburger, no, I want pizza….
(HOBBES' PHONE RINGS)
HOBBES: Hello? This is Hobbes from Hobbes Appraisals, how can I help you?
SHAGGY: Hello Hobbes. My name is Shaggy and I was referred to you by Velma over at MM Bank.
HOBBES: Oh yes, Hello Shaggy. Calvin, please tell the man what you want for lunch and stop playing around. Scooby stop running around the restaurant and come over here and place your order as well.
SHAGGY: Did I call at a bad time?
HOBBES: No it's fine, I am taking the kids out to lunch right now. How can I help you today?
SHAGGY: I am contemplating building a phase two for my self-storage facility in Kansas City.
HOBBES: Scooby! Stop pulling Calvin's hair. Tell the man what you want for lunch.
CALVIN: I want a hot dog with chili on top. I want mustard but no onion, I hate onions. Ow! Stop it Scooby.
SCOOBY: I want a pizza with pepperoni and green….Ow! Stop that Calvin!!
HOBBES: Boys! Will you just go sit down so I can talk to this man on the phone?

CALVIN: But we want drinks too!

SHAGGY: I can call back later if that works better.

HOBBES: Oh no, it's perfectly alright. We can talk now. So you said you were looking at buying a self-storage facility?

SHAGGY: Well I own it now. We are almost fully leased and we have some land adjacent to the property that would make for a great second phase. Right now we are using the land for recreational vehicle storage.

HOBBES: Oh, right you own it already. Where is the property located? Did you say it was in Kansas?

SHAGGY: No, it is in Kansas City. It is a 250-unit climate-controlled facility. I am looking to add another 150 units if you think that makes sense when you come out here.

HOBBES: How long have you owned the property?

SHAGGY: I have owned it for ten years. There has been so much new home construction in the area that I think it's time to build a second phase.

HOBBES: Calvin, put that down! Scooby, leave those people alone. And give them back their ketchup bottle! Shaggy, what is your current occupancy rate? Also is the second phase on the same site or nearby?

SHAGGY: We are almost full. We offer both traditional and climate-controlled space. The land for new construction is located right next to the current phase. It is actually across the street, but the land does have good visibility from the road.

HOBBES: Oh that is great, it's always good to be able to get a good look at that raw land while driving down the road! I am kidding, of course. Since I live in St. Louis, I am about three and a half hours away from where your self-storage site. Maybe we can schedule a time next week to meet there and I can review your blueprints? Also please provide me with a current rent roll and the historical financial statements on the current facility. I will also need you to itemize all of your construction costs as I will be doing a cost approach valuation in this appraisal along with the income and sales approaches to value.

SHAGGY: Yes that sounds good. I will email you the details and we can set up a time to meet next week.

HOBBES: Excellent. Calvin, watch out! You just spilled your drink all over me! Go and get some napkins and clean this mess up.

SHAGGY: Ok, well, talk with you later Hobbes.

(END SCENE ONE)

Scene two: site inspection detour

CALVIN: Where are the white squirrels?

SCOOBY: Ooh I want to see some of those too!

HOBBES: We are almost in Marionville, Missouri now, kids. I am so glad that you both could come on this site inspection given your paper on "strange nature" in your biology class, Calvin. I have always wanted to come to this town where they claim to have white squirrels.

CALVIN: I'm hungry. How long until we see some white squirrels?

HOBBES (THINKS TO HIMSELF): Oh, look, I just received a text from Velma over at MM Bank. It looks like she is really interested in how we value this self-storage property in Kansas City today. Looks like Shaggy has been pressing her for an answer as to how much of a loan she might consider.

SCOOBY: Oh boy! We are almost in Marionville now. I wonder where you can go to see those white squirrels?

HOBBES: Hopefully this pit stop will not take too long, as we have to be in Kansas City later this afternoon.

CALVIN: Ow, Scooby! Stop pulling my hair. I don't like this radio station, can we change it?

HOBBES: Yes, but let me call Shaggy and let him know that we might be delayed. It looks like there is a storm coming in anyway.

(Hobbes dials Shaggy while driving and looking at Calvin and Scooby fighting in the back seat.)

HOBBES: Hi, Shaggy, I am hoping to be able to see you at the site at 3 o'clock this afternoon, but I decided to take the kids to Marionville to see some white squirrels.

SHAGGY: What? I have never heard of white squirrels. Did you get a chance to look at the financial plans that I sent over for the second phase of the self-storage facility?

HOBBES: Yes, thank you for sending those over. Based on the acreage that you are utilizing in the first phase, it would appear that you might be able to increase your units in the second phase up to around 200, if that makes sense.

SHAGGY: I was wondering about that. I know the bank will only do a larger project if the financial plan looks good. I do have some equity in the first phase that might serve to collateralize the second phase.

HOBBES: Yes, I have seen banks do this sort of thing. Typically they will want to take any equity in the first phase and secure it along with the second-phase property, at least until such time as the second phase stabilizes.

SHAGGY: What does stabilize mean?

HOBBES: Calvin! Calm down, we are going to see the white squirrels in a minute.

CALVIN: I'm hungry ….I 'm bored …..and I want to see some white squirrels.

SCOOBY: I bet we can't even see any squirrels today as it is raining. (Smack!) That's what you get Calvin for pulling my ponytail earlier.

HOBBES: Boys! Knock it off. What was your question, Shaggy?

SHAGGY: What does stabilize mean? Also has Velma been in contact with you yet regarding the timing of the appraisal?

HOBBES: I wish I knew, we are far from stability over here at the moment. Ha, no seriously, stabilization just means when the property reaches its projected occupancy rate. And yes, Velma did email me just a few moments ago. Hopefully after I see the site for both phases, I will be able to get started on the valuation in short order. I am working on a few other self-storage appraisals as well as some multifamily properties, but hopefully this will not take too long.

SHAGGY: When you come into town you will see that a new national self-storage company has just put up a sign down the street from my location. I had heard that they were looking at coming into the area for the past few years, and apparently, they found a suitable site.

HOBBES: Thank you for letting me know about this. I will see how this new entrant might impact your demand for the second phase. Self-storage unit demand is often hard to predict. I will need to better understand the existing competition and what the market occupancy and rental rates are currently.

SHAGGY: To be honest, I am hoping that I do not have to get into a price war with this new competitor. But if I am to keep my existing customers happy, I may have to offer lower rental rates for a while, especially for the second phase.

CALVIN: Oh my goodness! Is that a white squirrel?

SCOOBY: No that is a cat, what is wrong with you Calvin?

HOBBES: Well Shaggy, once we get done seeing white squirrels or whatever they are, we can meet at your site and consider the impact of the new entrant on your plans for a second phase at your self-storage facility.

SHAGGY: Yes, please do hurry. Time is of the essence in this market.

Questions for discussion

1. How would you classify the relevant project experience and risk tolerance of Hobbes and Shaggy?
2. How do you think Velma at MM Bank will react to the new entrant in the market?
3. Expand on how Shackle's blueprint model is at play in this case.
4. Elaborate on how the provocation of time is influencing Hobbes and Shaggy in this case.
5. Construct a revised investment process flow for Hobbes' current universe of activity. How likely is Hobbes to get this valuation done quickly?

Bibliography

Castelli, M., et al. (2020) Predicting Days on Market to Optimize Real Estate Sales Strategy. *Complexity*, 2020, 1–22. doi:10.1155/2020/4603190.

Gassemi, K., Papastamatelou, J., & Unger, A. (2021) Time Perspective Influence on Management Leadership Styles and the Mediating Role of Self-Efficacy. *Leadership, Education, Personality: An Interdisciplinary Journal*, Springer Nature, Ludwigshafen, Germany. https://doi.org/10.1365.s42681-020-00018-x

Goddard, G. J. (2014) Kierkegaard and Valuation in a Business Context. *Business and Economics Journal*, 5(2), 1–7.

Goddard, G. J. (2020) Digital Finance Book Review. *Journal of Asia Pacific Business*. doi: 10.1080/10599231.2020.1745052

Goddard, G. J. & Gargeya, V. B. (2019) Managing in the Credit Analyst Universe. *RMA Journal*, April, pp. 24–28.

Goddard, G. J. & Marcum, B. (2011) the Good, the Bad and the 1031 Exchange. *RMA Journal*, April, pp. 44–47.

Han, B. C. (2015) *The Transparency Society*. Stanford Briefs, Stanford University Press, Stanford, CA.

Han, B. C. (2017a) *In the Swarm: Digital Prospects*. MIT Press, Cambridge, MA.

Han, B. C. (2017b) *The Scent of Time*. Polity Press, Cambridge.

Han, B. C. (2020) *The Disappearance of Rituals*. Polity Press, Cambridge.

Hayek, F. A. (1972) *Individualism and Economic Order*. Henry Regnery Company, Chicago, IL.

Johnson-Groh, M. (2018) Dark Matter Mystery. *Astronomy*, 46(10), 18–25.

Lamond, J. E., Bhattacharya-Mis, N., Chan, F. K. S., Kreibich, H., Montz, B., Proverbs, D. G., & Wilkinson, S. (2019). Flood Risk Insurance, Mitigation and Commercial Property Valuation. *Property Management*, 37(4), 512–528. doi: 10.1108/pm-11-2018-0058

McKeown, G. (2014) *Essentialism: The Disciplined Pursuit of Less*. Currency Books, Westport CT.

Shackle, G. L. S. (1949) *Expectations in Economics*. Cambridge University Press, London.

Shackle, G. L. S. (1969) *Decision Order and Time in Human Affairs*, 2nd ed. Cambridge University Press, Cambridge.

Shackle, G. L. S. (1970) *Expectation Enterprises, and Profit*. Aldine Publishing Company, Chicago, IL.

Shackle, G. L. S. (1979) *Imagination and the Nature of Choice*. Edinburgh University Press, Edinburgh.

Shackle, G. L. S. (1983) *Time in Economics*. Greenwood Press, Westport, CT.

Sinn, H. W. (1983) *Economic Decisions under Uncertainty*. North-Holland Publishing Co., London.

Wanjagi, J. & Fatoki, O. I. (2020), Blockchain Technology: Smart Contract Application in the Real Estate Industry in Kenya. *International Journal of Research and Scientific Innovation*, VII(VIII), 13.17.

Glossary

Absorption—Leasing or purchasing a property after its construction or renovation.

Agency guarantees—External credit enhancement for mortgage pools where the government explicitly or implicitly guarantees the credit offering.

Amenities—Amenities can include specific features in a particular unit, such as vaulted ceilings and fireplaces, or could consist of things offered in the complex as a whole, such as tennis courts, swimming pools, or laundry facilities.

Anchor tenant—Tenant in an investment property that serves as the primary draw for customers. The anchor tenant occupies the largest square foot in a given property, and the leases for in-line tenants may contain domino clauses.

Apartment property—Investment property that contains at least five third-party residential tenants. This is also known as multifamily property.

Artificial intelligence—Theory and development of computer systems able to perform tasks that normally require human intelligence.

Average daily rental (ADR) rate—Average rental rates per day at a hotel.

Band of investment—Income property appraisal technique where the overall capitalization rate is derived from weighting mortgage and equity rates.

Basis points—One one-hundredth of one percentage point.

Blockchain—Digital peer-to-peer network that allows transactions between two parties without the need for an intermediary.

Break-even analysis—Sensitivity analysis to determine the required interest rate or vacancy factor required in order for the net operating income to equal the annual debt service.

Break-even interest rate—The maximum interest rate paid on debt before leverage becomes negative. Break-even occupancy rate—Where the gross revenue is equal to the sum of the annual operating expenses and annual debt service requirements.

Build-to-suit—Properties constructed for a particular use or tenant.

Business parks—Master-planned developments that encompass a group of predominantly industrial buildings on large acreage tracts.

Cap rate—The ratio of projected net income relative to sales price.

CDO—Collateralized debt obligation.

CMBS—Commercial mortgage-backed securities.

Collateralized mortgage obligation (CMO)—A mortgage-backed security that generates separate cash flows for different classes of securities called tranches. Tranches have varying loan maturities and prepayment risks and offer varying expected returns for investors.

Collection loss—Reduction in expenses due to trouble collecting rent, or possibly due to lease rate concessions during the year.

Commencement date—When a commercial lease takes effect.

Common area maintenance (CAM)—An agreement for tenants to reimburse the landlord for their pro-rata share of certain expenses.

Concessions—Benefits granted by a seller or lessor to induce a sale or lease.

Condominium—A system of ownership of individual units in a multiunit structure, combined with joint ownership of the commonly used property.

Convexity—Measure of the nonlinear relationship of bond prices to changes in interest rates.

Correlation—Statistical measure of how two securities move in relation to each other.

Cost approach—A method of appraising property based on the depreciated reproduction or replacement cost (new) of improvements, plus the market value of the site.

Covered bonds—Securitization model utilized in Europe and Asia whereby the lender keeps the loans on their balance sheet and has the flexibility to change the loans within the portfolio which is eligible for investment.

Credit enhancement—Techniques used to improve the creditworthiness of a borrower.

Debt service coverage ratio—The relationship between net operating income (NOI) and annual debt service (ADS). The formula is NOI divided by ADS.

Debt yield—Net operating income divided by the purchase price. From a loan underwriting perspective, it can also be defined as the mortgage constant multiplied by the desired debt service coverage ratio.

Digital swarm—Han term used to describe the mass of incessant communication in a digital world.

Direct capitalization model—One year projected net operating income divided by a capitalization rate in order to estimate value.

Discount rate—Required rate of return (or rate of interest) for the investor taking into account opportunity costs, inflation, and the certainty of payment.

Discounted cash flow (DCF) model—Income approach valuation methodology utilizing a multiyear view of the revenues and the expenses for a property which are received during the defined holding period of the investment.

Discounted sellout—Valuation model used in for-sale investment scenarios.

Easement—A non-possessory interest in land by an entity other than the owner of the property.

Effective age—The effective age of a property is the remaining economic useful life of the property given the quality of construction and improvements made to the property since it was originally constructed.

Effective gross income (EGI)—Stabilized income a property is expected to generate after a vacancy allowance.

External credit enhancements—Techniques used to enhance a borrower's, or securitization structures', creditworthiness that involves third-party guarantees such as a letter of credit or monoline insurance.

Fee simple—Absolute ownership of real property; owner is entitled to the entire property with unconditional power of disposition.

Five C's of credit—Character, capacity, collateral, capital, conditions.

GOPPAR—Gross operating profit per available room for a hotel.

Gross income multiplier (GIM)—A blend of the sales and income approaches, and is typically utilized in appraisals for single-family residences or for generally smaller properties with stable income streams.

Gross potential income (GPI)—The total income that the investment property can produce based on full occupancy at market rental rates.

Gross rent multiplier (GRM)—Same as the gross income multiplier.

Ground lease—Lease agreement concerning renting the land only.

Herfindahl index—Effective loan count concentration measure in CMBS; also known as Herf score.

Highest and best use—Appraisal term meaning the legally and physically possible use that, at the time of appraisal, is most likely to produce the greatest net return to the land and/or buildings over a given period.

Holding period of the investment—The time span of ownership.

Homeowner association (HOA)—Organization of the homeowners in a particular subdivision or condominium; generally for the purpose of enforcing deed restrictions or managing the common elements of the development.

Housing boom—An increase in housing prices fueled by demand, speculation, and exuberant spending.

Housing ladder—Model used to describe the differences in housing from the cheapest to more expensive housing.

Housing life cycle—Model used to describe how the changes in the size, composition, and housing preferences are correlated to the different stages of the nuclear family.

Housing life course—Model used to describe housing preferences based on familial considerations, education, and career choices.

Income approach—A method of appraising real estate based on the property's anticipated future income.

Income-producing property—Real estate held as investment where the tenants have different ownership than the owner of the property.

Inflation—A loss in purchasing power of money; an increase in the general price level.

In-line tenants—Supporting players relative to the anchor tenants.

Industrial property—Property used for industrial purposes, such as manufacturing, warehousing, and storage.

Internal credit enhancements—Techniques used to enhance securitization structure's creditworthiness that involves injections of capital by the securities' issuer or originator.

Internal rate of return (IRR)—The true annual rate of earnings on an investment. It is the rate that equates the present value of the cash inflows with the present value of the cash outflows.

Investment holding period—The time span that the investor owns the property. The holding period begins once the property is purchased and ends once the property is sold. The length of the holding period will vary according to the investment objectives and investment horizon of the investor.

Investment horizon—The going-in assumption as to how long a property will be owned after purchase.

J-Factor—Associated with Ellwood's cap rate derivation model. It is a mathematical equation focusing on a curvilinear change in income over the projection period.

K-Factor—Associated with Akerson's cap rate derivation model. It is a mathematical equation focusing on a linear movement up or down in the property value over the projection period.

Lease rollover risk—Risk that tenants will not renew their leases.

Leased fee—Landlord's ownership interest of a property that is under a lease.

Leasing commissions—Commissions paid by investor to a broker in order to obtain a tenant in an investment property.

Lender's yield—Cap rate derivation model utilizing the debt service coverage ratio as the equity component, and the mortgage constant and LTV as the debt components.

Lessee—Tenant.

Lessor—Owner.

Loan constant—See "Mortgage constant".

Machine learning—Use and development of computer systems that are able to learn and adapt without following explicit instructions, by using algorithms and statistical models to analyze and draw inferences from patterns in data.

Market abstraction—Cap rate derivation model which uses sales from the market.

Market comparison approach—See "Sales approach".

Market equilibrium—The level of occupancy, lease rates, and property expenses per property type in the region when supply equals demand.

Mini-storage—A building separated into relatively small lockable individual units, typically with a garage-door-styled opening that provides storage. Also known as mini-warehouse and self-storage.

Minksy moment—Sudden, major collapse of asset values which marks the end of the growth phase of a cycle in credit markets or business activity.

Modified internal rate of return (MIRR)—The MIRR assumes a reinvestment rate equal to the required rate of return, or some other realistic rate rather than at the IRR.

Mortgage constant—Fractional annual rate that will pay off a loan of a given amount, interest rate, and amortization period. Also known as loan constant.

Mortgagee—One who holds a lien on a property or title to property, as security for a debt; the lender.

Mortgagor—One who pledges property as security for a loan; the borrower.

Net operating income (NOI)—Income from property or business, after operating expenses have been deducted, but before deducting income taxes and financing expenses.

Net present value—A method of determining whether expected performance of a proposed investment promises to be adequate. It is a technique that discounts the expected future cash flows at the minimum required rate of return.

News from the field—Shackle concept where market information can sway an investor's value perception.

Non-recourse financing—Where no personal liability is available to the lender for a loan.

Note—A document that serves as evidence of debt and a promise to pay between a borrower and the lender.

Opinion of value—Official definition of an appraisal of real estate.

Over-collateralization—An internal credit enhancement technique in which the originator transfers a pool of collateral loans to the SPV that has a higher par value (usually 5–10%) than that of the issued securities. This means that the SPV holds a larger pool of assets than would be necessary if the loans in the pool pay as expected.

Payback ratio—In for-sale projects, it is the relationship between the required loan repayment per unit and the amount of loan per unit.

Portfolio lender—A financial institution that holds a portfolio of loans and earns profit from origination and the difference (spread) between the interest they charge on the loans and the interest they pay on deposits.

Prepayment risk—Risk associated with the desired rate of return being impacted by the early repayment of loan principal.

Private-label securities—A mortgage-backed security or other bond created and sold by a company other than a government-sponsored enterprise (GSE). The security frequently is collateralized by loans that are ineligible for purchase by Freddie Mac or Fannie Mae.

Pro-forma statement—Projection of the income and expense statement for a property for the current year.

QQD framework—Framework which includes analysis of the quantity, quality, and durability of the income stream for an investment property.

Qualified presale—In a for-sale project, where a prospective buyer has put down deposit toward purchasing a unit and has been approved for a loan by a financial institution.

Real estate mortgage investment conduit (REMIC)—A type of special-purpose vehicle, created by the Tax Reform Act of 1986, that holds commercial and residential mortgages in trust and issues interests in these mortgages in the form of securities to investors.

Rent roll—Document which lists all of the current tenants in the subject property, the amount of square footage for each tenant, the annual lease rate paid per square foot for each tenant, and the expiration dates of the current leases.

Replacement cost—The cost of erecting a building to replace or serve the functions of a previous structure.

Replacement reserve—An amount set aside from net operating income to pay for the eventual wearing out of short-lived assets.

Reversion—Sale of the property at the end of the holding period.

RevPAR—Revenue per available room in a hotel.

RMBS—Residential mortgage-backed securities.

Sales approach—One of the three appraisal approaches to value. Value is estimated by analyzing sales prices of similar properties recently sold. Also known as the market comparison approach.

Self-storage—See "Mini-storage".

Sensitivity analysis—A technique of investment analysis whereby different values of certain key variables are tested to see how sensitive investment results are to possible change in assumptions. It is a method of evaluating the riskiness of an investment.

SERVQUAL—Service quality measures for a hotel.

Shackle possibility curve—Economic model theorized by George Lennox Sharmin Shackle illustrating the universe of potential value choices that might exist for a given situation.

Single-family residence—A type of residential structure designed to include one dwelling.

Smart contracts—Contract where an asset is transferred between buyer and seller without the need for a human interaction.

Speculative investment—Investment where the profit potential comes solely from the eventual resale of the property. This would be the case for investment properties where there is no tenant, or for various owner-occupied properties such as single-family residences. An alternative definition would be where income from the property exists, but where there is a shortfall of monthly income relative to the debt service for the loan that is secured by the property. In either case, the investor has purchased the property for reasons other than the annual cash flow produced after debt service is paid.

Standard deviation—A measure of dispersion about the mean.

Structural credit enhancements—Techniques used by securitizations to distribute risk among bonds, such that some of them provide protection to those that enjoy a higher priority.

Supportable loan amount—What the lender is willing to lend on an investment property. It is traditionally calculated by taking the net operating income and dividing by the mortgage constant, and dividing by a desired debt service coverage ratio.

Terminal cap rate—The cap rate based on the eventual sale of the investment at the end of the holding period.

Third-party tenants—Tenants in income-producing property that have ownership other than the ownership of the real estate. These tenants could be unrelated parties in an apartment complex, or operating companies located in an office, retail, or warehouse property.

Underwriter—Banks, investment banks, and brokers that sell the securities in a public offering or place them privately, often retaining a portion of the issuance for their own account.

Variance—Statistical measure of how far a set of numbers is spread out from the average value.

White squirrels—Rare species of squirrels typically seen in locations such as Brevard, NC.

Xystus—Garden walk embarked by trees.

Yield capitalization—Method of converting future income from an investment into present value by discounting each year's income using an appropriate discount rate.

ZAM—Zero amortization mortgages; interest-only mortgages with principal due at maturity.

Zoning ordinances—Limitations on ownership owing to government mandated uses of a property given its location or other distinguishing characteristics.

Index

Made in the USA
Columbia, SC
09 January 2023

75785323R00130